IMAGES
of America

WEST MILWAUKEE

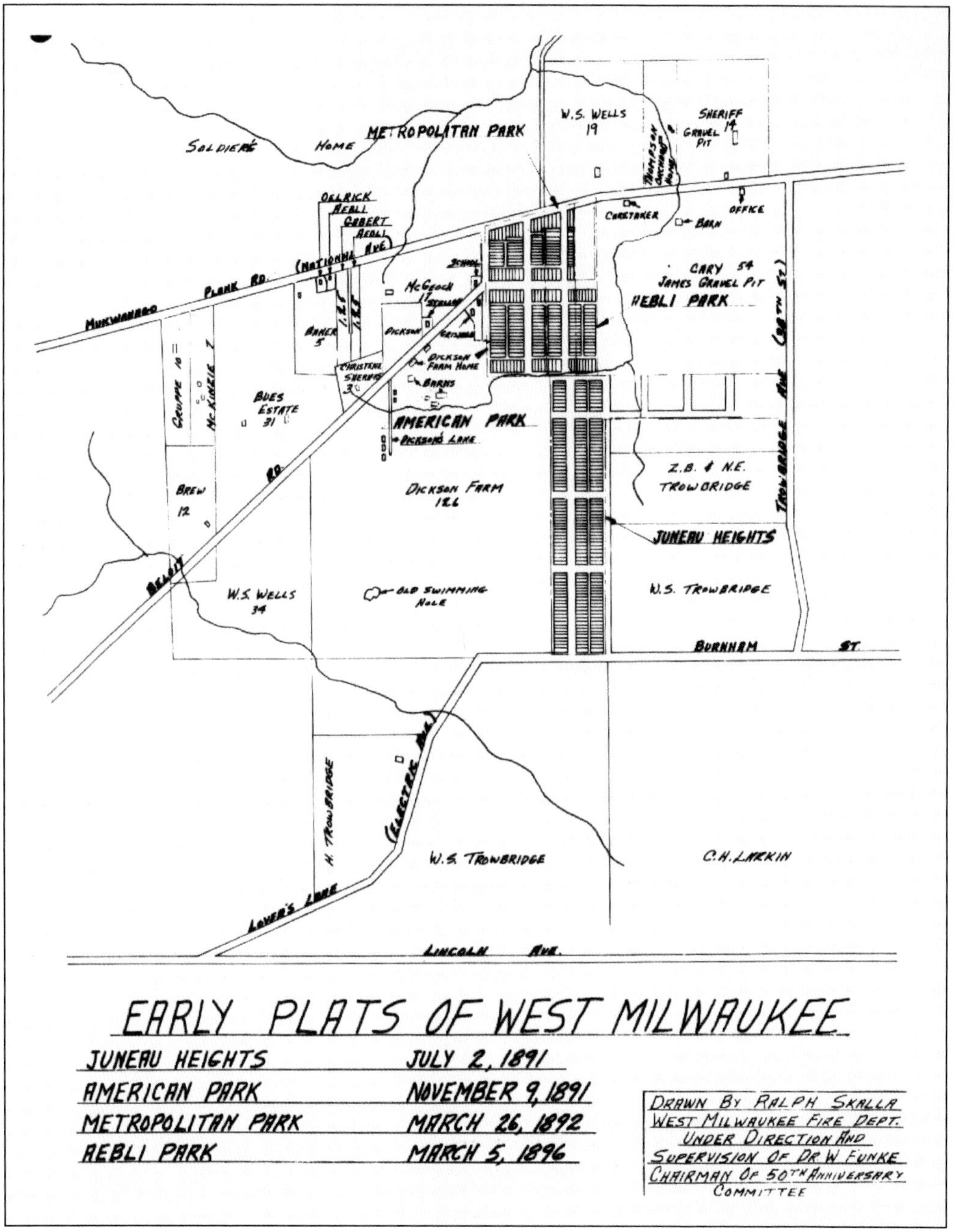

Drawn for the village's 50th anniversary in 1956, this map shows plats of farms, estates, and the first subdivisions, as well as the original roadways.

IMAGES
of America

WEST MILWAUKEE

West Milwaukee Historical Society

ARCADIA
PUBLISHING

ISBN 978-0-7385-3365-0

Published by Arcadia Publishing
Charleston, South Carolina

Printed in the United States of America

Library of Congress Catalog Card Number: 2004115834

For all general information contact Arcadia Publishing at:
Telephone 843-853-2070
Fax 843-853-0044
E-mail sales@arcadiapublishing.com
For customer service and orders:
Toll-Free 1-888-313-2665

Visit us on the Internet at www.arcadiapublishing.com

On the cover: This scene reveals the back of Druml's Saloon. A front view of the tavern can be seen on page 11.

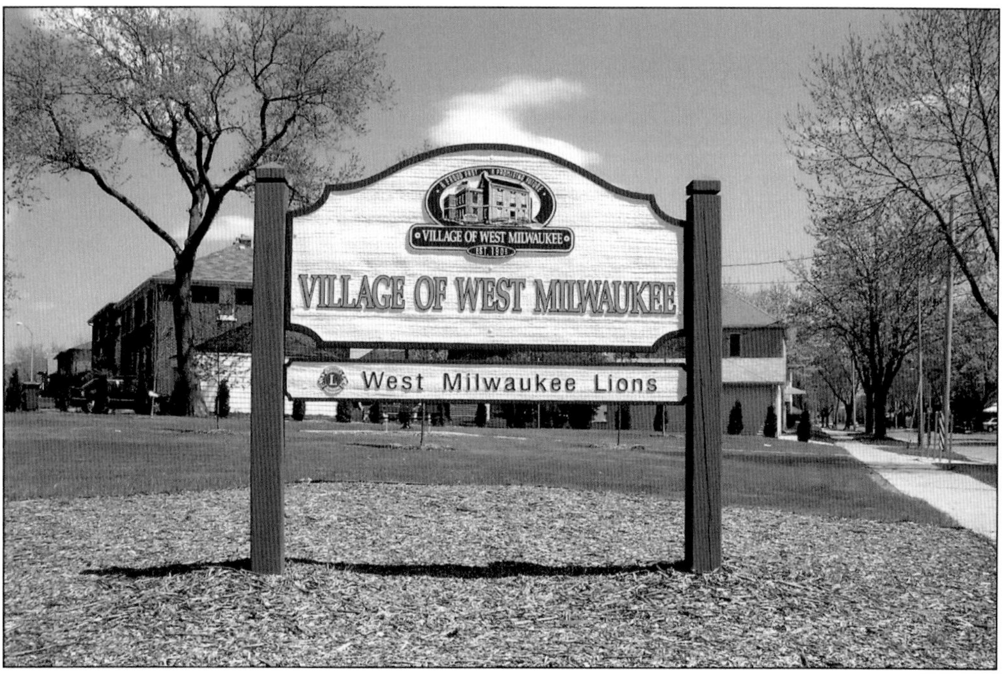

Welcome to West Milwaukee! The sign in Lions Park, at South Fifty-fifth Street and West Beloit Road, welcomes those entering the village. The little corner park was established in 2004 on the site of a former gas station.

Contents

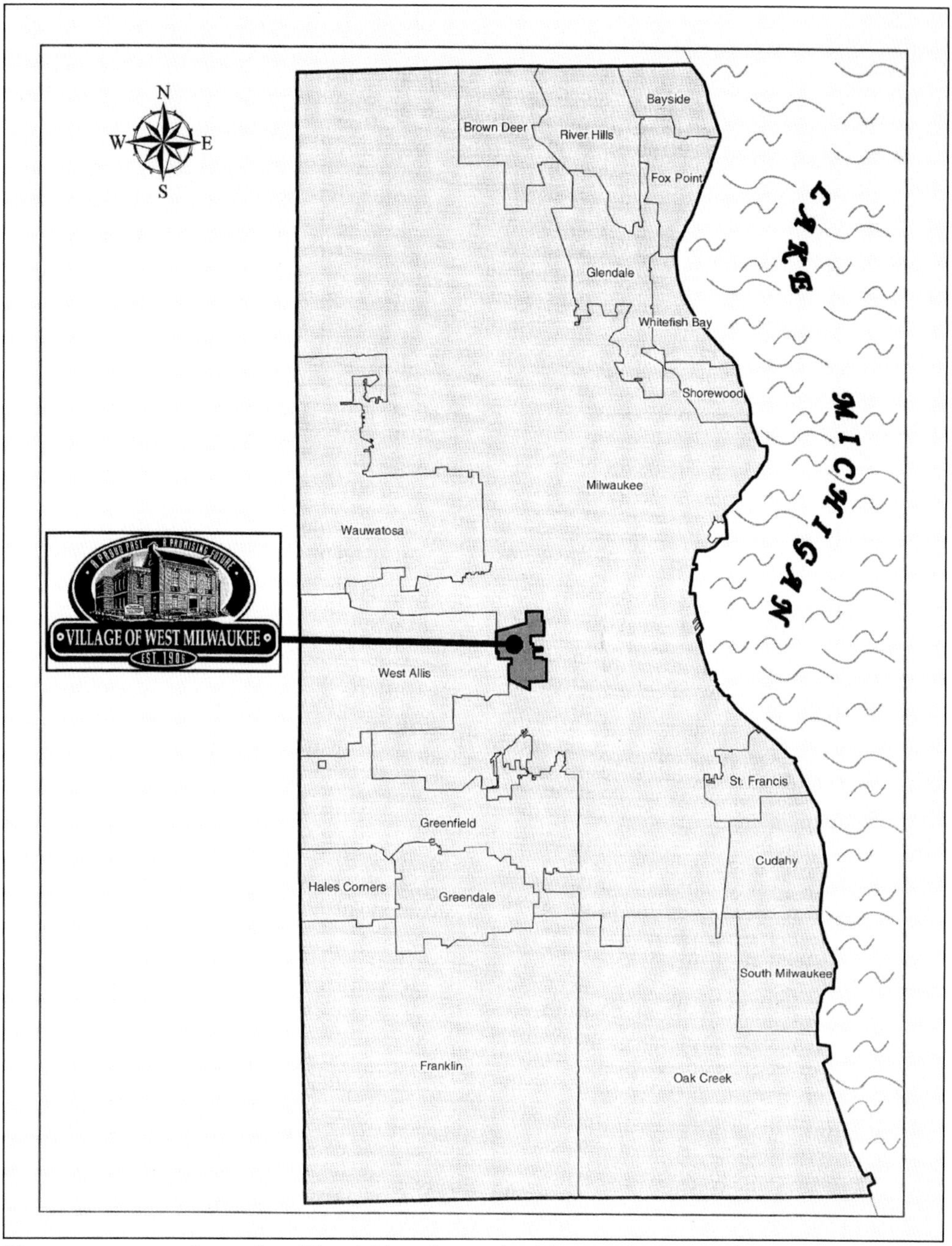

This current map shows that West Milwaukee indeed lies in the heart of Milwaukee County, surrounded by the city of Milwaukee, city of West Allis, and the Clement J. Zablocki Veterans Affairs Medical Center. (Map courtesy of Len Roeker, village engineer.)

INTRODUCTION

The year 1906 was a momentous one. The average worker earned $500. A tremendous earthquake hit San Francisco, the supposedly unsinkable Lusitania was launched, the Statue of Liberty was rededicated after being lit with electricity, and the Village of West Milwaukee was born and has been rolling forward for 100 years.

American Indian tribes prior to the Potawatomi were drawn here, as evidenced by mounds in the shape of lizards and other animals in the "Indian Fields" south of Greenfield and west of Forty-third Street. The area boasted rolling hills, meadows, thick forests, and fish so numerous they could be seen jumping in the Menomonee River. Rare black swans were said to inhabit the ponds in the Soldiers' Home. Settlers were also drawn by cheap land. The story is told of members of the settlers' union threatening to throw into the river anyone bidding over the $1.25 per acre price.

The face of West Milwaukee in 1906 was quite different than today. Its less than one square mile boasted many taverns, a gravel pit, a 28 room mansion, small and large farms, and even a pickle factory owned by the father of George Brew (who became the first village president). Well remembered is the Dickson farm where children came to get milk in the morning before going off to school and had great fun exploring in the after school hours.

After incorporation, elections were held annually until 1920. They were then held in even-numbered years, except for three of the trustee positions. Since 2001, trustees have been elected to three-year terms. Past candidates for office belonged to various political groups including the Socialist Party, the Citizens' Party, the Peoples' Party, and the Workers' Party. Since the 1960's, candidates have run independently. Since 1977, West Milwaukee has had a non-elected full time administrator. At times, the course of politics has been tumultuous, perhaps indicating a very strong concern for the welfare of the village.

Initially, West Milwaukee had no fire protection services. There was a fire that destroyed the entire block between Forty-fifth Street, Forty-sixth Street, and National Avenue. In 1912, West Allis began providing fire protection. In 1926, Milwaukee assumed that role, serving until West Milwaukee formed its own department in 1952. Because of fiscal considerations, West Milwaukee discontinued its fire department in 1991 and now contracts with Milwaukee for fire protection. The police department was at first served by one lone marshal, then deputy marshals, and now has a staff of 18 officers. The DPW ably maintains village streets, alleys, and other properties, as well as providing garbage collection.

West Milwaukee Middle School opened in 1997. The school colors changed to red and black from blue and gold; and the "Mustangs" became the "Panthers." The West Milwaukee name remains on the remodeled building, whose beautiful exterior has been preserved. The children once again are under the guidance of capable and caring educators, and citizens are very glad to have both an elementary school (Pershing) and a middle school. St. Florian's, the village's Catholic Church, provided parochial education from 1913 until 2004. St. John's Lutheran Church holds regular worship services. Both have been an integral part of the community.

An annexation in 1951 extended village limits to just south of Lincoln Avenue, increasing its size to almost two square miles. At one time, West Milwaukee was 80 percent industrial. Industry paid 80 percent of the taxes and West Milwaukee's taxes were the lowest in the state. West Milwaukee has always had a close relationship with industry; its small size meaning less bureaucracy, and factories meaning more jobs. Business leaders have been active members of the Rotary Club, the Business and Advancement Association, and the Chamber of Commerce. They have also contributed to many village events and efforts. During the Depression, when West Milwaukee could not meet its payroll, Henry Harnischfeger stepped in and paid his taxes early. Post-proms were held at Chain Belt. The machinery and equipment exemption from taxes and the loss of some industry due to obsolescence contributed to a big bump in the road for West Milwaukee. This and the loss of the Forty-third Street corridor, caused taxes to escalate. (Note that 250 homes and businesses were demolished for a north-south freeway which was never built.)

West Milwaukee residents like the location, small size, and moderate home prices. About growing up in West Milwaukee, many have commented "Wasn't it fun?" Indeed, village life has been interesting and varied—from skinny dipping in Dickson's Pond, to singing in the church choir. Movies and dances were once part of an extensive recreation program at Pershing Elementary School. Night classes and swimming were offered at West Milwaukee High. A large Austrian group met regularly and even had a welfare league. There was a Gun Club, a Garden Club, a Golden Agers group, and a Lions Club, which still serves the community today. Despite the high school's closing, a booster club still exists. Baseball has been popular throughout the years. Professional ball fans have been able to walk on over to nearby County Stadium and later to Miller Park. Football practices were once held in Chain Belt field (now the Rexnord parking lot). The players joined in to mow the field, fill in the pot holes, and erect the goal posts.

The Soldiers' Home, with its bucolic setting, provided a place to promenade, picnic, and listen to concerts. The hills there were also perfect for winter sports. Then there was music, music, and more music. Liberace was, of course, West Milwaukee's most famous musician, but many other villagers played in bands, or sang at home gatherings. A glass or two have been lifted in the taverns of West Milwaukee. Card playing and bowling were common in our town, too. All in all, West Milwaukee was and is a lively village.

The spirit of West Milwaukee is best discovered through a look at the individual West Milwaukee resident. We are a small village, so close to our neighbors that we can often shake their hands and often do. Here, in our little space, the individual more easily stands out. Some personalities mentioned herein have left their mark on the world, among them aviators, athletes, wild game hunters, politicians, and musicians. Some have been influential in more quiet ways, for example, by helping a neighbor, nurturing children, or volunteering. Civic leaders have influenced both the schools and government. To quote William Testdorf, village president from 1975 to 1982, "As long as we keep dedicated people running the Village, there will always be a West Milwaukee."

Into the 21st century, West Milwaukee is literally exploding with development. The barren and contaminated land along old Forty-third Street, as well as Electric Avenue, has been made over. The wheel has come full circle. Where residents' first homes stood, condominiums, apartments, restaurants, banks, credit unions, and retail stores of all types stand ready to serve. Equally appealing are village staff and residents whose caring keep West Milwaukee a great place to live. After 100 years, we are here to stay. We are West Milwaukee!

One

The Early Years

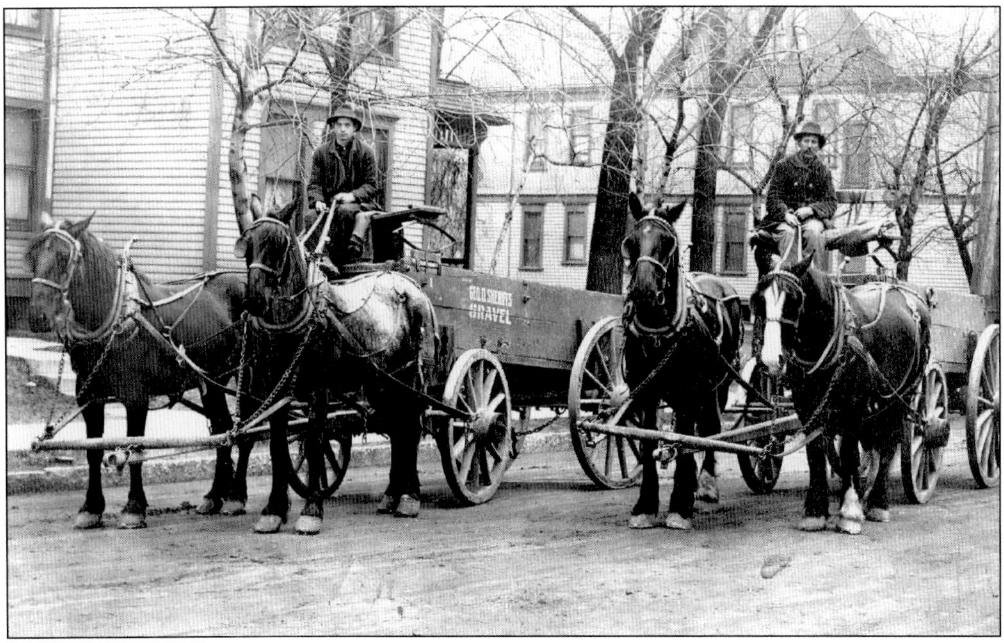

George Sheriff's horse-drawn gravel wagons pause along a delivery route. Sheriff operated a gravel pit bounded by National Avenue to the south, the Milwaukee Road tracks to the north, South Thirty-ninth Street to the east, and South Forty-first Street to the west. He was also part owner of the Sheriff Manufacturing Company, which produced marine propellers. In 1906, he platted a portion of his property as the Sheriff subdivision. Another of Sheriff's land parcels, opposite the Robert Johnston Company, became a recreational area known as Carney Park, where carnivals were held. A baseball field was located there in 1908, with the first lighted game illuminated with kerosene.

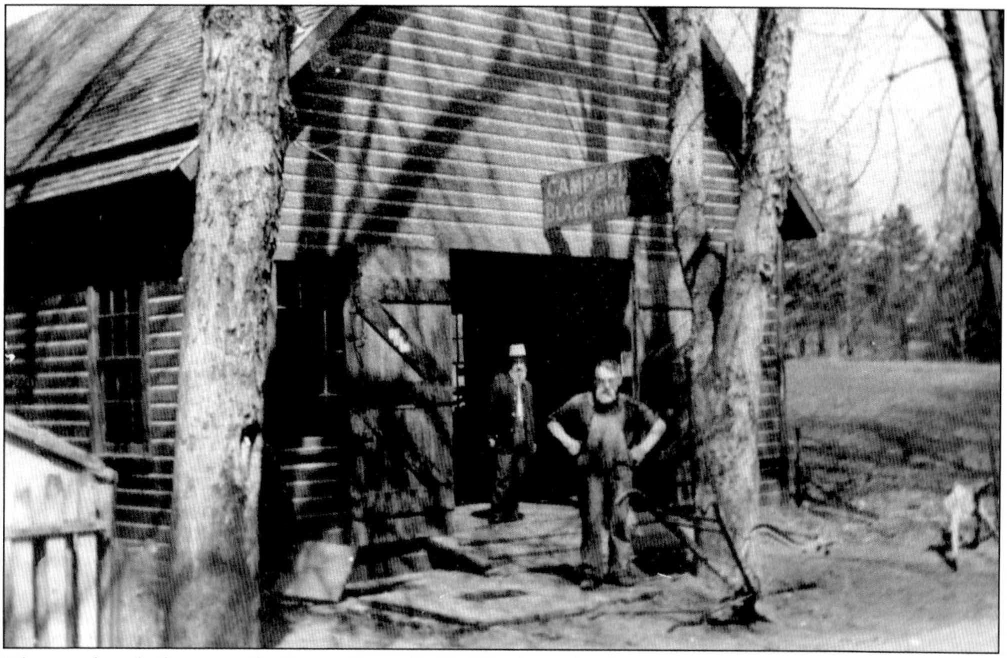

This undated photograph shows Campbell's Blacksmith Shop, at South Forty-sixth Street and West Beloit Road. Around 1900, Robert Roberts purchased this horse-shoeing business from a man named Griffin, whose home was near the alley on South Forty-fifth Street. Children used to go sledding on the long, steep hill at the rear of the shop.

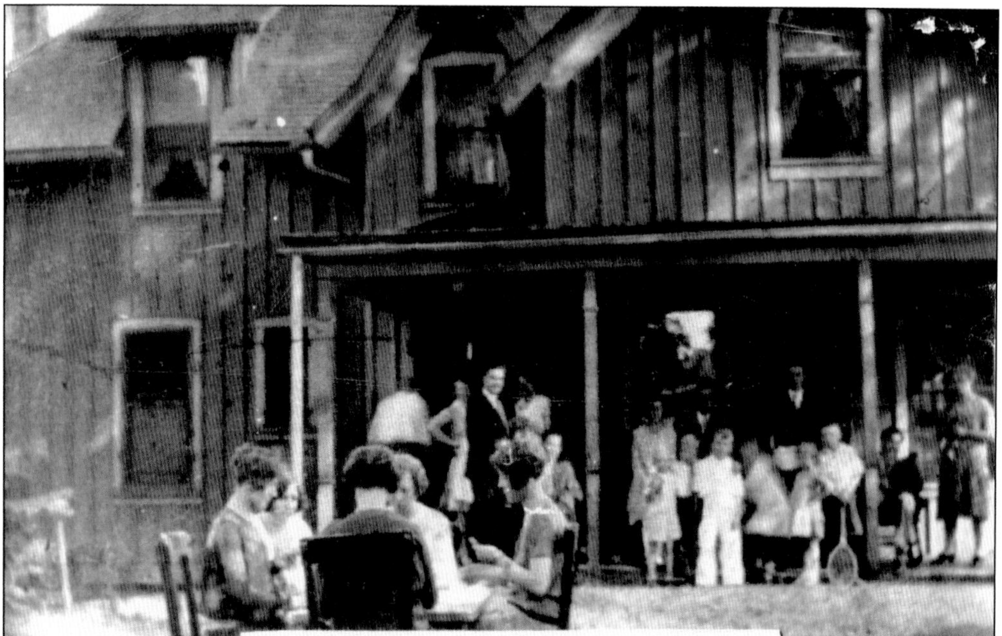

The oldest house in the village still stands at its original site at 4623 West Beloit Road, east of the Pershing School grounds and about 50 yards south of Beloit Road. A Mr. Barber, a Civil War veteran, lived there for many years. A later resident was Fred Runkels, a Soldiers' Home band leader.

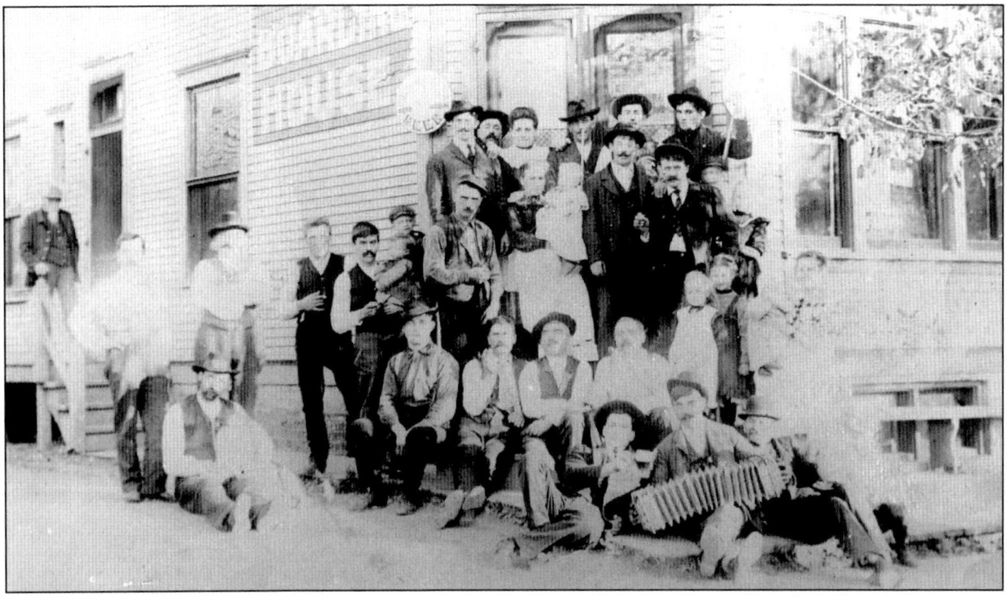

This 1905 view reveals Druml's Saloon and Boarding House, the rear of which can be seen on the cover. Included in this merry crowd is M. Schwei, Mike Rahoy (with concertina), George Wiegele, Paul ?, Laurence Grafenauer, Martin Yahnke, Martin Erat, John Zimmerman, Martin Tschabuschnig, Mike Schnabl, Val ?, Andrew Metzgar, Paul Druml, Agnes Druml, Frank Kuglitsch, Theresa Grafenauer, John Grafenauer, John Moertl, and Pete Mackey. The tavern was later named Hintz's and is currently J. D.'s Hideaway, at 1218 South Forty-fifth Street.

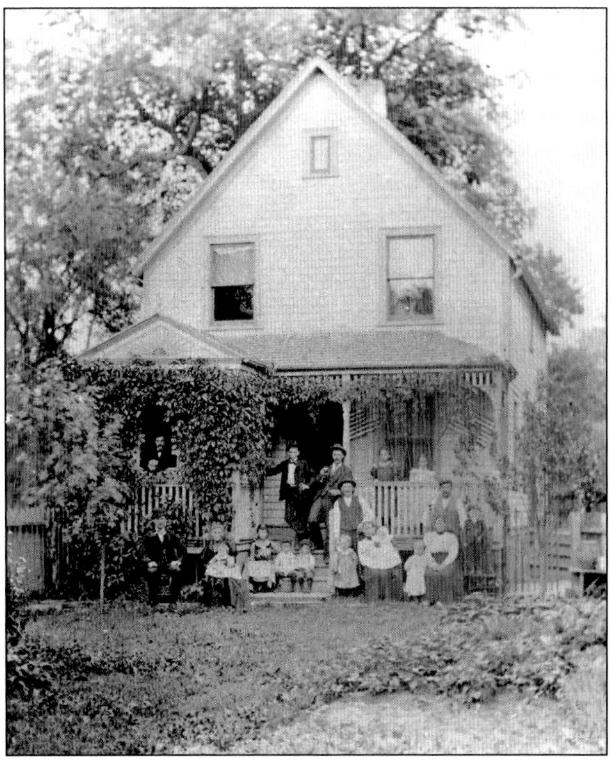

The Mark Druml home, erected prior to the tavern, was located at the rear of the saloon and directly across the street from St. Florian's Catholic Church. Pictured in the first row are Mr. and Mrs. Markus Druml, with their baby Anton. Mr. and Mrs. Schnabl (first row, seventh and eighth from left) are also seen with their daughters Kate (held) and Ann. The others are not identified.

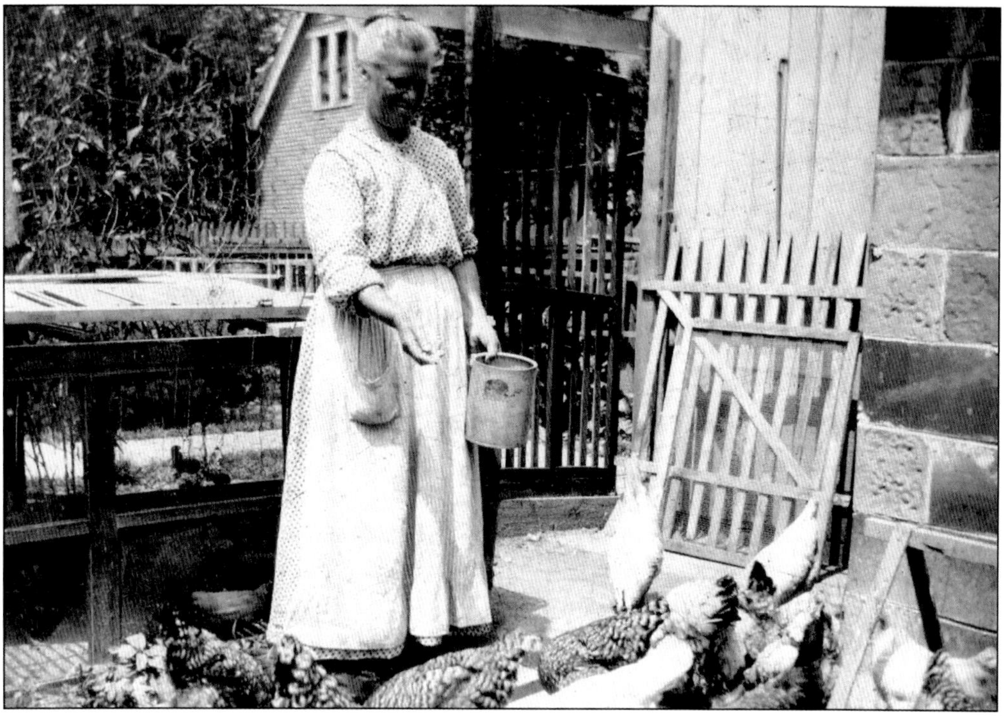

Frances Boiger, the mother of Frances Gebhard, feeds chickens in the backyard of 486 South Thirty-ninth Avenue (presently 1248 South Forty-fifth Street). A 1928 village ordinance stated, "No horses, mules, cattle, sheep, goats, swine, geese, ducks, turkeys, chickens, or any other poultry are to run at large within this village."

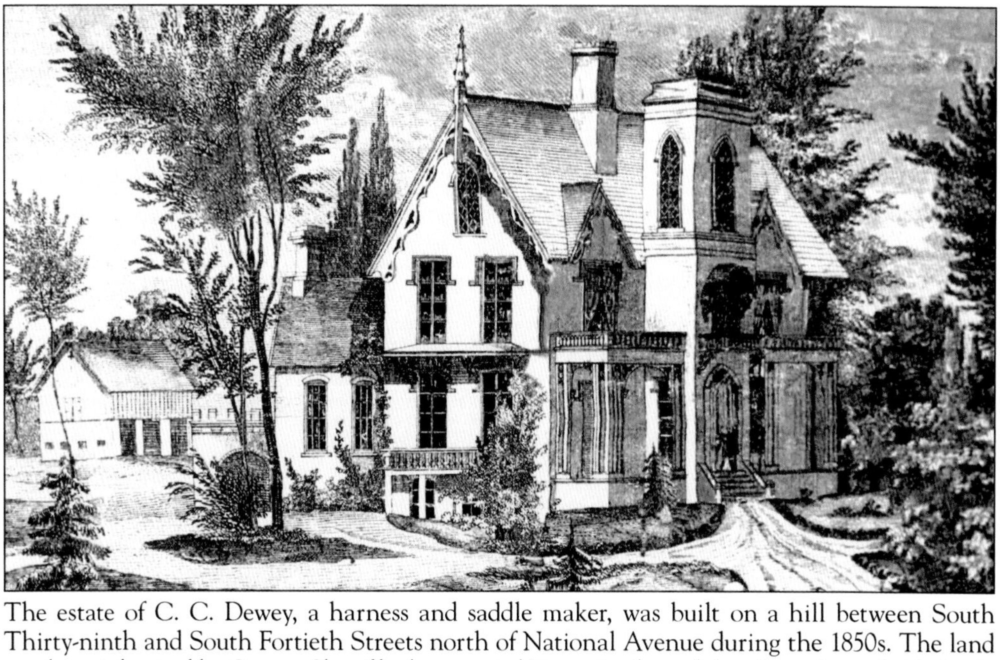

The estate of C. C. Dewey, a harness and saddle maker, was built on a hill between South Thirty-ninth and South Fortieth Streets north of National Avenue during the 1850s. The land was later inherited by George Sheriff, who married Dewey's adopted daughter, Anna Stickels. By the early 1900s, the home had been replaced by a cement block house.

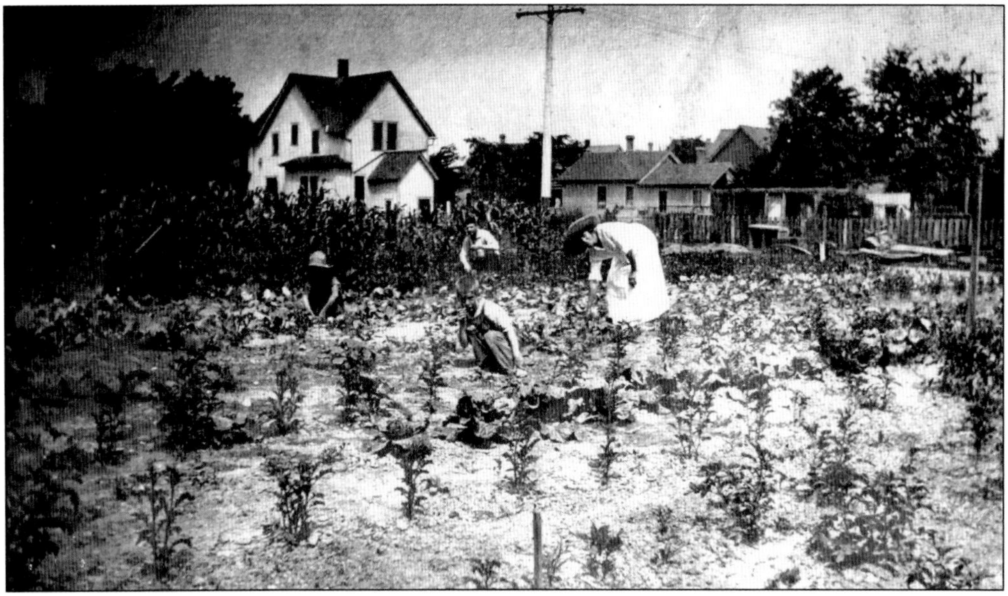

Mr. and Mrs. August Pinske and their sons August and Roland work a victory garden on the northwest corner of South Forty-seventh Street and West Beloit Road in 1918. In the background are the homes of the Alpners and Vasil and Mary Nick.

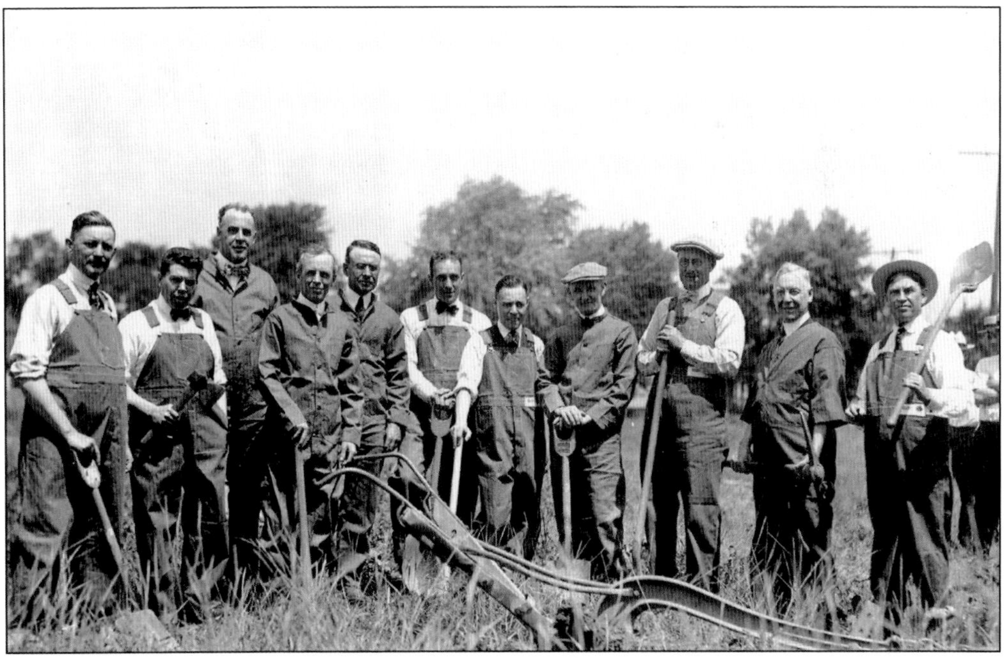

A crew of gardeners pose while tending a victory garden during World War I. Victory gardens were grown to supplement home front food supplies during wartime.

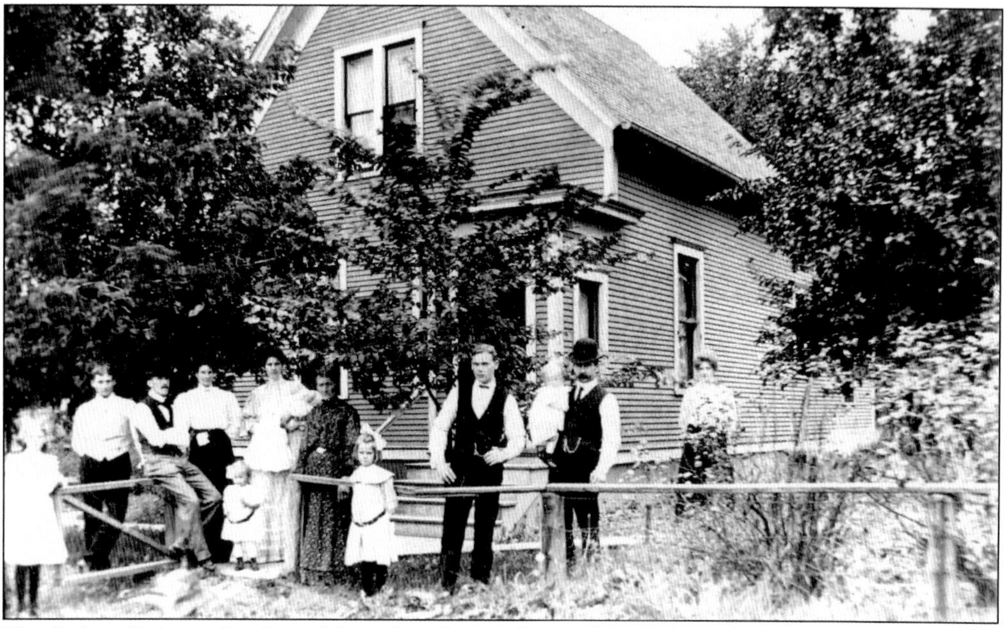

The Robert Roberts family and friends gather in front of the Roberts home at 4611 West Beloit Road. Pictured here, from left to right, are Mary Jane Roberts, Smith Emanuelson, Mr. and Mrs. Gordon Martini, an unidentified toddler, unidentified woman and baby, Grandmother Emanuelson, Eunice M. Roberts, unidentified man, unidentified man holding an unidentified child, and an unidentified woman. An apartment building now stands on the site. In 1936, Mary Jane Roberts became the first deputy clerk in the village.

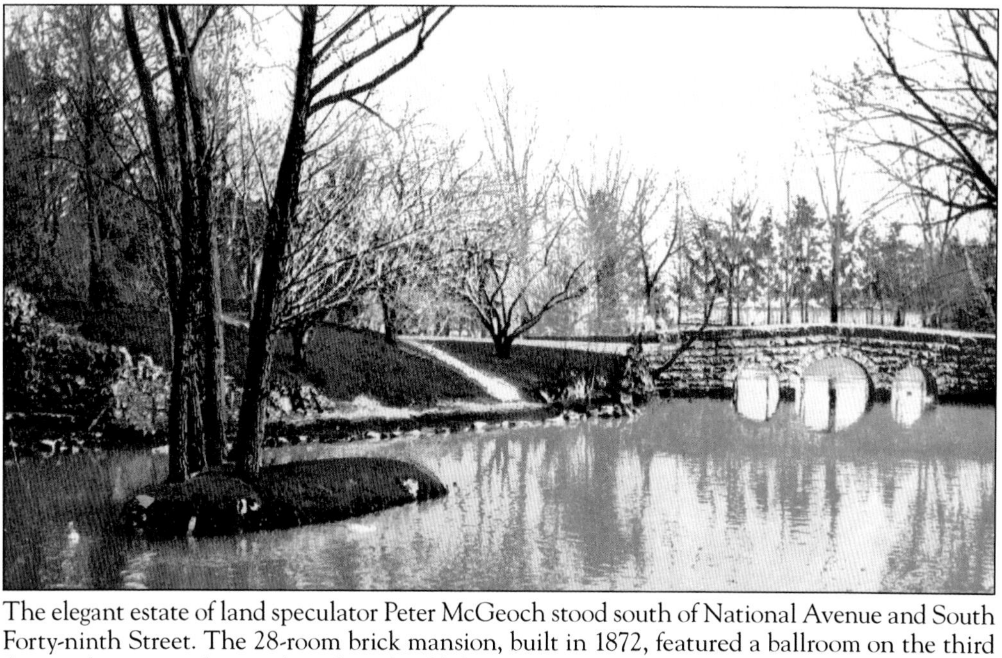

The elegant estate of land speculator Peter McGeoch stood south of National Avenue and South Forty-ninth Street. The 28-room brick mansion, built in 1872, featured a ballroom on the third floor and a surrounding park and artificial lake. In 1904, the mansion was razed and McGeoch's son Arthur began selling the homestead as the Red Brae subdivision. "Red Brae" means the slope of a hill of red clay.

Paul and Lena Schwei pose with their daughter, Mary, at their 446 Forty-first Avenue home about 1910.

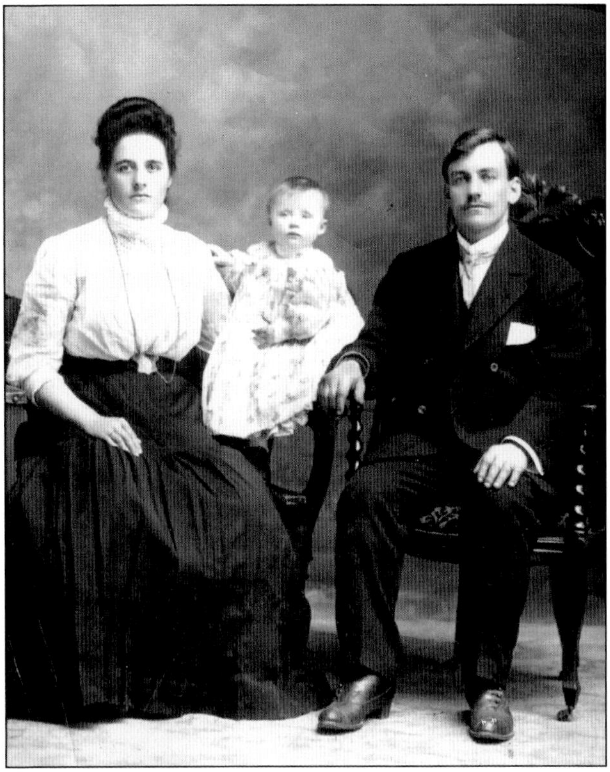

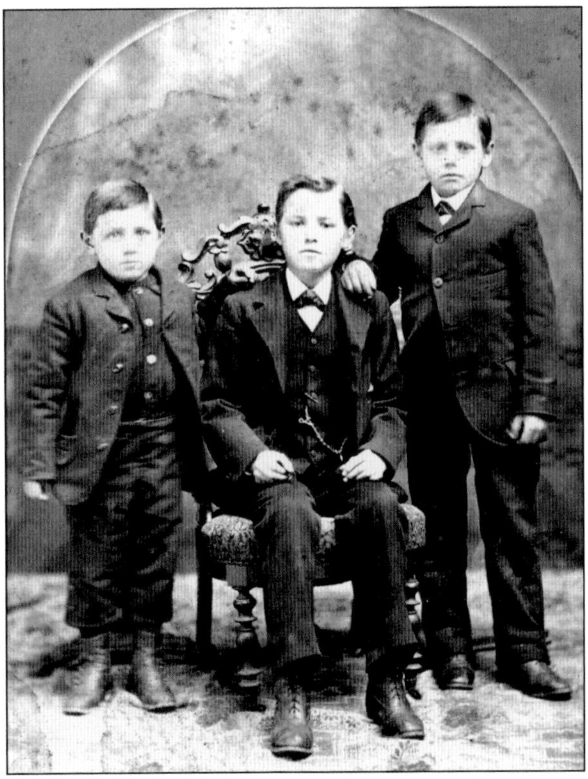

This late-1800s portrait depicts the Baker boys, from left to right, Henry, Charles, and Walter—sons of Albert and Gusta of 5133 West National Avenue. The 1906 census also lists a daughter, Ida. The family name was shortened from Backhaus, that of Albert's father, Carl. Charlie Baker later became the plumbing inspector for the village. The Bakers owned a celery farm at South Twenty-seventh Street and West Greenfield Avenue. They were forced to leave that area and come to the village, where Albert purchased the land where the high school now stands, from Greenfield Avenue north to National.

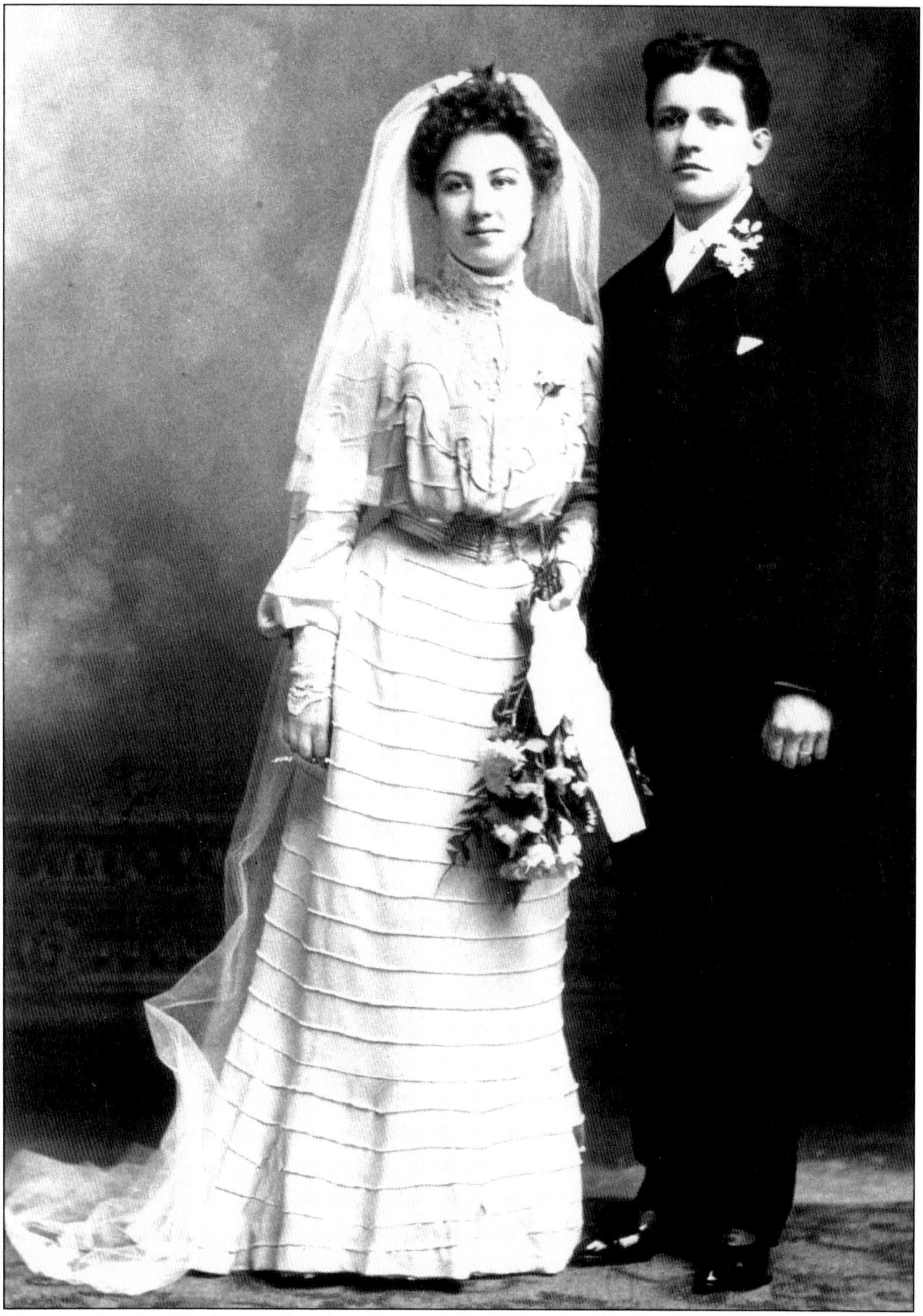

Max and Sophie Thekan strike a handsome pose in their undated wedding photograph. Both came to America from Saak, Austria—Max to West Milwaukee in 1883, and Sophie to Iron Mountain, Michigan, in 1886. Their two daughters, Sophie "Lillian," and Doris, were raised in West Milwaukee.

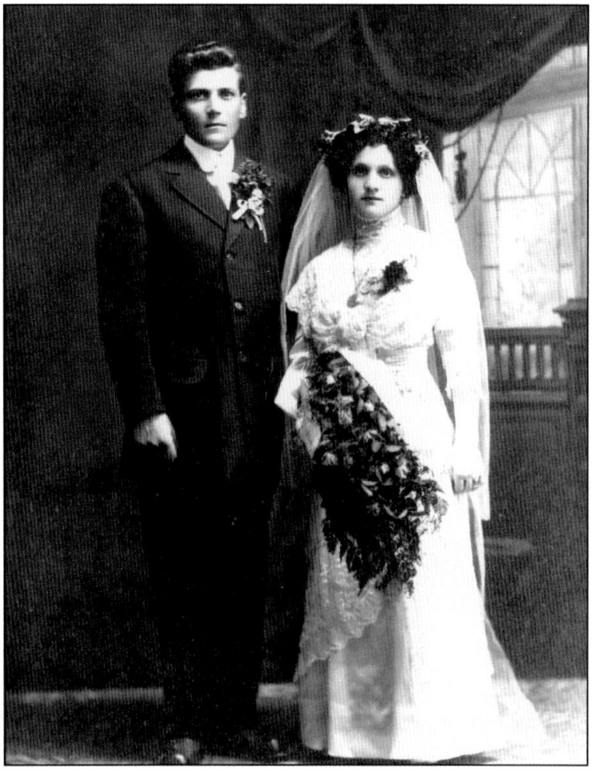

Pauline (Maier) and Anton Wurzer (later changed to Wurcer) immigrated to America from Notsch and Feistritz in Karnten County, Austria, in the early 1900s and settled in West Milwaukee. Anton was employed as an electrical worker at Allis-Chalmers. Pauline worked as a charwoman for over 30 years in the old Federal Building on Wisconsin Avenue in downtown Milwaukee. The couple raised three children, with the third generation still residing in the village. (Courtesy of Edie Wurcer.)

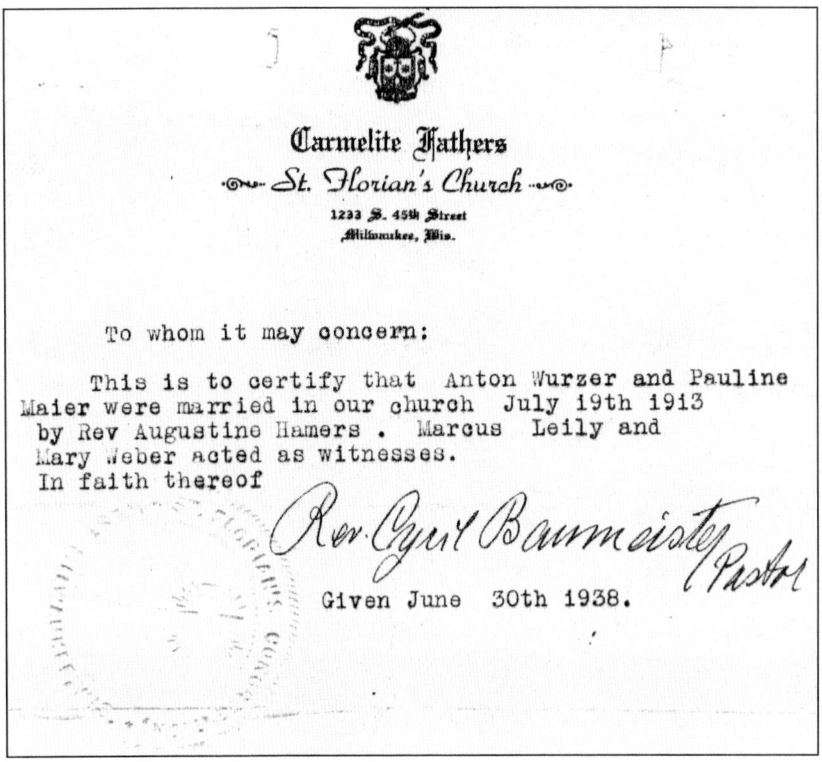

Carmelite Fathers

St. Florian's Church

1233 S. 45th Street

Milwaukee, Wis.

To whom it may concern:

This is to certify that Anton Wurzer and Pauline Maier were married in our church July 19th 1913 by Rev Augustine Hamers. Marcus Leily and Mary Weber acted as witnesses.

In faith thereof

Rev. Cyril Baumeister Pastor

Given June 30th 1938.

Seen here is the 1938 certification of the Wurzer marriage at St. Florian's Church. (Courtesy of Edie Wurcer.)

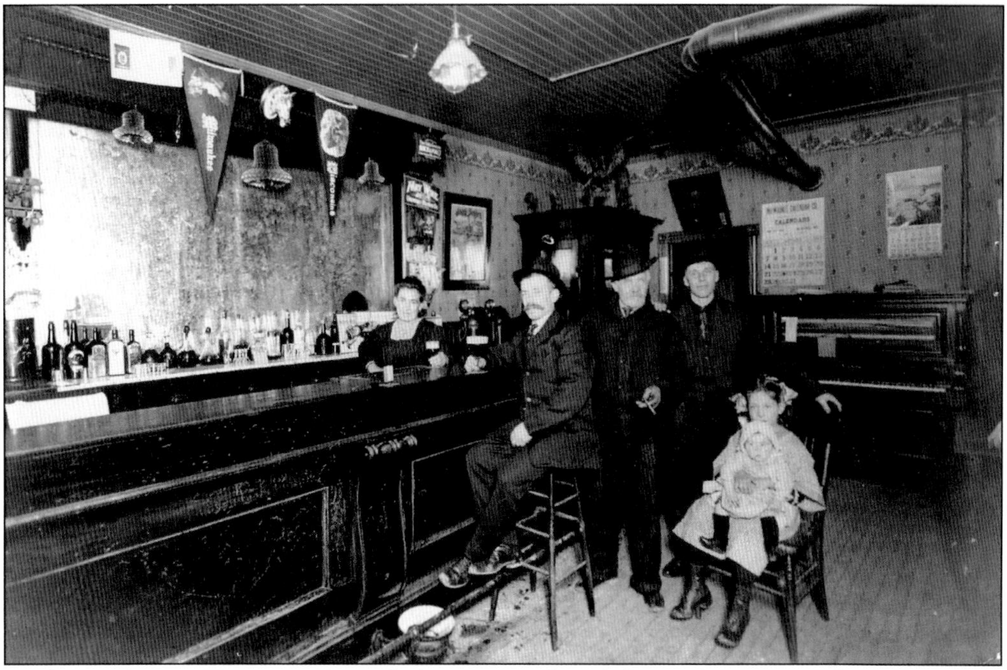

At the Grafenauer Tavern on Fortieth Avenue are, from left to right, Mrs. Grafenauer (back of bar), Markus Druml, unidentified, Grandpa Mike Grafenauer, and Theresa Grafenauer, holding baby Fran.

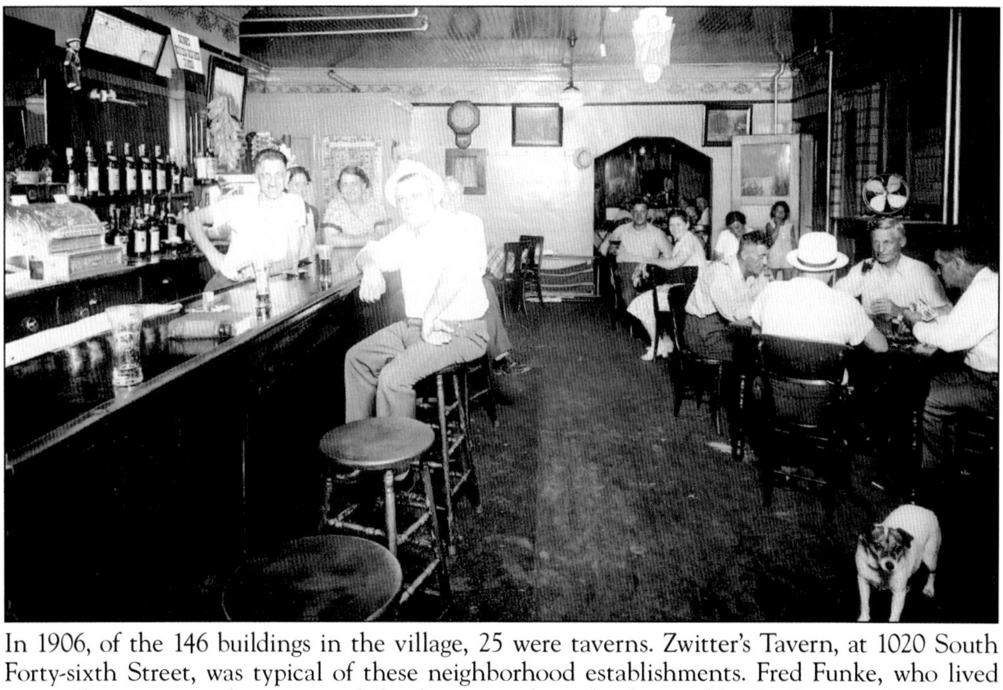

In 1906, of the 146 buildings in the village, 25 were taverns. Zwitter's Tavern, at 1020 South Forty-sixth Street, was typical of these neighborhood establishments. Fred Funke, who lived across the street, smokes a pipe while playing cards at the front table. Funke served as village president from 1915 to 1917. Behind the bar, from left to right, are Paul Zwitter; his wife, Theresa; and his mother-in-law, Theresa Grafenauer. Sitting at the bar is Anton Wurcer.

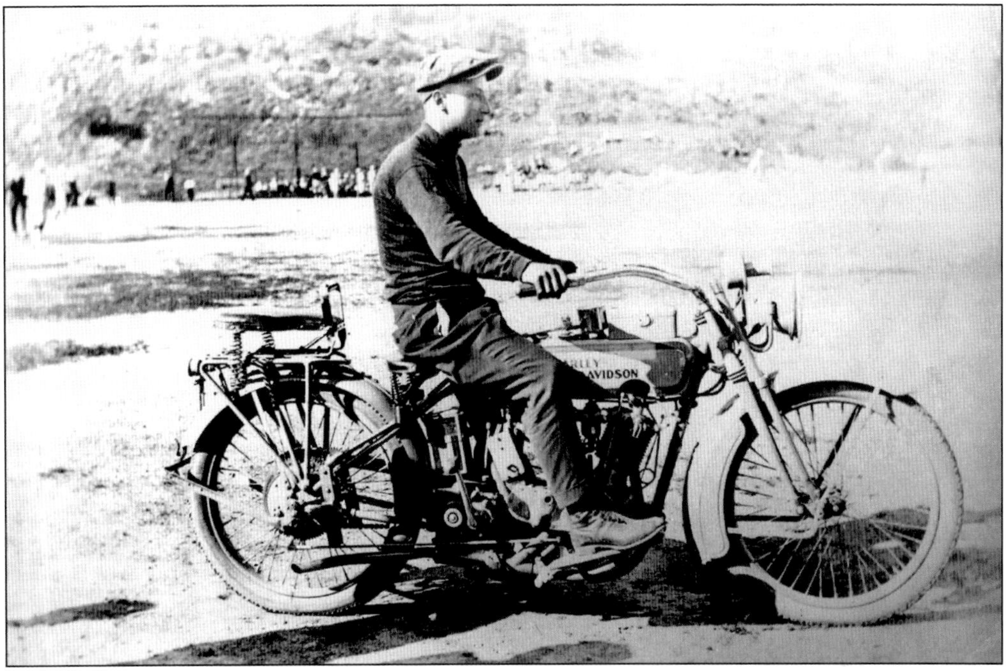

Mark Druml sits on his Harley-Davidson motorcycle in 1914. Harley-Davidsons were first manufactured in Milwaukee in 1903 and are still locally produced.

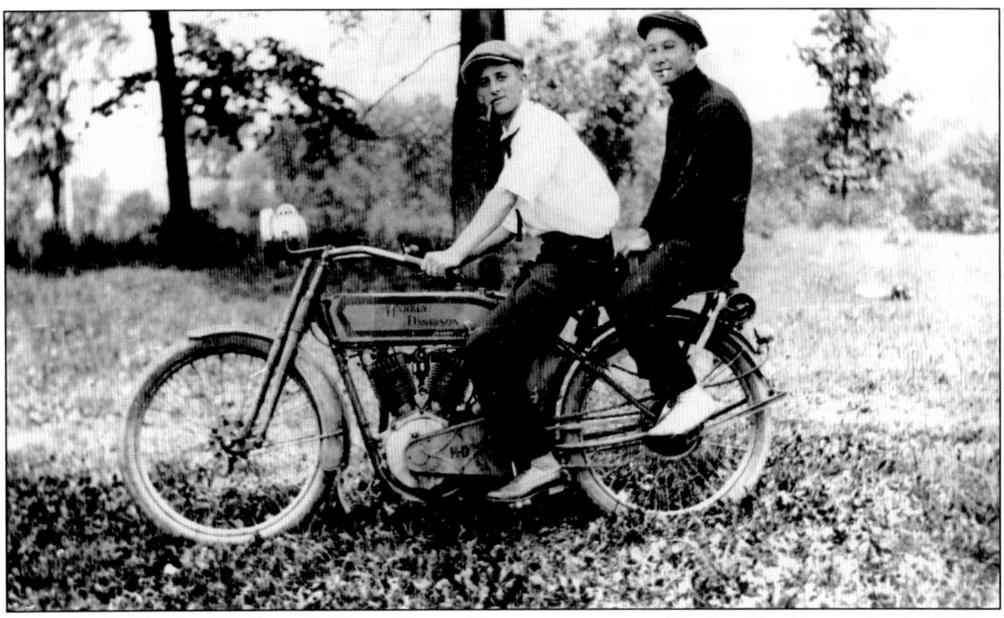

"Speeders" Charles Thekan (left) and Louis Brenner pose on a Harley-Davidson, also in 1914.

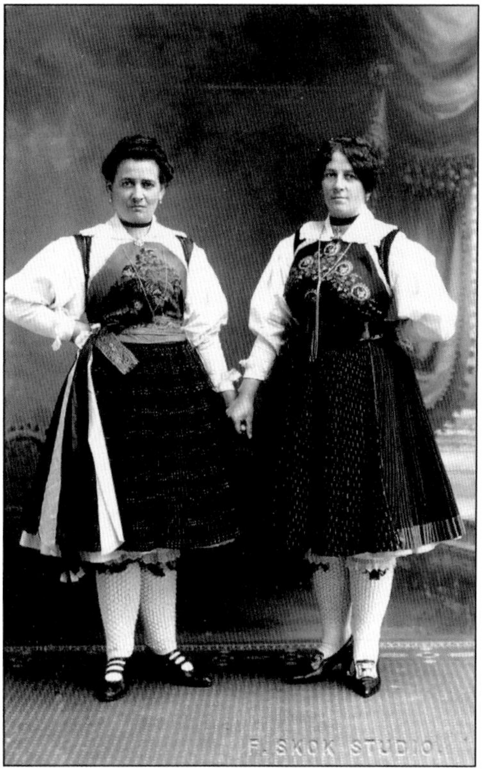

These two Austrian women in folk costume represent the large, closely knit group of Austrians who settled in West Milwaukee. On the left is Theresa Grafenauer and on the right, her good friend Frances Brunner. Daughter Fran Grafenauer remembers her delight in visiting the Brunners because they had an entire cigar box full of marbles to play with. (Courtesy of Fran Grafenauer.)

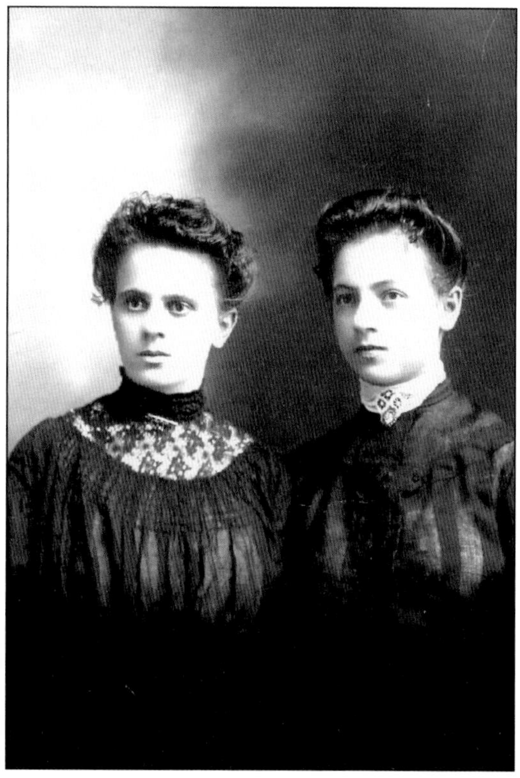

Theresa Tschabuschnig (left) and Mary Rahoy, members of an early village family, are dressed in fine attire. A sister, Johanna, was married to Valentine Brugger, the owner of a village tailor shop. Another sister, Pauline Wurcer, still has grandchildren living here. (Courtesy of Edie Wurcer.)

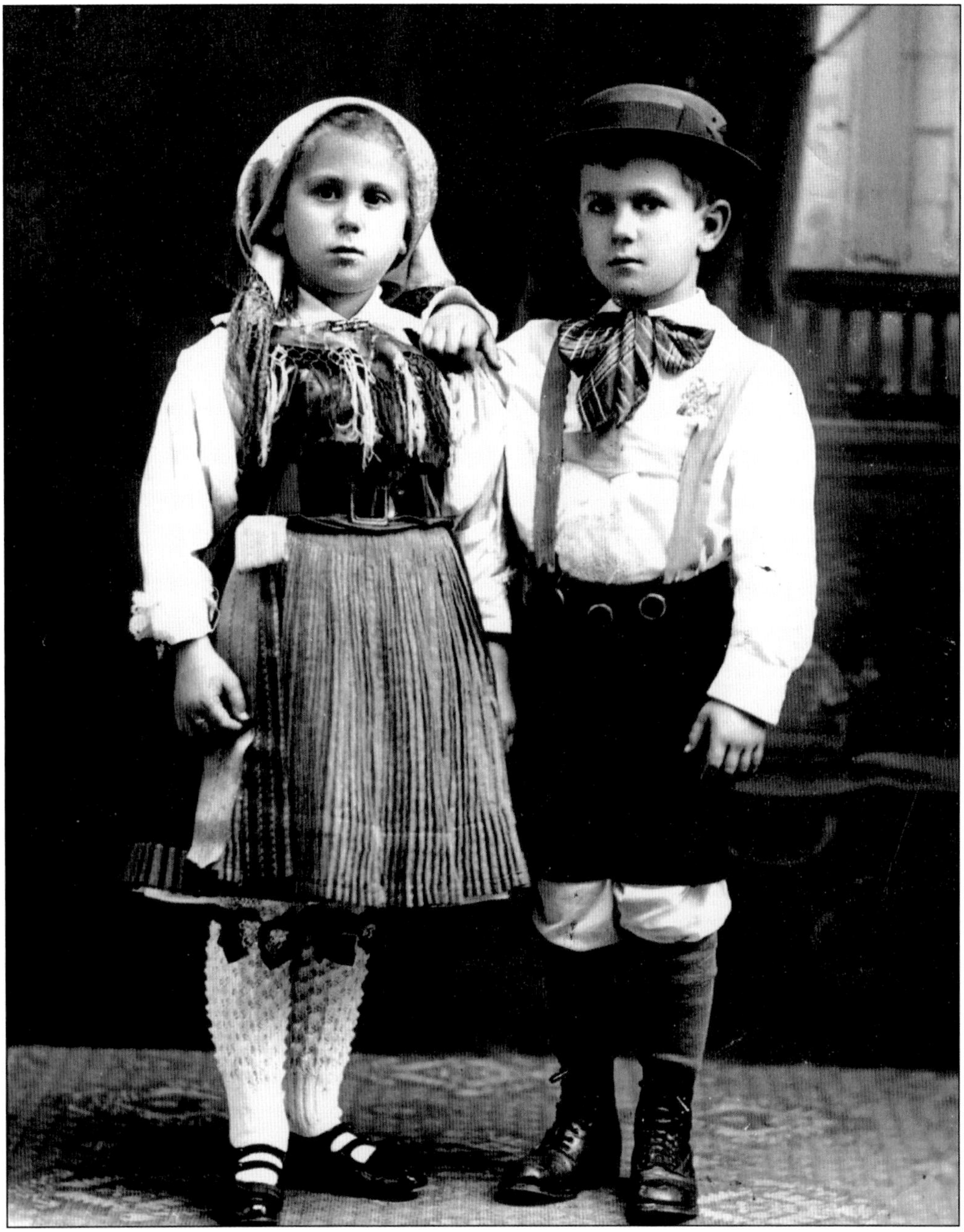

Theresa's children, Joseph and Mary Tchabushchnig (later Tabushing), appear in their Austrian finest. Joseph served as village clerk from 1960 until 1982, and Mary grew up to wed Walter Bode.

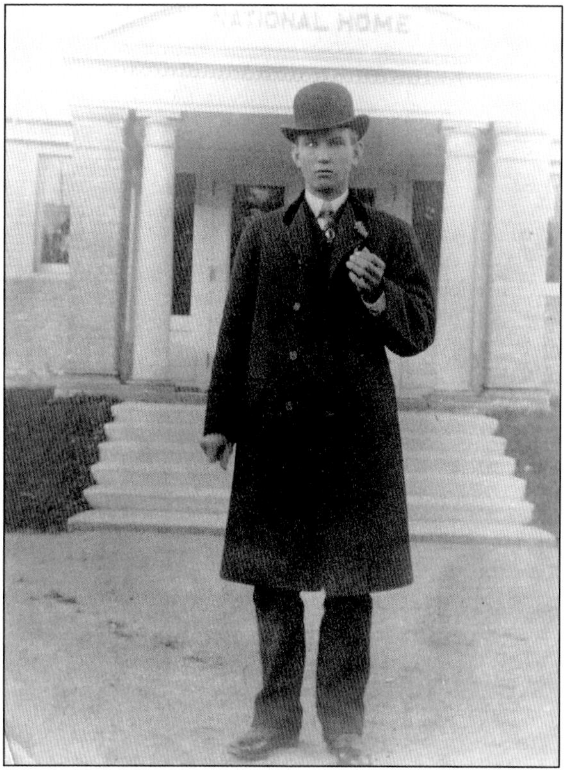

Gustave Niederstadt was a longtime village trustee and later clerk of West Milwaukee schools. As a young man in 1903, he stands in front of the flower house at the Soldiers' Home.

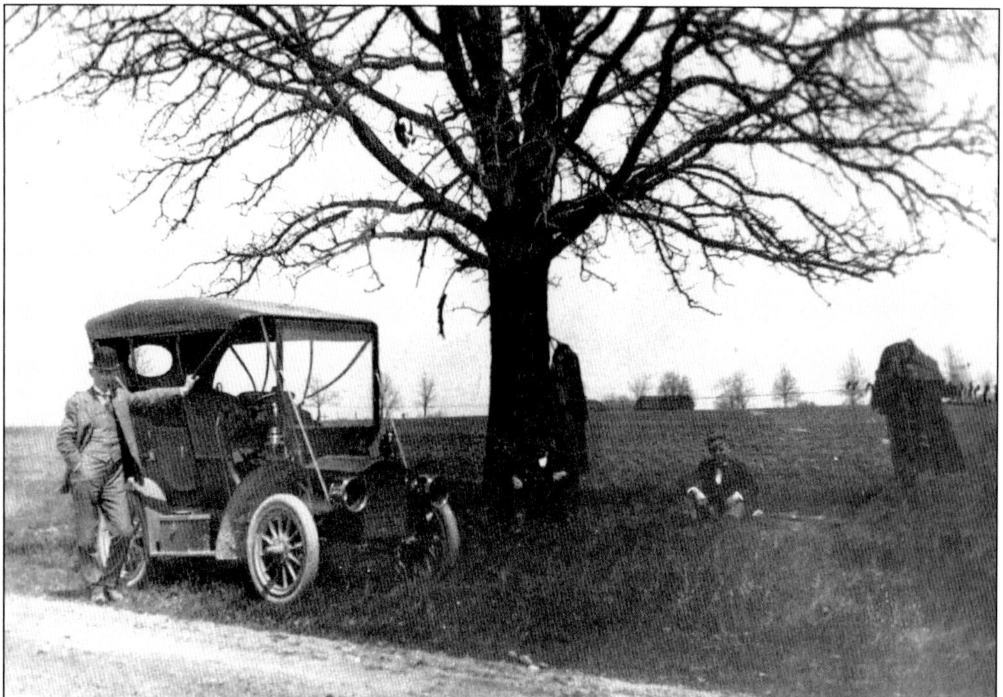

In this early-1900s photograph entitled "On the Road to Waukesha," Gus Niederstadt poses with a Cadillac. It must have been a rough ride!

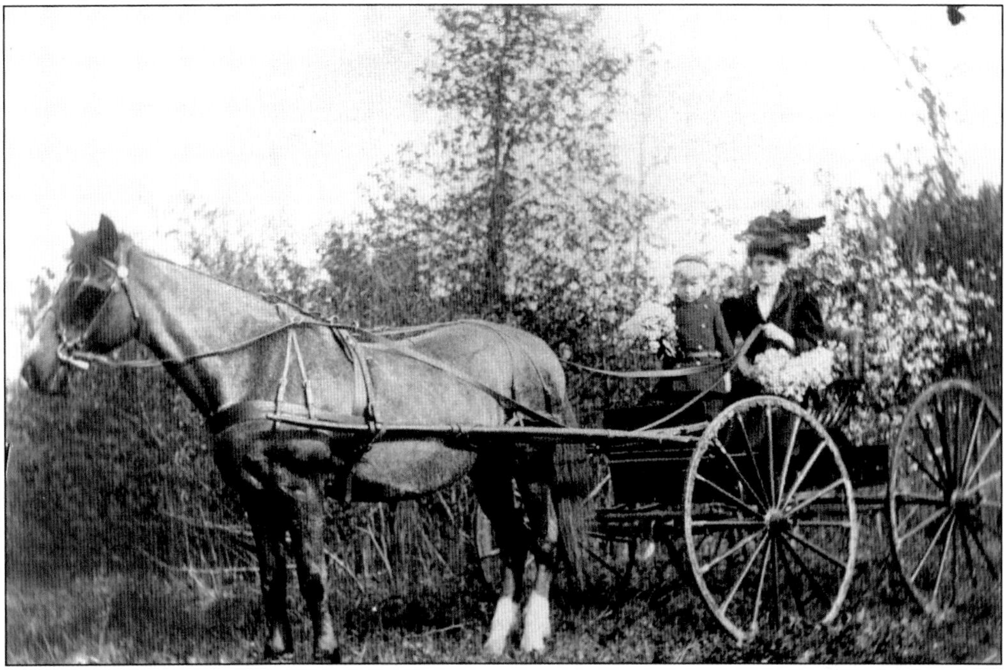

Bertha Niederstadt (Gus's mother) and her young son Elmer take a carriage ride in 1907.

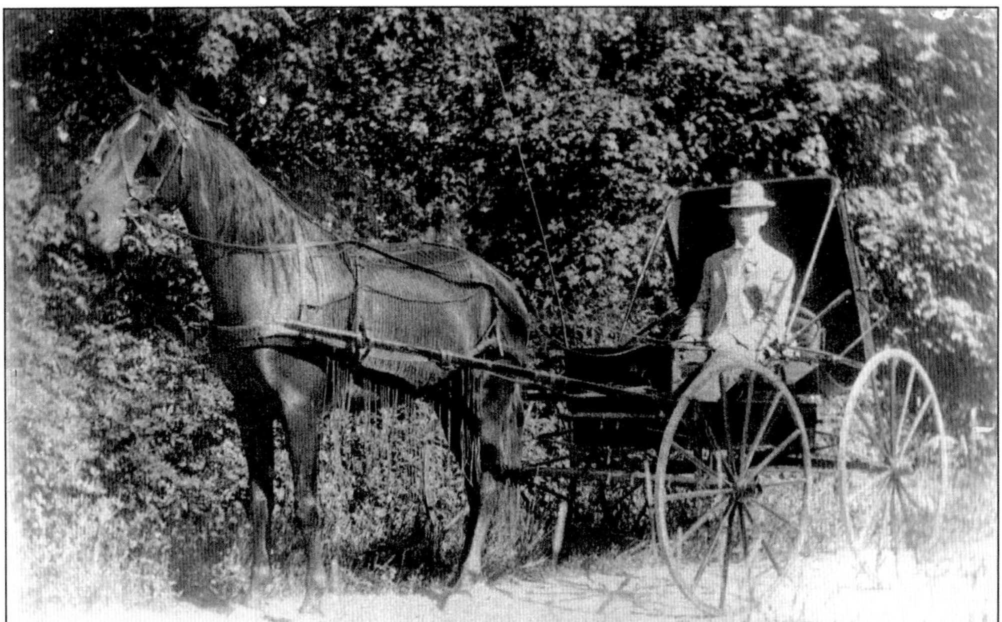

Gus Niederstadt appears in his horse rig in 1908. The horse is sporting "fly chaser" fringes. A poem found on saloon walls at the time reads in part, "Horses you are a wonderful thing, No horns to honk, no bells to ring . . . your frame is good for many a mile, your body never changes style."

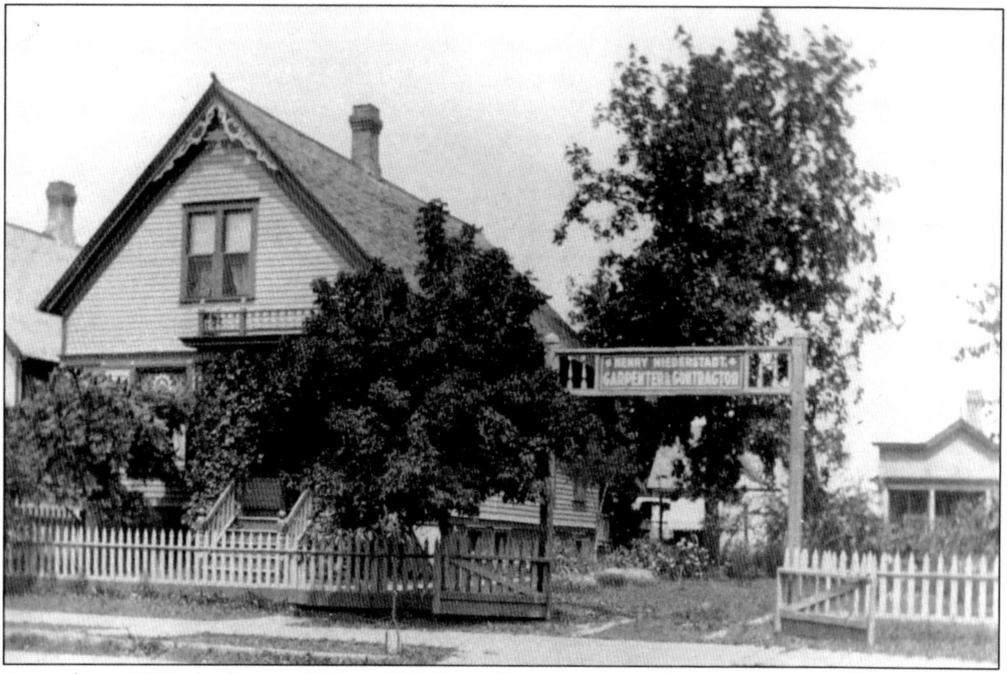

Seen about 1905, the home of Henry Niederstadt, carpenter and contractor, stood at 4416 West Scott Street.

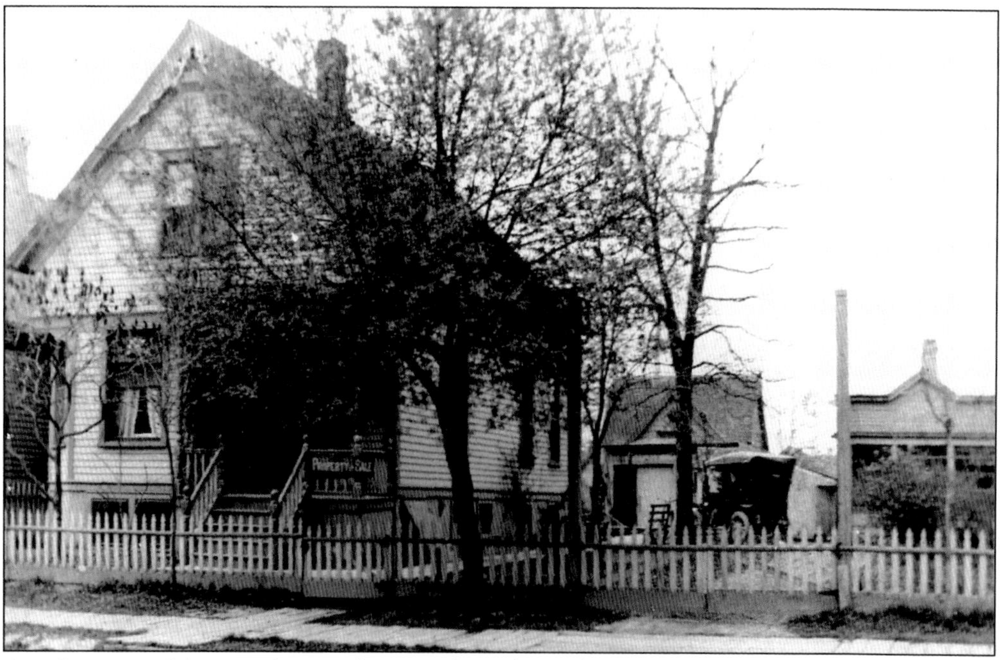

Another view of the same home a few years later shows the property for sale. Notice the Cadillac parked in the yard, the same automobile seen on page 22. The home no longer remains.

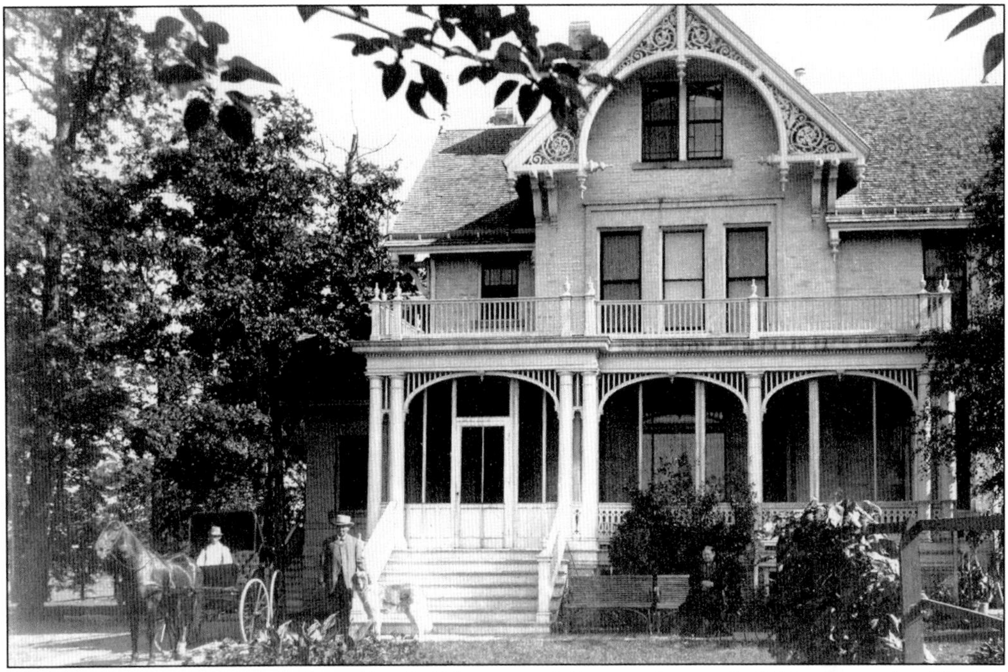

The Bues estate was located on South Fifty-second Street about a half-block north of Beloit Road. In 1885, Fred Bues, president of the Stark Dredge and Dock Company of Milwaukee, purchased 25 acres of farmland stretching from Beloit Road to National Avenue and from South Fiftieth to South Fifty-fourth Streets. Well-known landmarks on the estate were a windmill and a lily pond. In 1919, the land was sold to the Evangelical Lutheran Synod of Wisconsin for the construction of a seminary. This plan was never carried out. The property was purchased by Hillview Realty in 1924 and platted shortly thereafter.

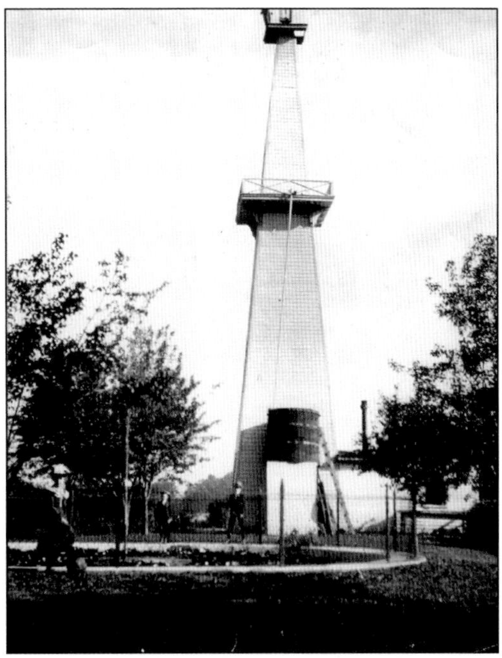

Shown here is the noted windmill of the Bues estate.

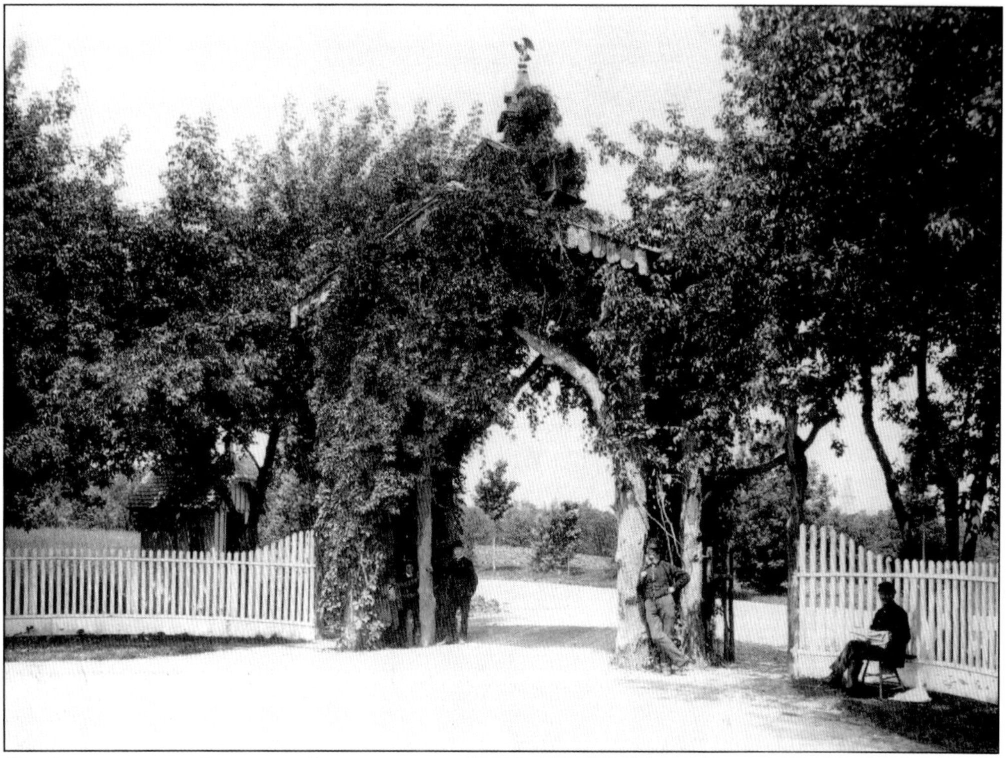

Shade trees grace the original entrance to the National Soldiers' Home on National Avenue, known today as the Clement J. Zablocki Veterans' Affairs Medical Center. Established as a home for displaced Civil War veterans, it still serves veterans today. On the grounds are the original Old Main building, Wadsworth Library, Ward Theater, chapel, Wood National Cemetery, and other structures.

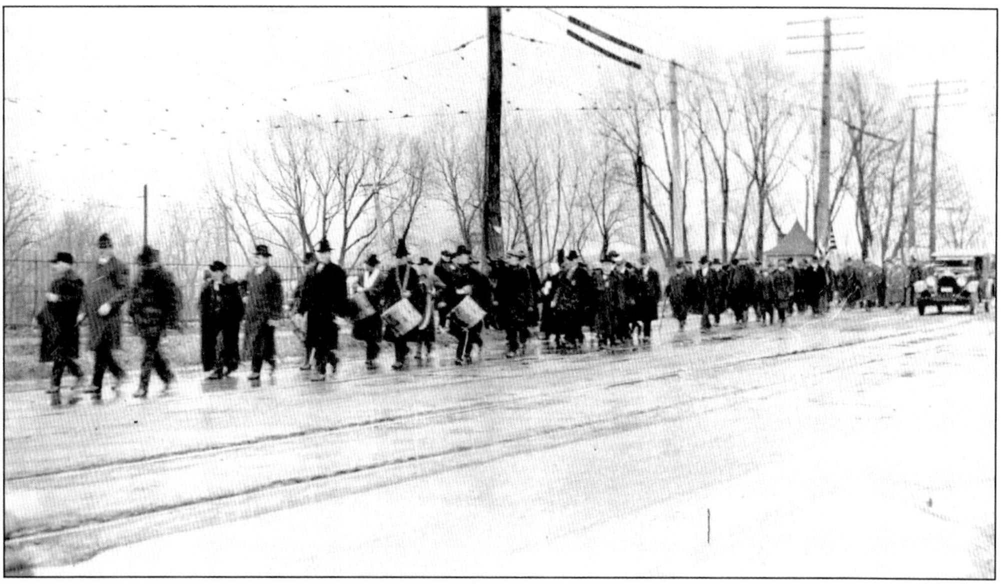

Veterans march along National Avenue at the dedication of the Soldiers' Home Tuberculosis Hospital about 1924.

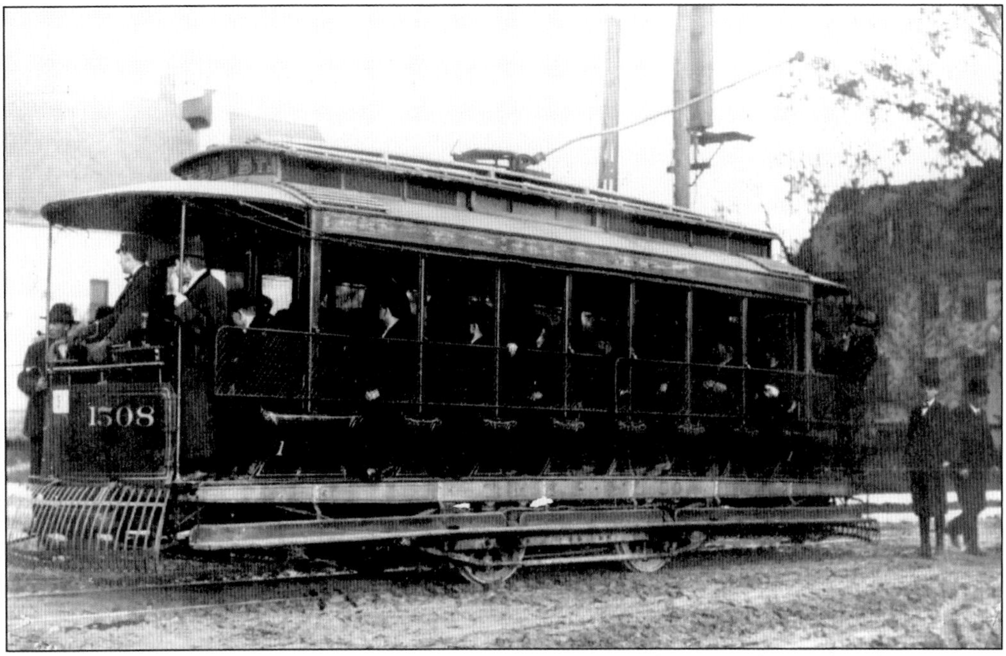

A Milwaukee streetcar travels on National Avenue around 1900. The Milwaukee County Transit Company's Route 18 still serves the Zablocki Medical Center, formerly the National Soldiers' Home.

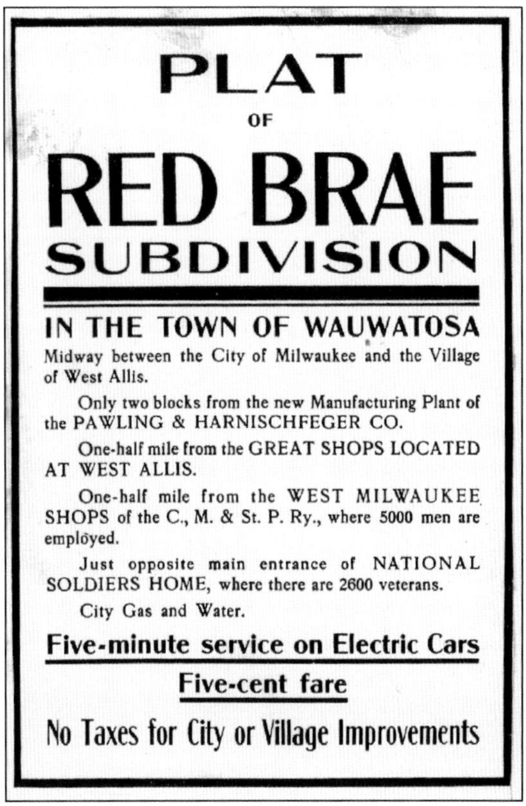

PLAT

OF

RED BRAE

SUBDIVISION

IN THE TOWN OF WAUWATOSA

Midway between the City of Milwaukee and the Village of West Allis.

Only two blocks from the new Manufacturing Plant of the PAWLING & HARNISCHFEGER CO.

One-half mile from the GREAT SHOPS LOCATED AT WEST ALLIS.

One-half mile from the WEST MILWAUKEE SHOPS of the C., M. & St. P. Ry., where 5000 men are employed.

Just opposite main entrance of NATIONAL SOLDIERS HOME, where there are 2600 veterans.

City Gas and Water.

Five-minute service on Electric Cars

Five-cent fare

No Taxes for City or Village Improvements

This advertisement promotes the Red Brae subdivision, originally part of the Peter McGeoch estate. Red Brae was sited in the town of Wauwatosa before West Milwaukee's incorporation.

LOTS
$1 DOWN ..
$1 A WEEK
NO INTEREST

BREW MANOR

LOTS
$1 DOWN ..
$1 A WEEK
NO INTEREST

THE NEW WEST MILWAUKEE HOME PLACE

THIS beautiful subdivision is situated on Beloit Road (one of the finest thoroughfares running south-west of the city) between 45th and 47th Avenues. It is south of National Avenue and north of Burnham Street and is therefore within a couple of blocks of either of these Car Lines — one fare downtown. This property lays high, overlooking the many large manufacturing plants in the great "South-West Factory District." There are already twenty thousand men employed within easy walking distance of this property, and twenty million dollars are invested in factories and shops. More large factories are to be built in this section in the near future. This means rapid growth, and rapid growth has always made real estate values rise. Soldiers Home, one of the most beautiful parks near Milwaukee, is only a few blocks away.

TERMS, $1 DOWN $1 A WEEK

No Interest At Any Time

LOW PRICES **$275 to $470** A FEW HIGHER

WARRANTY DEEDS 10% discount on $25 or more. Taxes paid for 2 years (except when deed is given) CERTIFIED ABSTRACTS FREE

COME OUT AT ONCE—COME OUT SUNDAY

Take the Burnham Street Car (marked West Allis.) These cars cross Grand Avenue at 3d Street; thence out Reed St., Greenfield Ave. and Burnham St. Be sure and get off at **47th Ave.,** walk one short block north to Beloit Road. YOU WILL SEE THE SIGN ON THE RIGHT

L. A. KINSEY & SON

Phone Grand 547

202 Empire Building
Corner GRAND AVENUE and WEST WATER ST.
MILWAUKEE, WIS.

A land agent's advertisement describes the new Brew Manor subdivision in glowing terms. A pickle factory was located on the original farm, owned by Richard Brew. Richard's son, George, was West Milwaukee's first president.

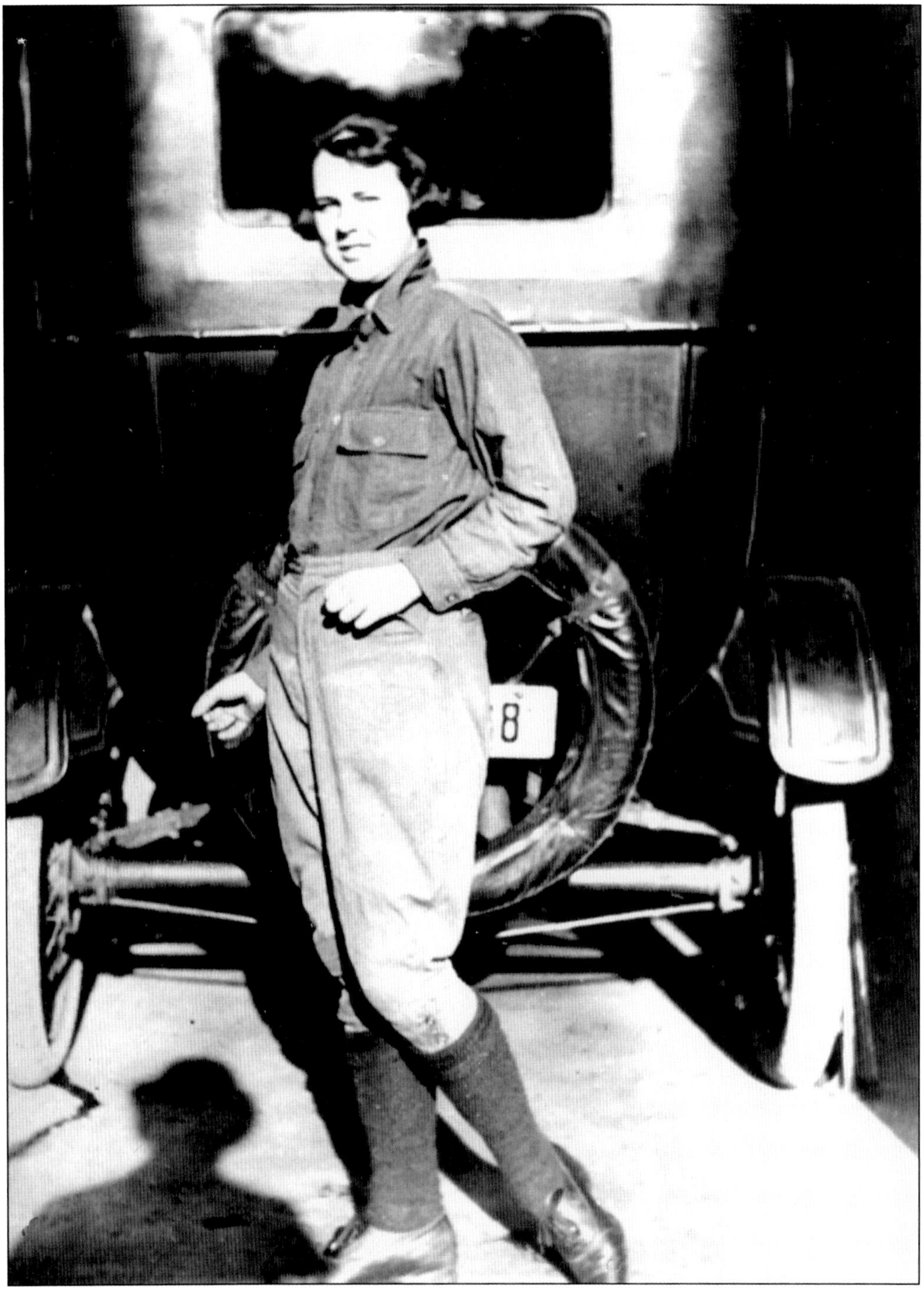

Ruth Whitcomb is described as a flapper in this 1923 scene. Notice the jack on the car behind her. Not much is known about Ruth, but perhaps "The Shadow" (lower left) knows.

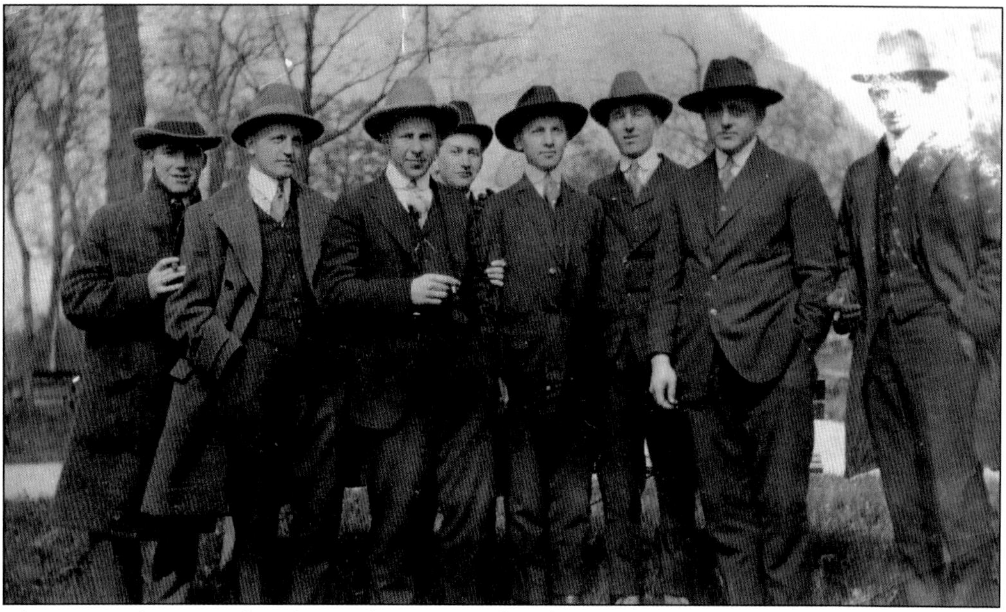

This group of men is referred to as the "West Milwaukee Gang." Pictured here, from left to right, are, Mike Cunningham, Tony Thekan, Charlie Schultz, Bruno Reinhold, John Schmidt, Paul Thekan, John Wagner, and Charles Thekan.

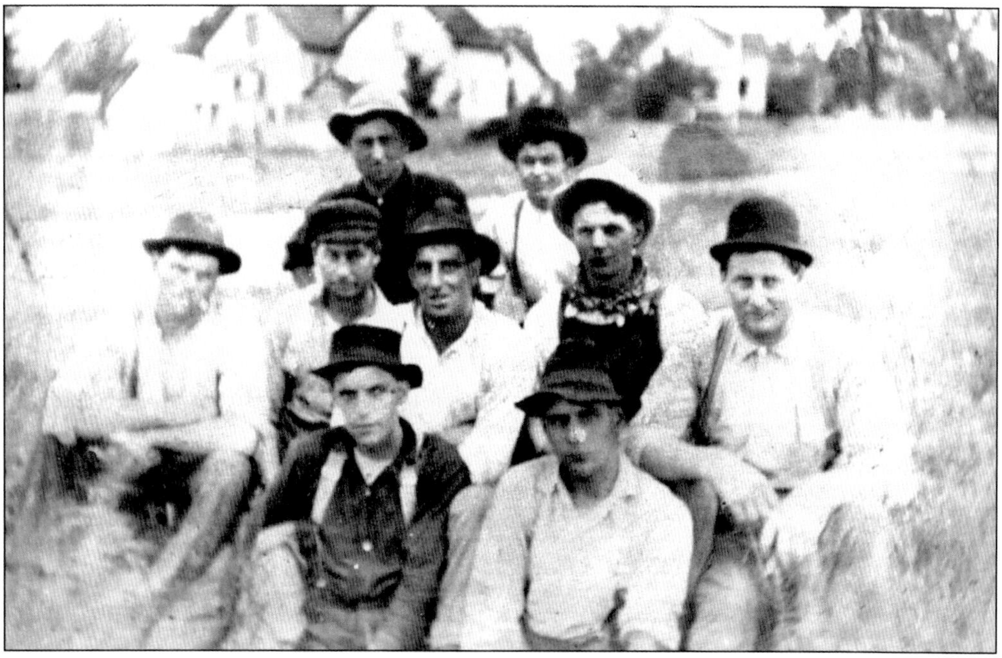

The "Ice House Group" may have been affiliated with the Ice House Tavern, originally a storage facility for block ice. Seen here, from left to right, are the following: (first row) Ziggy Emanuelson and Otto Zunker; (second row) Jocko Pipke, Oscar Emanuelson, Charles Baker, Fred Zunker, and Smith Emanuelson; (third row) two unidentified men.

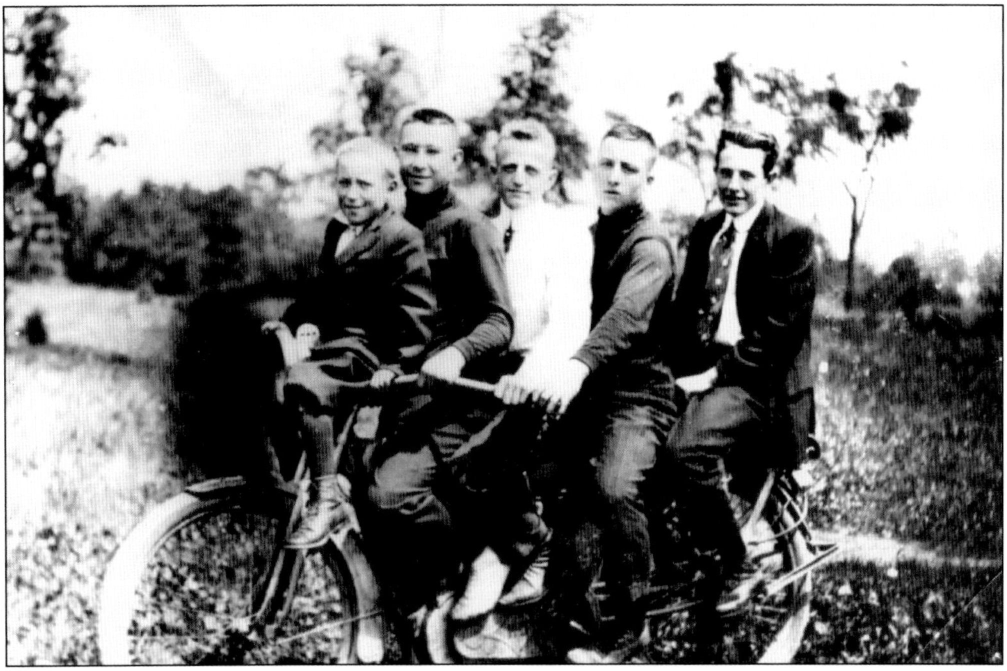

Five young men are dressed up for a motorcycle outing. Perched on the bike, from left to right, are John Druml, Louis Brenner, Tony Thekan, Max Druml, and Edward Klatt.

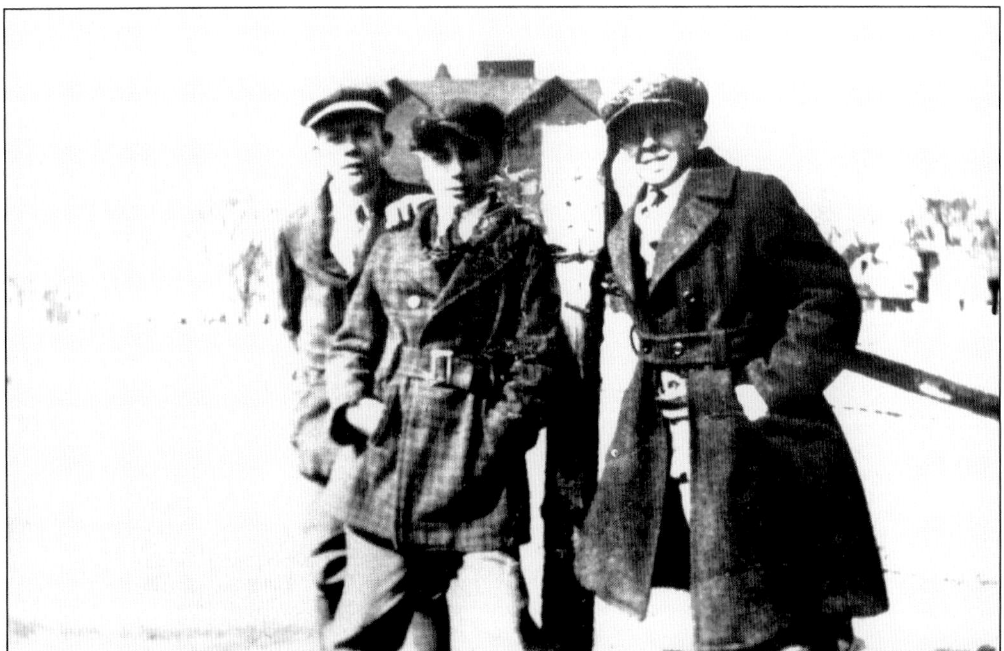

Buddies meet at the back of Pershing School in 1919. Clarence Anderson (left, a future druggist), Gordon Friauf (center), and Walter Funke (a future dentist and village historian) pose for the photograph.

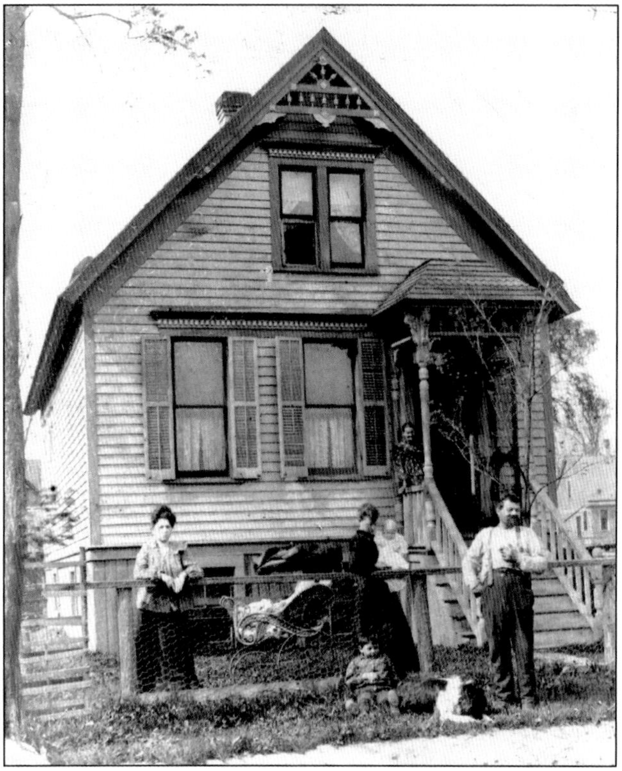

The Graf home, pictured in 1903, was located in the 4400 block of West Greenfield Avenue. Shown here, from left to right, are Frances Bunk, Gertrude Berghoefer (holding baby Al), Arnold Graf (sitting with dog Rover), and Mrs. Graf on porch. The man at right is not identified. Note the Victorian details: an ornate baby carriage, trim work at the peak of the house, and a wooden sidewalk.

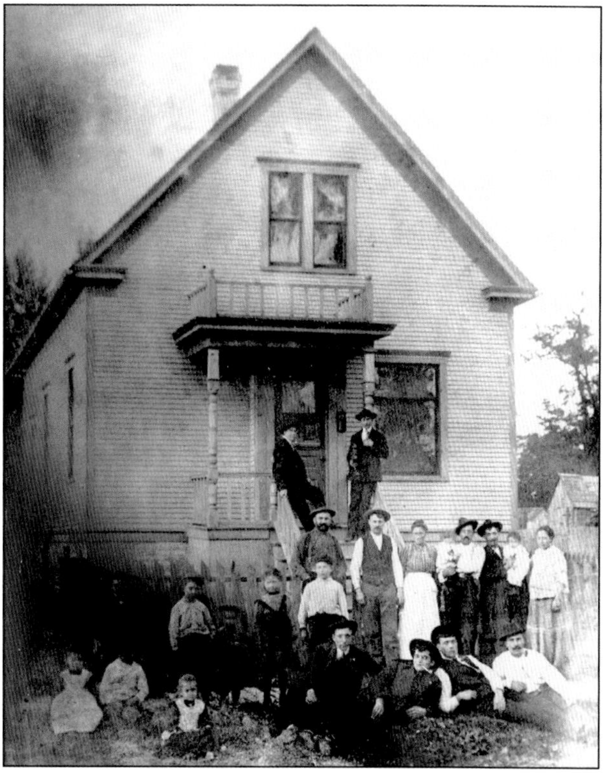

Joseph Lewein appears with family and friends at his home near South Forty-fifth and Scott Streets in 1905. Seen here are Vincent Lewein, Joseph Lewein, Agnes Lewein, Martin Tabushing (holding Mary Lewein), John Grafenauer (holding Kath. Lewein), Katy Lewein, Tim Ryan, Louis Brenner, George Lewein, Lena Brenner, Joe Brenner, Elizabeth Lewein, Jack Lewein, Mary Schnabl, Pete Mackey, Laurence Grafenauer, unidentified, and Val Mitsche. Above them, on the steps, are Vincent Brenner (left) and Rudy Schnabl.

The Michel home, at 4738 West Beloit Road, still stands today and has been recently renovated. Pictured left to right are its earlier residents Peter Michel, Roy Michel, Christina Stelloh (Ella's mother), Ella Michel, and Stella Michel.

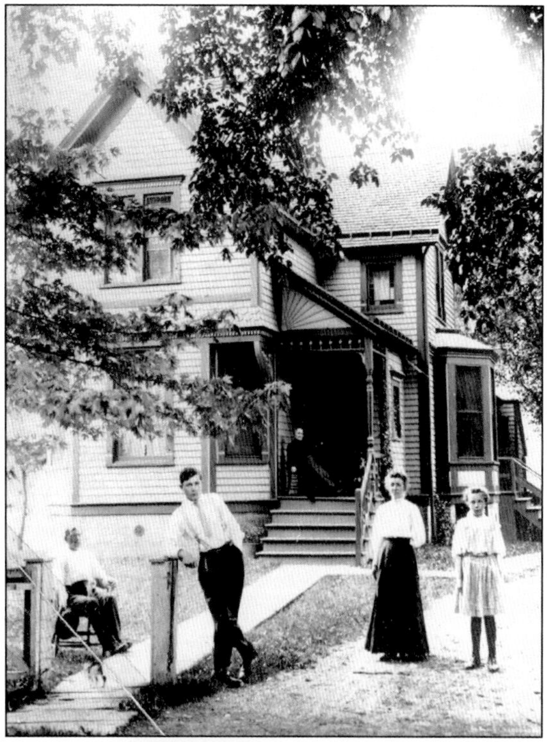

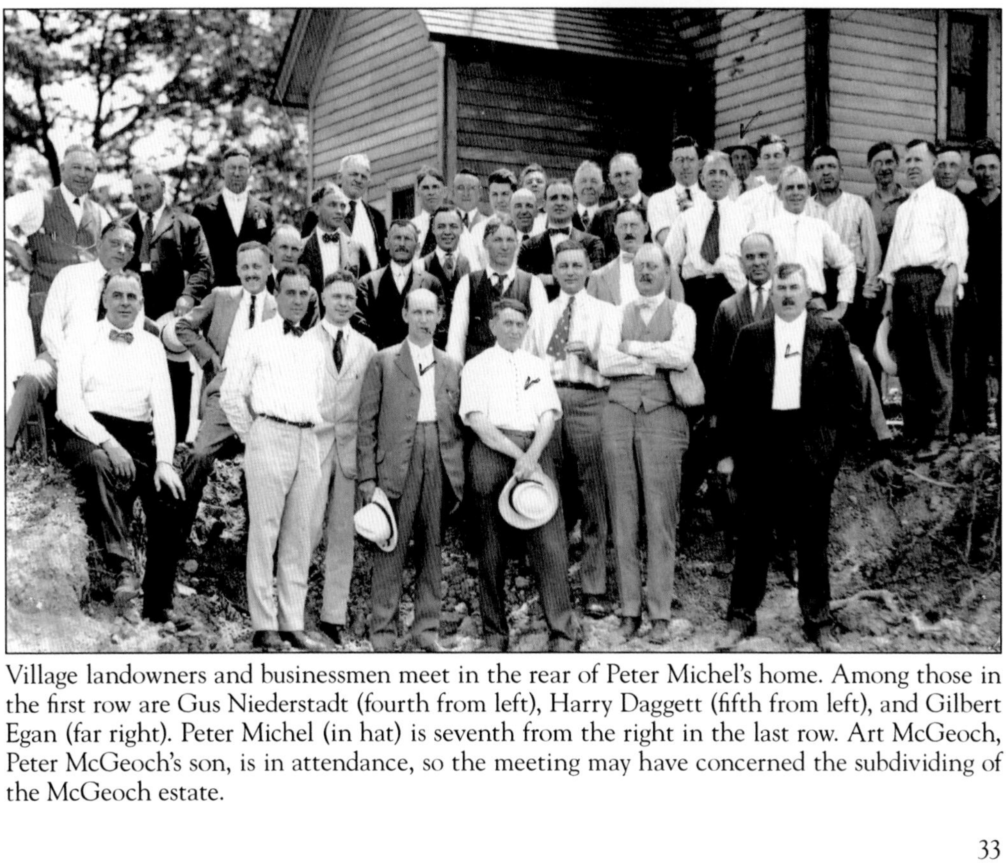

Village landowners and businessmen meet in the rear of Peter Michel's home. Among those in the first row are Gus Niederstadt (fourth from left), Harry Daggett (fifth from left), and Gilbert Egan (far right). Peter Michel (in hat) is seventh from the right in the last row. Art McGeoch, Peter McGeoch's son, is in attendance, so the meeting may have concerned the subdividing of the McGeoch estate.

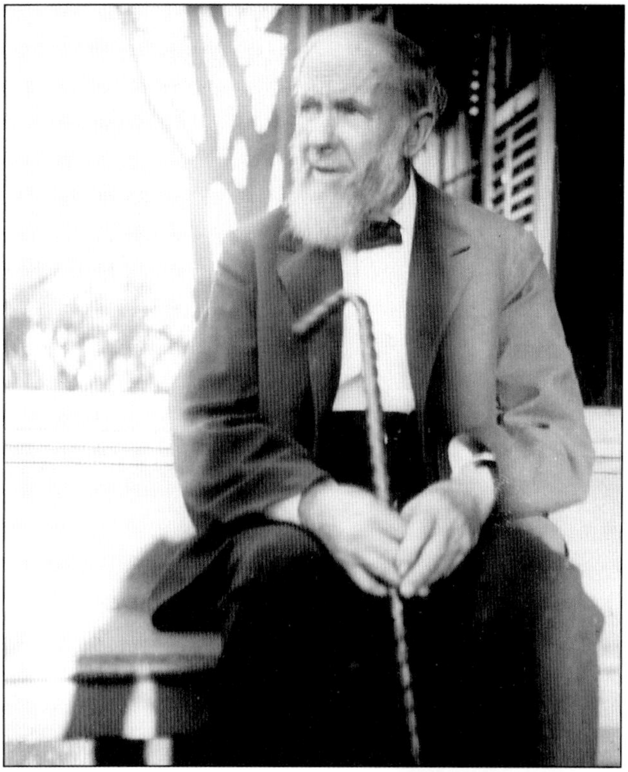

Andrew Dickson (left) and his wife, Marcia (below), were the owners of approximately 150 acres of farmland now occupied by the Rexnord Corporation. The Dickson home stood west of the present village hall, on the site of the Stana Apartments. Andrew died in 1900, and Marcia in 1932.

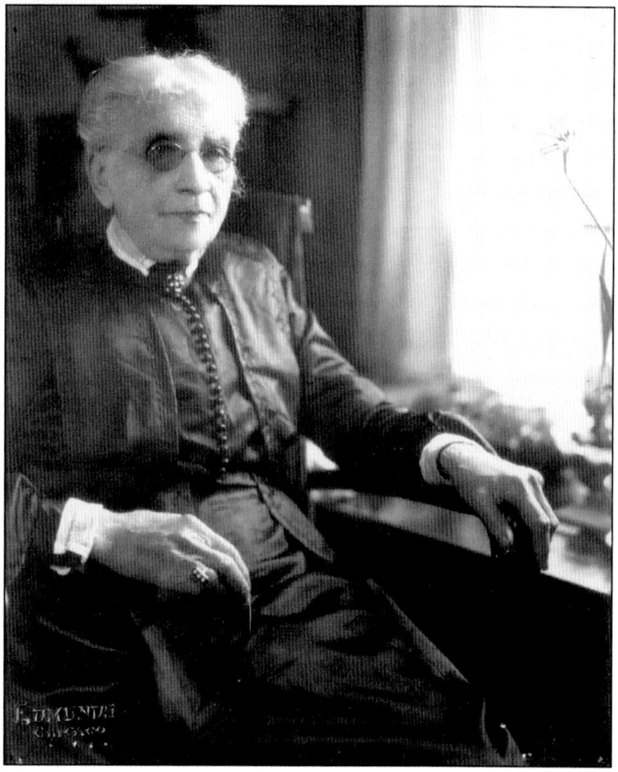

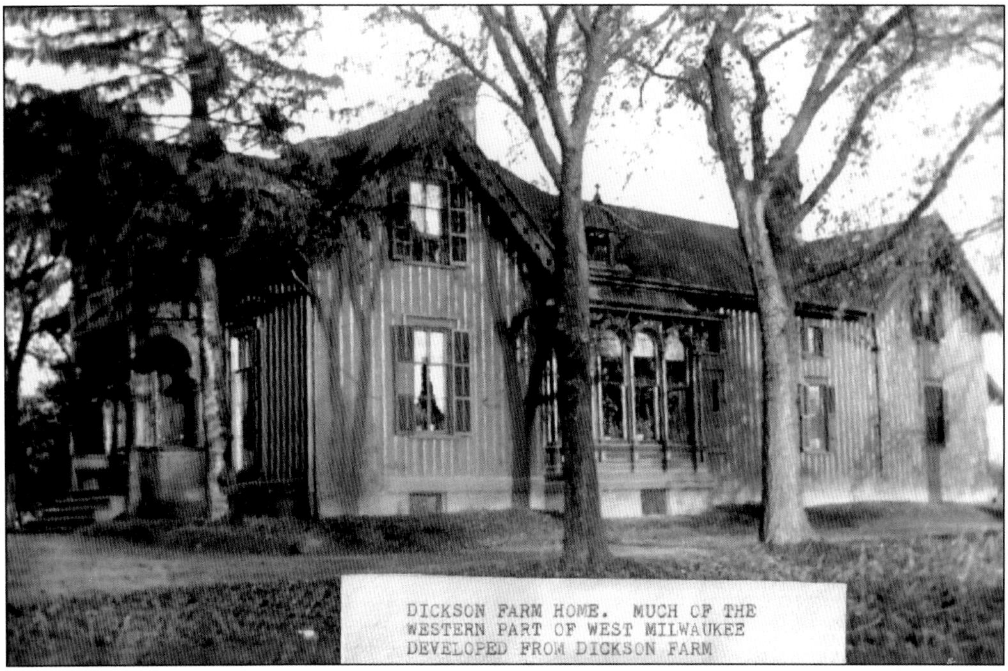

The 150-acre Dickson dairy farm covered much of the southwest portion of the village. Andrew and Marcia's son, Edgar, constructed a malleable iron foundry on the property, which later became the Chain Belt Company.

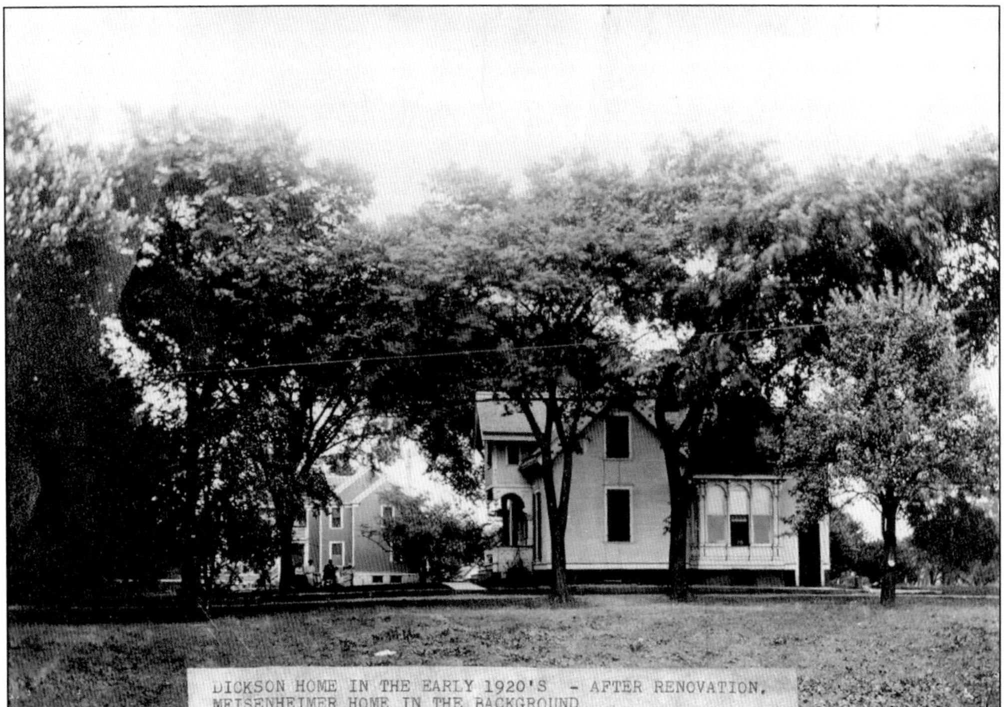

The Dickson home appears here in the early 1920s, following renovation. The southernmost portion of the house has been removed.

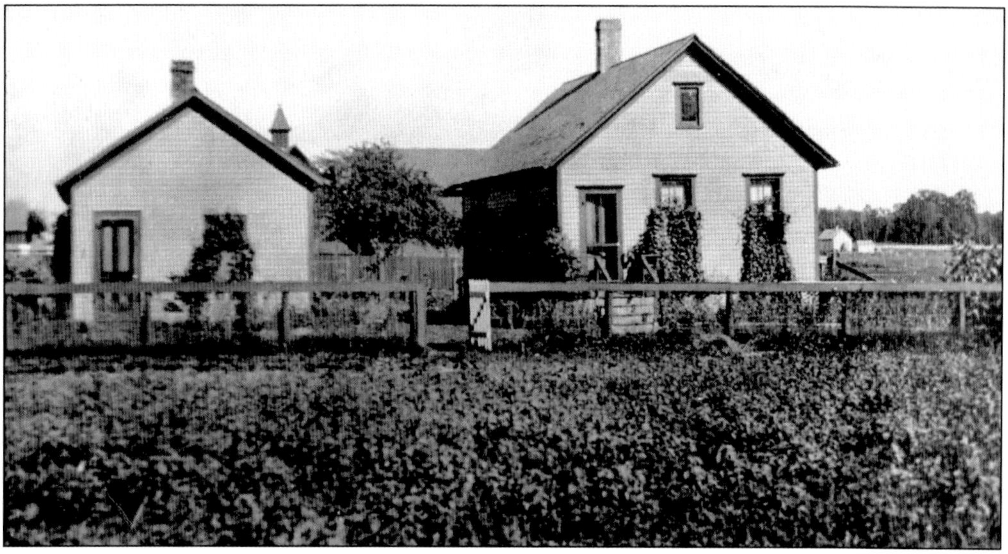

These houses are located on Dickson Lane, south of Beloit Road and Greenfield Avenue. A horse barn can be seen in the background. The house on the right belonged to Edward Richards, a Civil War veteran who regularly fired a cannon east of the Soldiers' Home main building at sunrise and sunset.

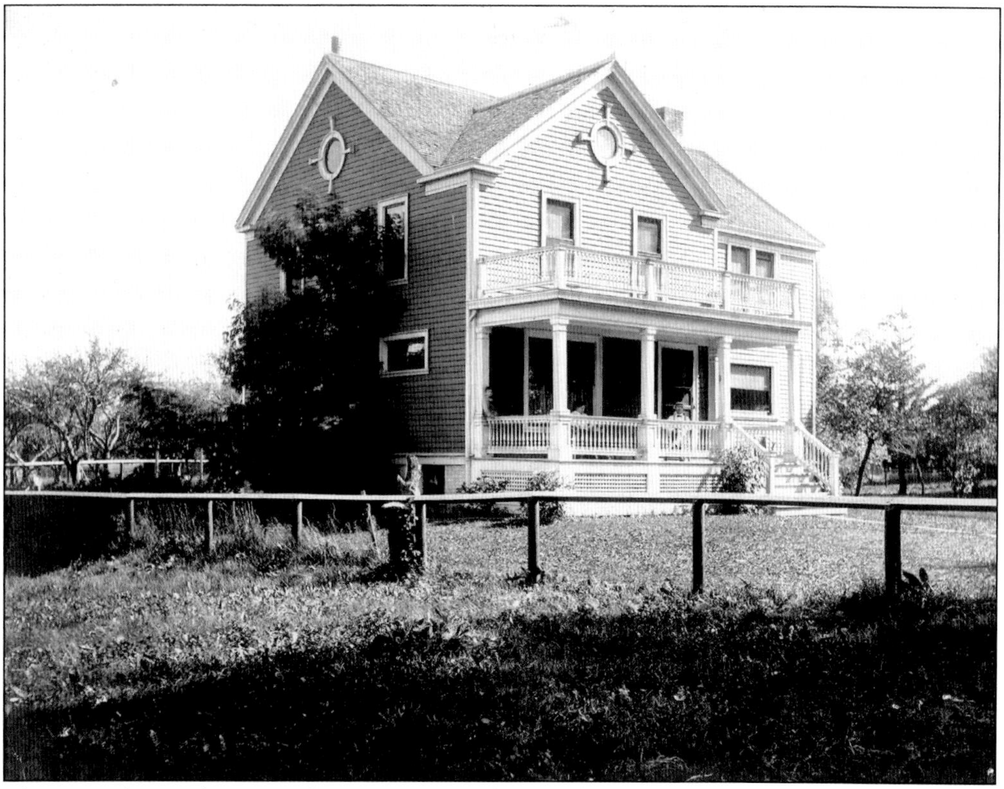

The Meisenheimer home stands at 4739 West Beloit Road, east of the Dickson farmhouse. Built for Andrew Dickson's son Edgar, the house was later occupied by E. J. Meisenheimer, the second village president, and his aviator son Gilles. The house remains today and is rented out as apartments.

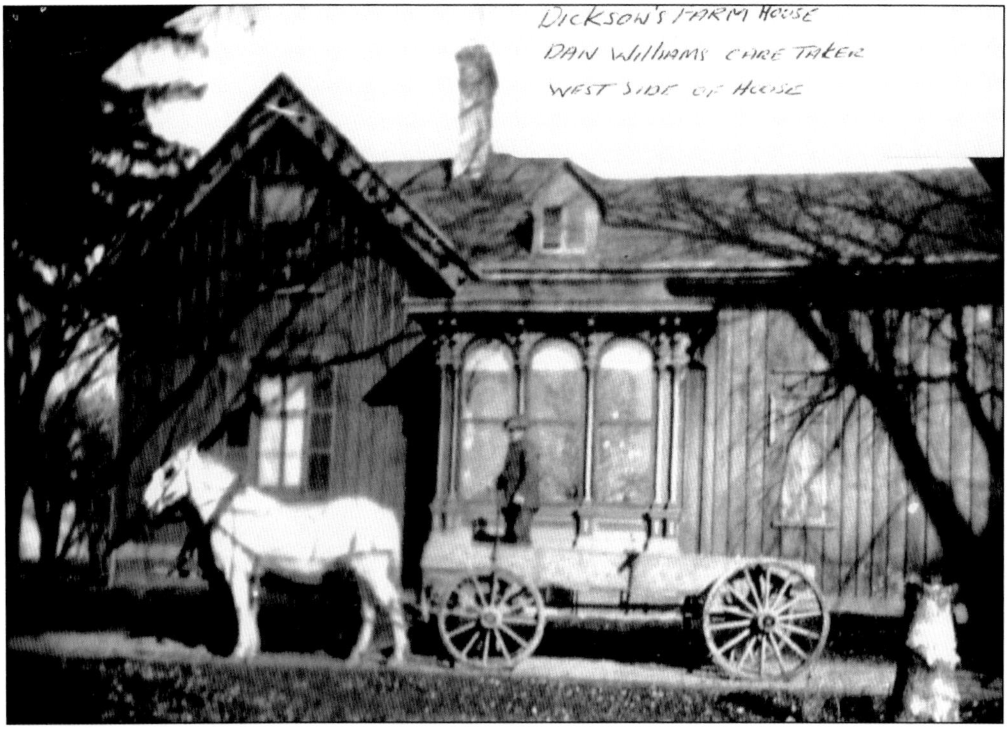

Dan Williams, the manager of the Dickson farm, is shown with a horse and wagon on the west side of the house. He later became a Chain Belt employee.

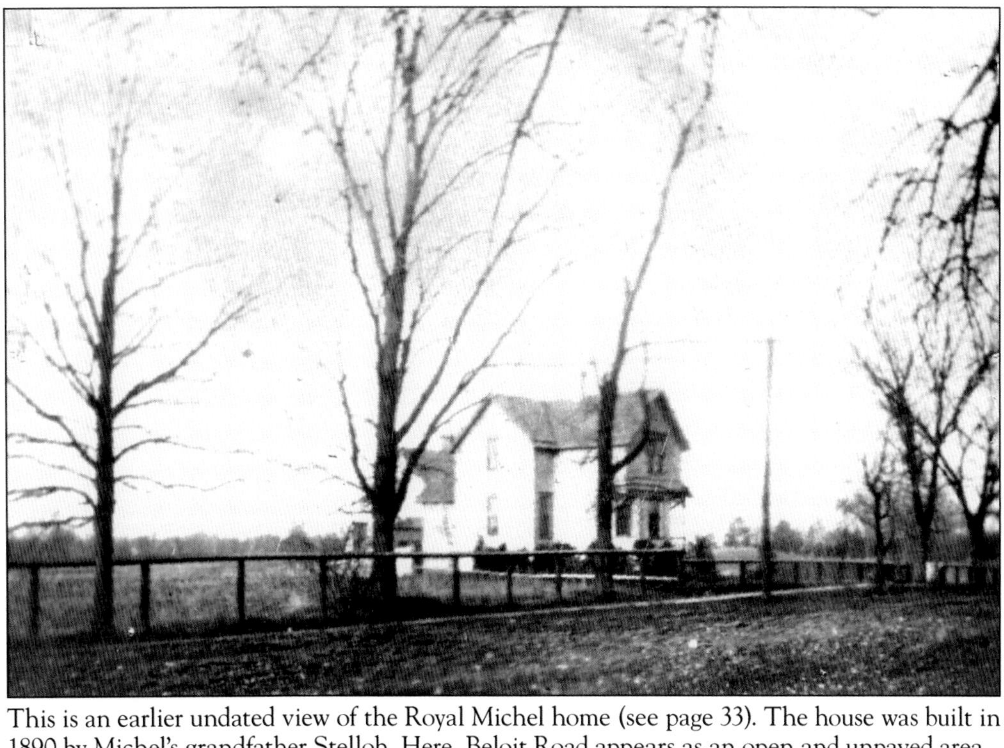

This is an earlier undated view of the Royal Michel home (see page 33). The house was built in 1890 by Michel's grandfather Stelloh. Here, Beloit Road appears as an open and unpaved area.

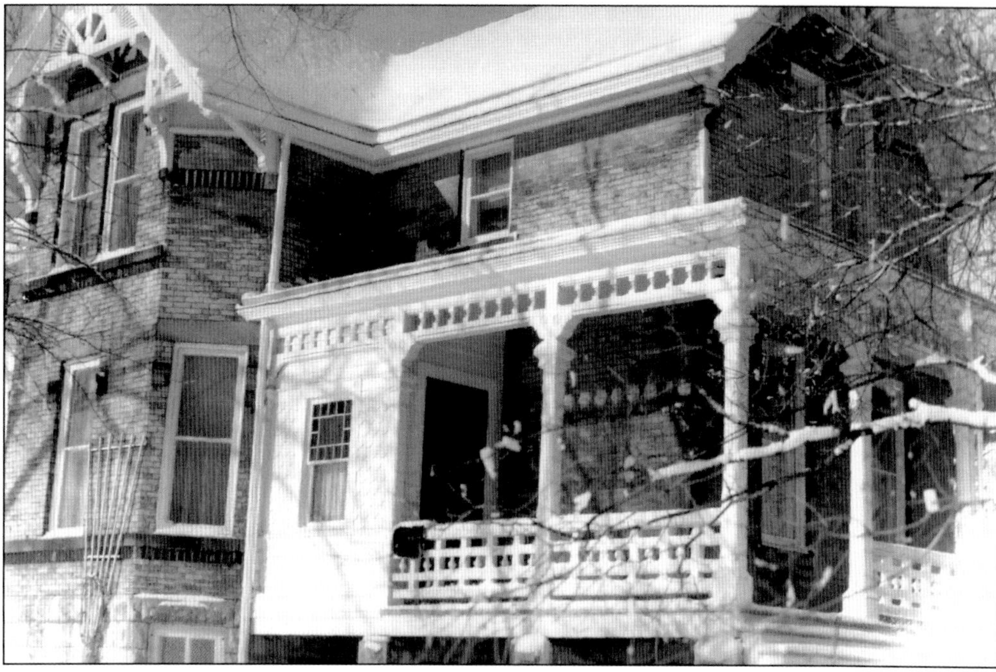

The Charles Gruppe home, at 5513 West National Avenue, was built in 1885 and featured a crystal chandelier. The house was razed in the 1960s, and the site is now part of St. John's Lutheran Church.

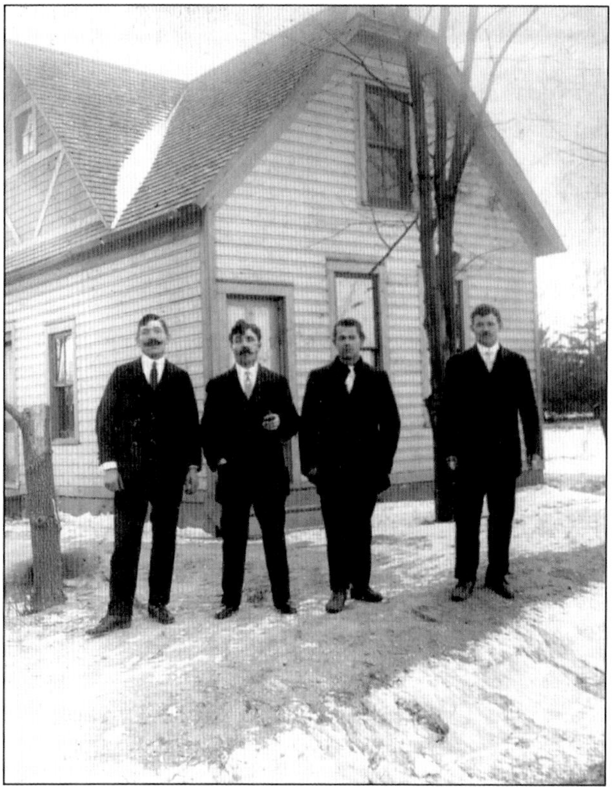

Four dashing gentlemen stand outside the David and Margaret McKinzie home, east of the Gruppe estate. The house burned in the late 1910s.

Dr. Rudolph Roethke, a prominent Milwaukee obstetrician, served the village from 1912 to 1917. He was born in 1884 in Mayville, Wisconsin, and spent most of his early life in nearby Chilton. Roethke interned in New York's Lying In Hospital and married a Pershing School teacher, Margaret Steinhagen, in 1918.

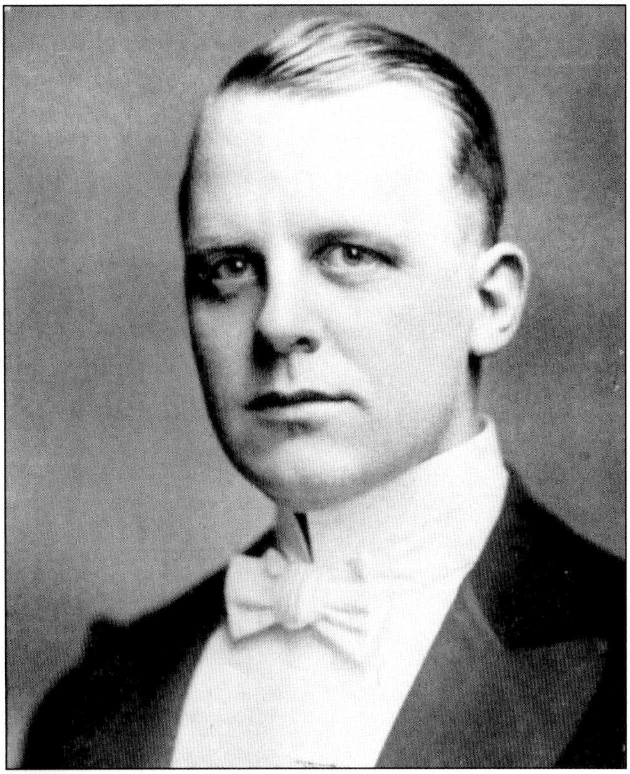

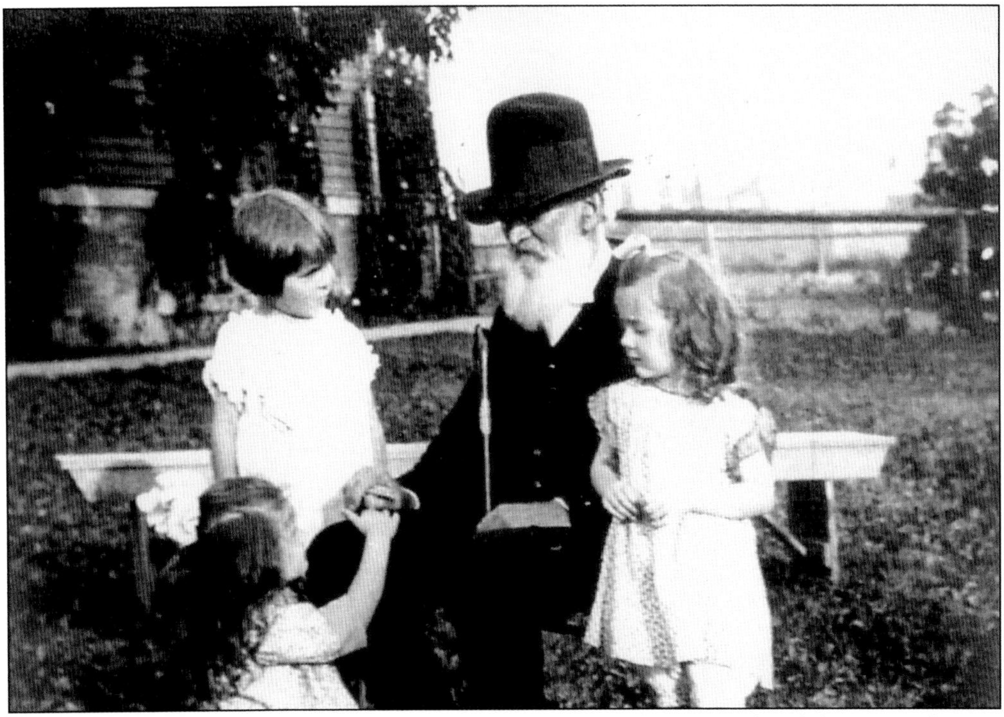

John Knurr's grandfather Bieres visits with three girls on the west side of the Meisenheimer home around 1924.

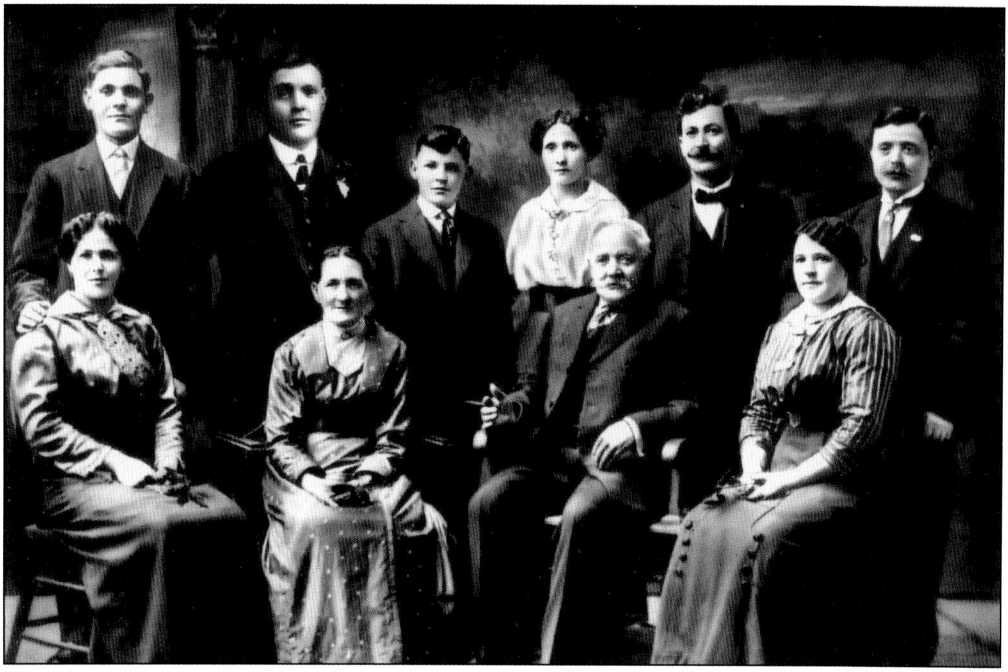

The Grafenauer family gathers for a portrait. Pictured here, from left to right, are the following: (first row) Liz, Grandma Gertrude, Grandpa Mike, and Mary; (second row) Lawrence, Frank, Matthew, Toni, John, and Mike.

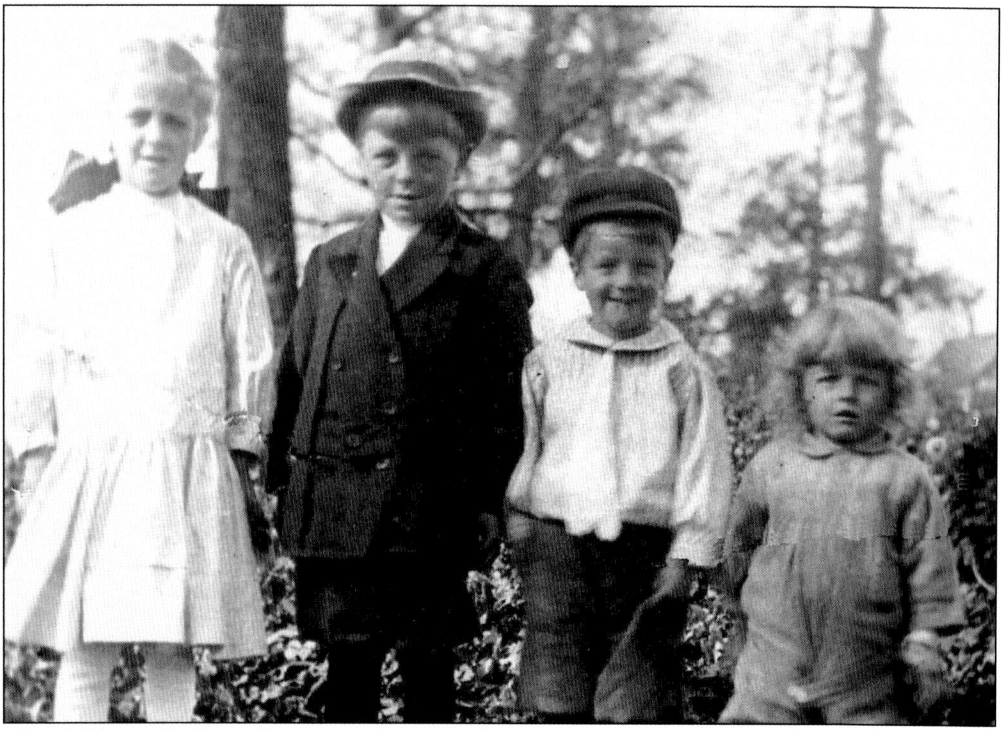

The children of Mike and Mary Grafenauer pose at 4458 West Beloit Road (now Fiftieth Street). Seen from left to right are Mary, Michael Jr., Lawrence, and baby Andrew.

Two

Government and Politics

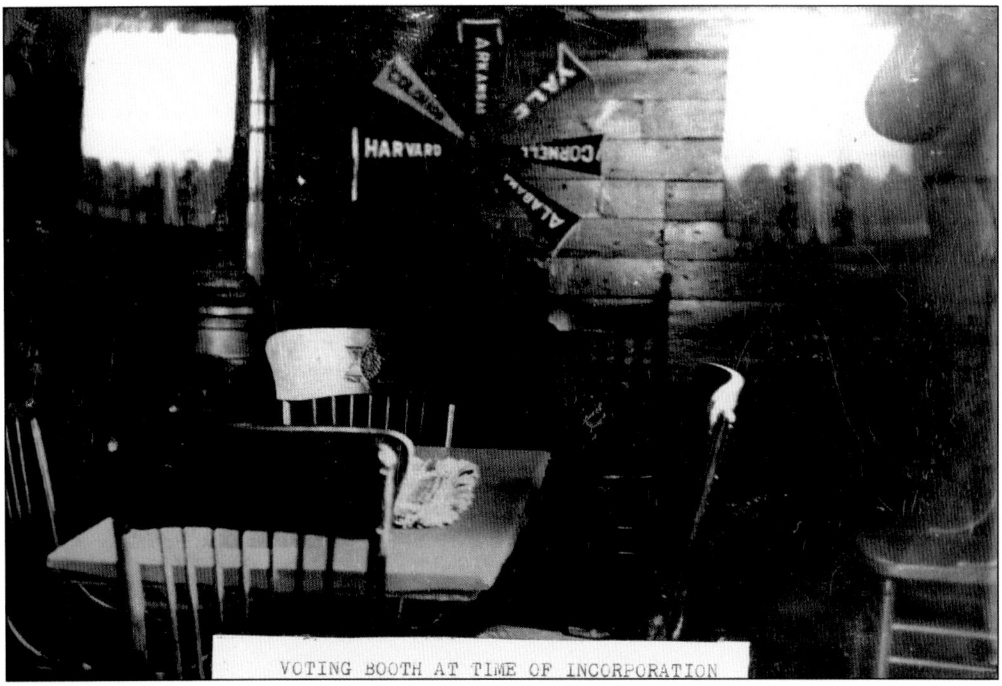

In 1906, at the time of incorporation, the voting booth was located in a barn behind what would now be 4435 West National Avenue. The vote was 119 in favor, 69 opposed, and 1 vote invalid. Thus, West Milwaukee became a village at 4:04 p.m. on April 4, 1906. A census showed 909 residents, 146 buildings, and 20 more buildings under construction. These buildings were assessed at $486,000. Personal property was valued at $59,110 and included more than 100 head of cattle, 57 horses, and 45 wagons and carriages.

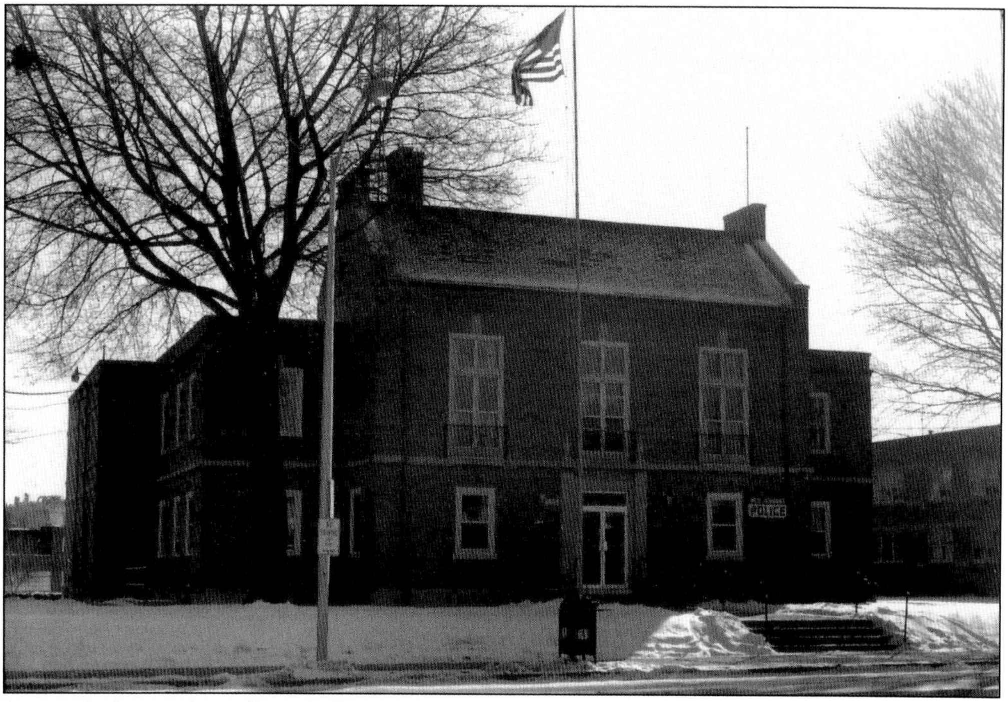

Pictured above, the village hall was brand new in 1928. Previously, administrative offices, including the police department, had been at several locales—from 1906 to 1913, in the National Home School building at Forty-sixth and Beloit Road; from 1913 to 1918, at 4409 West National Avenue; and from 1918 to 1928, at 4517 West National Avenue. The hall was renovated from 1998 to 1999 at a cost of approximately $1 million.

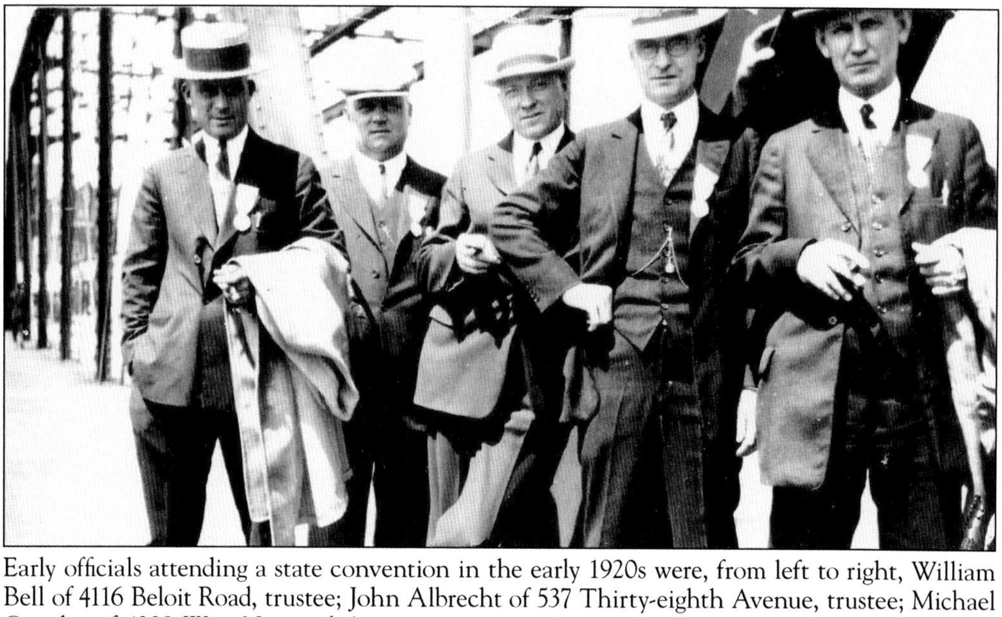

Early officials attending a state convention in the early 1920s were, from left to right, William Bell of 4116 Beloit Road, trustee; John Albrecht of 537 Thirty-eighth Avenue, trustee; Michael Crowley of 4209 West National Avenue, treasurer; George Garity of 481 Forty-third Avenue, trustee; and Gustave Niederstadt of 4117 Beloit Road, trustee.

An die Stimmgeber von West Milwaukee:

Wir, die Kandidaten, welche im öffentlichen Kaukus am 24. März 1916, in der Schulhalle für die verschiedenen Aemter nominirt wurden, für welche in der kommenden Wahl, welche in der Village Hall am 4. April 1916, gestimmt wird, ersuchen Sie achtungsvoll um Ihre Unterstützug.

Wir versprechen eine reine, ehrliche und sparsame Administration, jeden Bürger in der Village von West Milwaukee gerechte Behandlung und frei von Druck seitens irgend eines Einzelnen. Mache ein Kreuz (X) hinter jeden Namen, welche auf der einliegende Karte ist.

This German voting notice suggests that many early settlers may have understood German better than English. Translated, it states the following: "To the voters of West Milwaukee: We, the candidates nominated in public affairs in the school on March 24, 1916, for different positions for the coming election in the Village Hall on April 4, 1916, beg you faithfully for your support.

"We promise a pure, honest, and economizing administration, fair treatment of each citizen in the Village of West Milwaukee free of pressure of anybody. Make a cross (X) behind each name on the card inside."

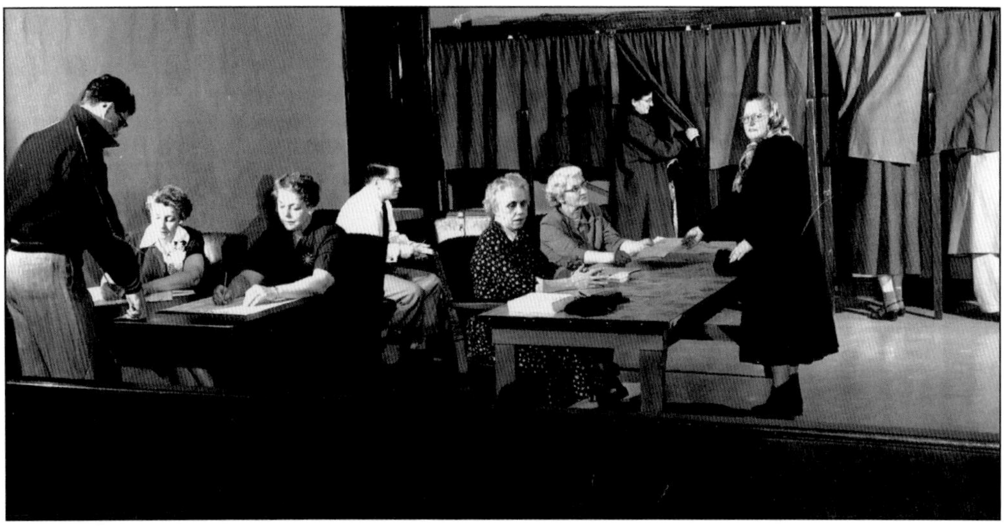

In this 1950s voting scene, Mrs. Berse is dressed very typically of the times, wearing a "babushka" and overshoes. Dresses with jewelry are part of the poll workers' attire, along with footwear of wedgies and socks. The cloth curtains assure privacy. Voting took place for Precinct 1 at the southwest corner of Forty-fourth and Greenfield Streets. Precinct 2 went to the village hall, and Precinct 3 to West Milwaukee High School. Presently, all voting occurs at the Community Centre.

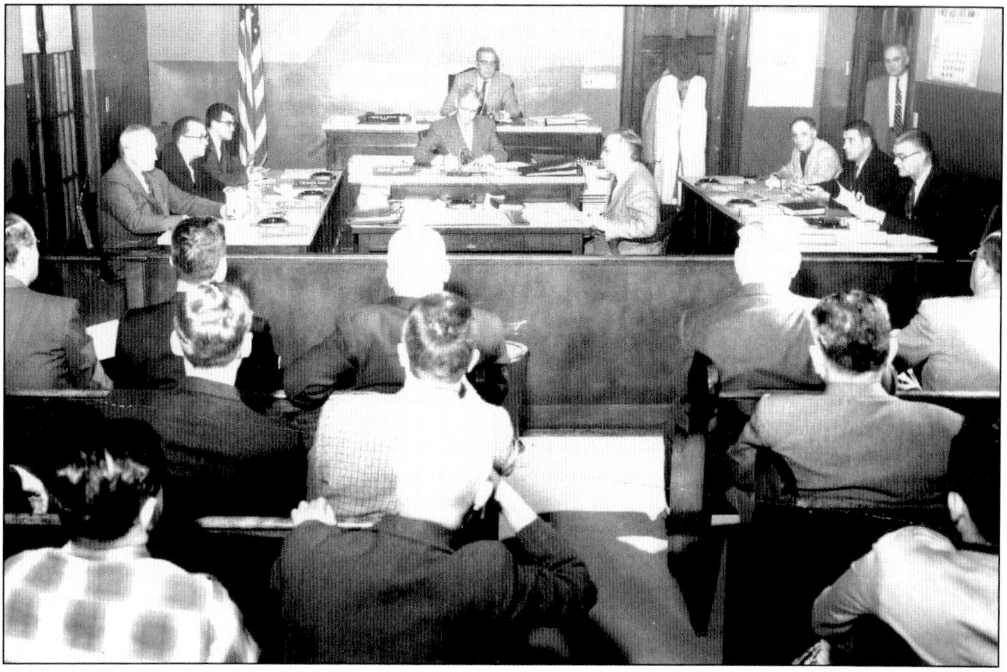

In this 1956 village board photograph, these men are identified, from left to right, as Sidney Tilley (trustee), John Hayduk (trustee), Clifford James (trustee), Herman Dieringer (village clerk), Charles Becker (president), Allen J. Busby (village attorney), Thomas Bell (trustee), Andrew Puschnig (trustee), Roy Bensene (trustee), and an unidentified man standing at the right. Note the large number of citizens in attendance.

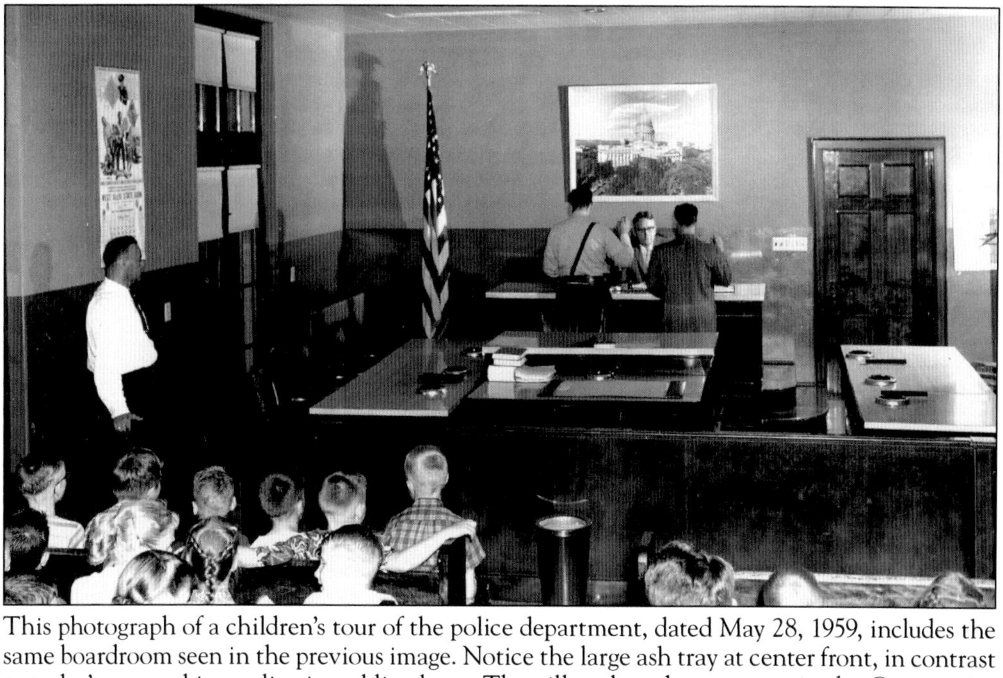

This photograph of a children's tour of the police department, dated May 28, 1959, includes the same boardroom seen in the previous image. Notice the large ash tray at center front, in contrast to today's no-smoking policy in public places. The village board now meets in the Community Centre, and the former boardroom has become the clerk's office.

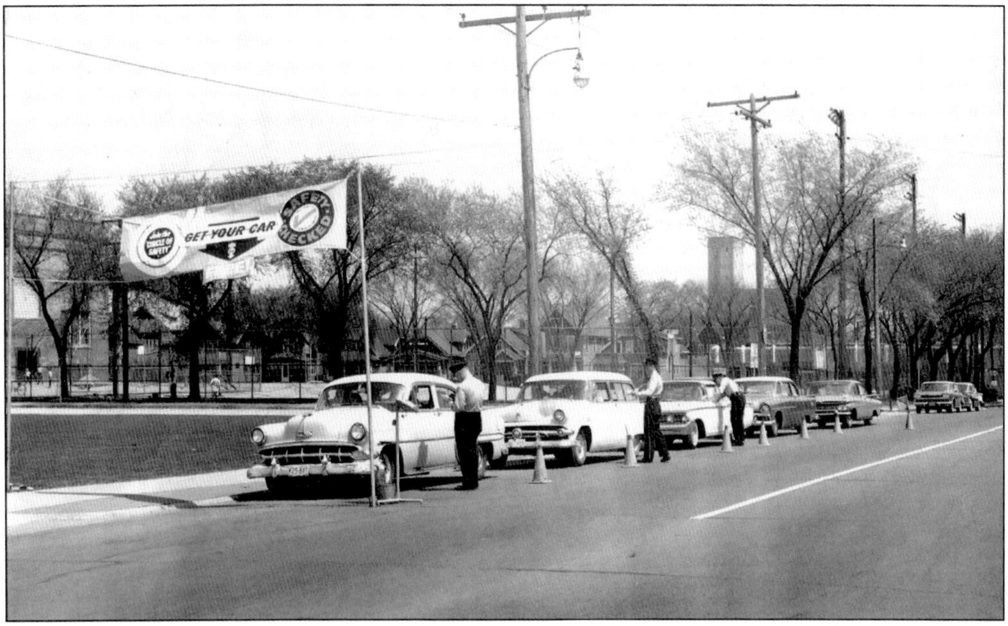

This car safety check at 4800 West Greenfield Avenue was conducted during the month of May in the early 1960s. Headlights, taillights, and horns were checked. Citations required a return to show that car lights and horns operated properly. The old Pershing School can be seen in the background.

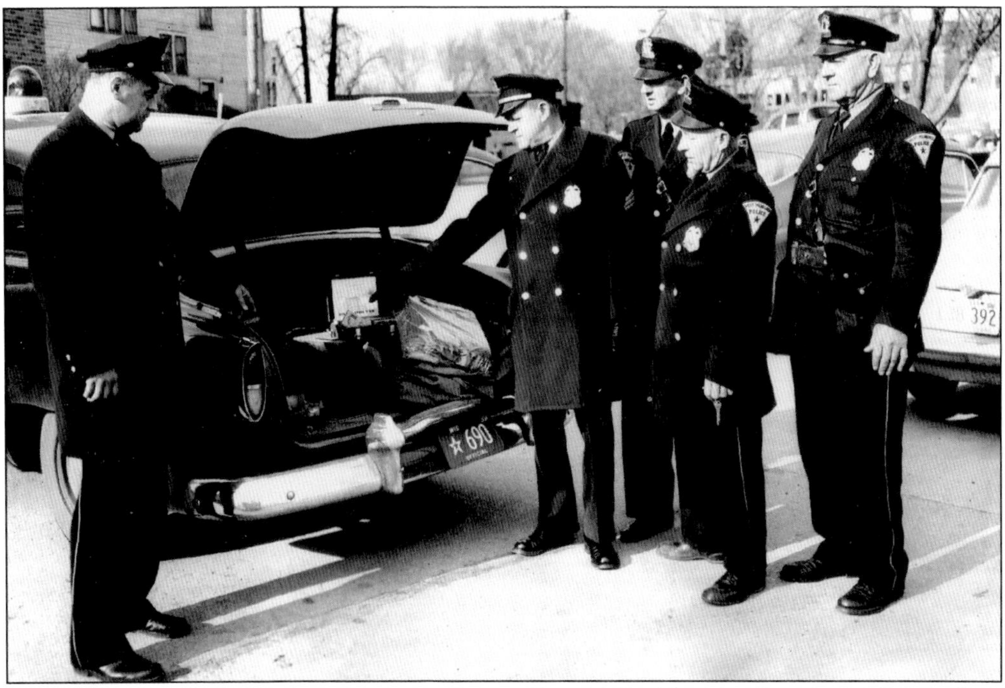

West Milwaukee police inspect equipment kept in the trunk of the patrol car in 1956. Seen from left to right are Jack Kuglitsch, Erv Raeglin, Tony Mersdorf, Art Uebelacker, and John Bensene. The site is the parking lot behind the village hall. The old Pershing School is again visible in the background.

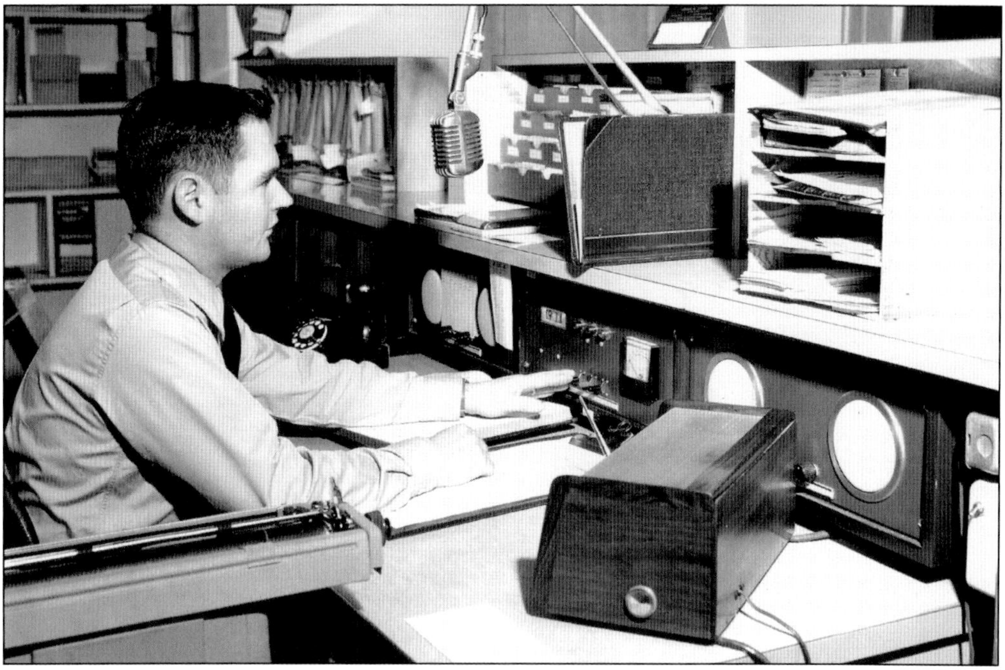

Direct communication is at the fingertips of dispatcher Charles Springer in this police department photograph, dated January 17, 1960. Calls were possible not only from the station to mobile units but also to other police agencies via the state radio and teletypes.

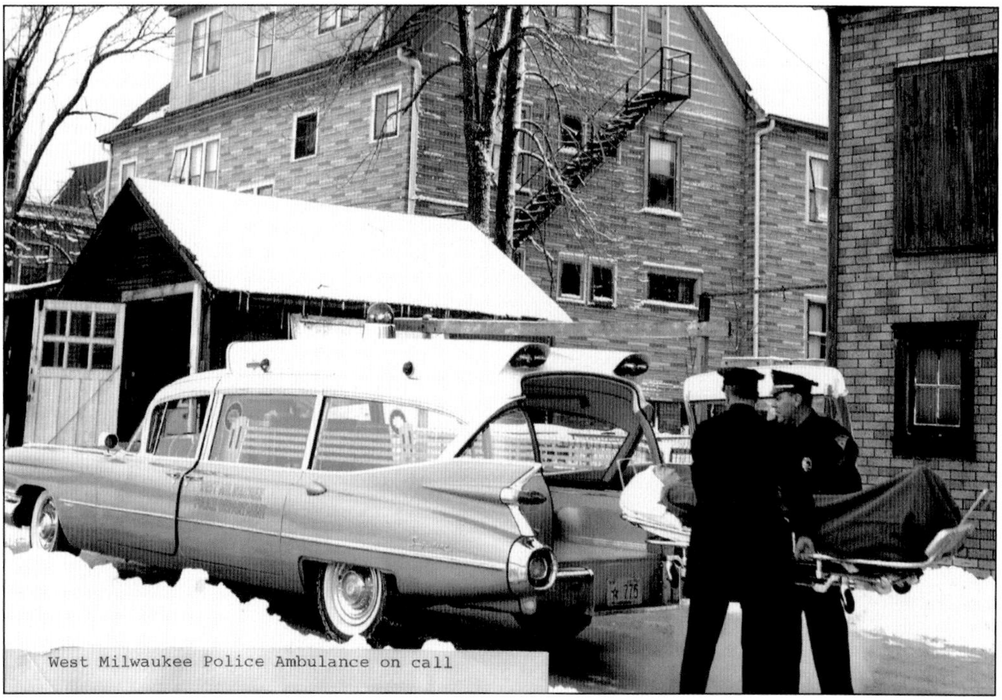

This photograph, taken in the alley behind the police station and also dated January 17, 1960, shows off the new Cadillac police ambulance. Officer Henry Peters faces the front. Extra officers were hired to man the ambulance.

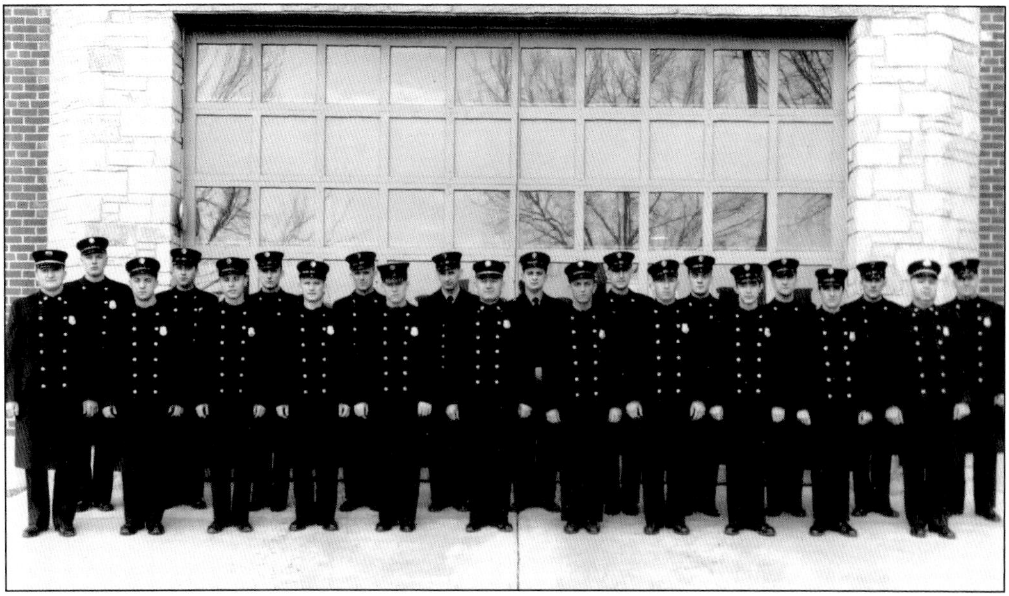

When the West Milwaukee Fire Department began in 1952, there were eight firefighters, with John Pavlik serving as chief (11th from the left). Some 400 young men were screened in three exams. From these, 14 more were added to the department and enrolled in the Milwaukee Firefighters School. The original eight worked for the Milwaukee Fire Companies for one month before the January 1 start of the department.

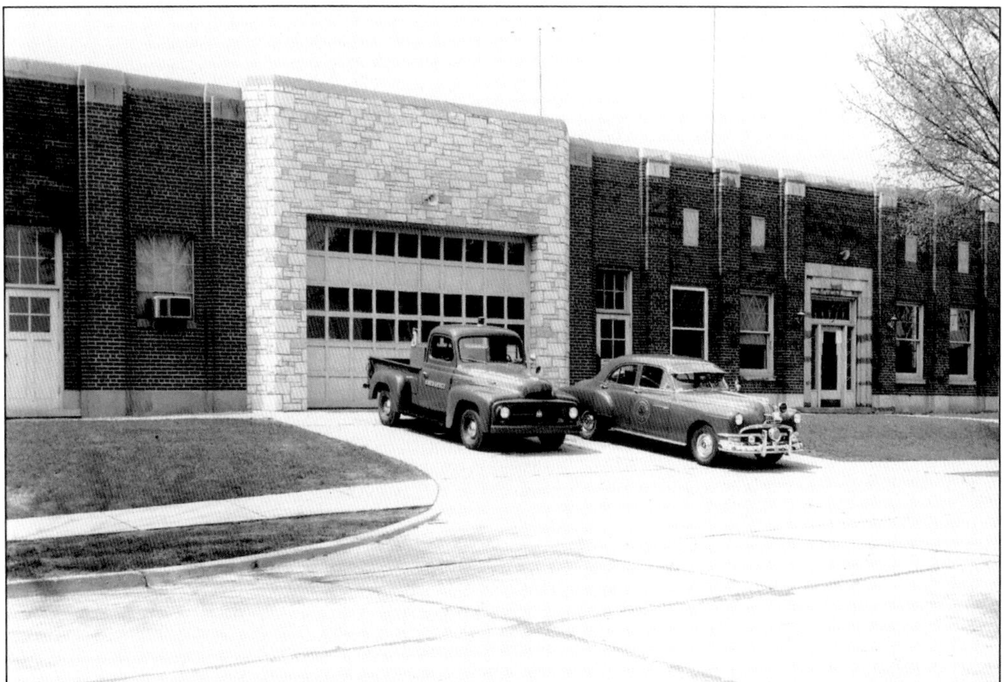

The West Milwaukee Department of Public Works, at 1225 South Forty-third Street, is seen with a $7,000 addition, $3,500 of which was paid for by the federal government as part of a WPA project. The building has since been demolished.

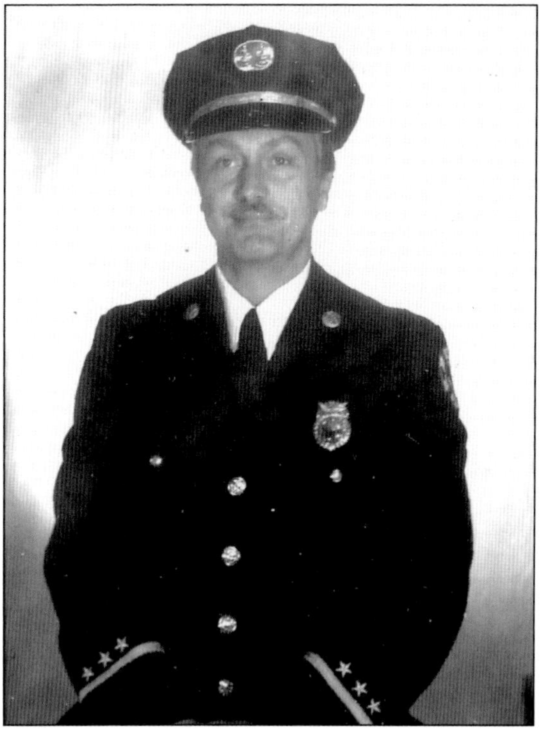

George Heuer, a 1957 graduate of West Milwaukee High School, served as the village's last fire chief, succeeding Clarence Quant in 1984. When Richard Plant retired in September 1989, a new position of public safety chief was created. Heuer served in that position when the very difficult decision was made to drop the fire department and contract out services. He also became acting village administrator when Fred Patrie resigned.

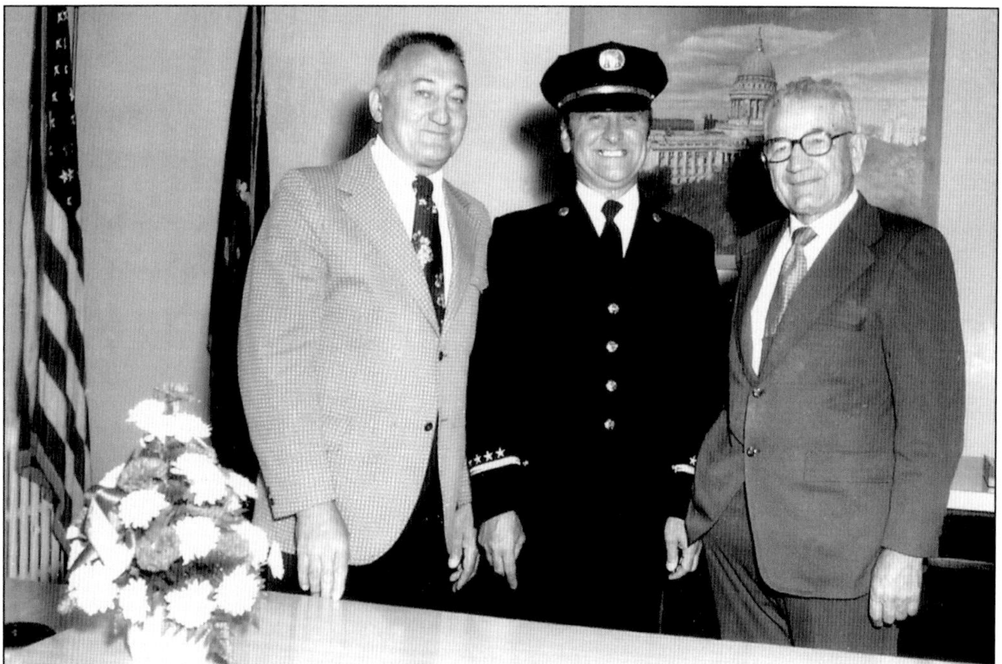

West Milwaukee's other three fire chiefs were Harry Rydlewicz (1966–1975), left; Clarence Quant (1975–1984), center; and John Pavlik (1951–1966). In 1957, West Milwaukee was awarded first place in its population class for fire prevention.

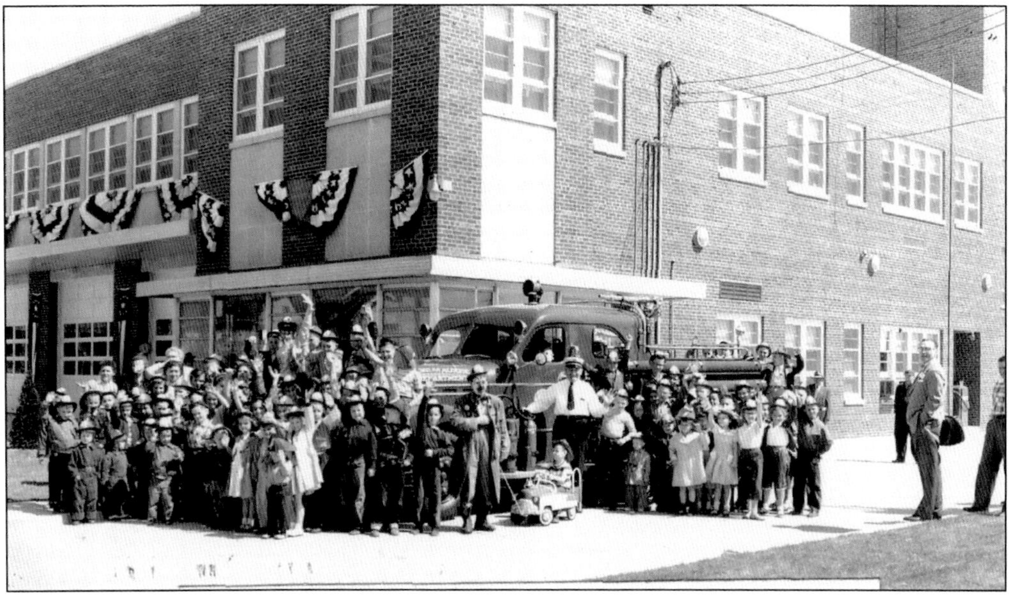

West Milwaukee's fire house dedication, shown above, occurred on May 20, 1956. The party included a clown, fire hats for all the kids, decorative bunting on the new building, and fun for Chief Pavlik (center). The fire house is located at 4515 West Burnham Street and is presently occupied by the Milwaukee Fire Department, which has provided service to West Milwaukee since 1991. The photograph below reveals a well-attended demonstration of a new aerial ladder truck.

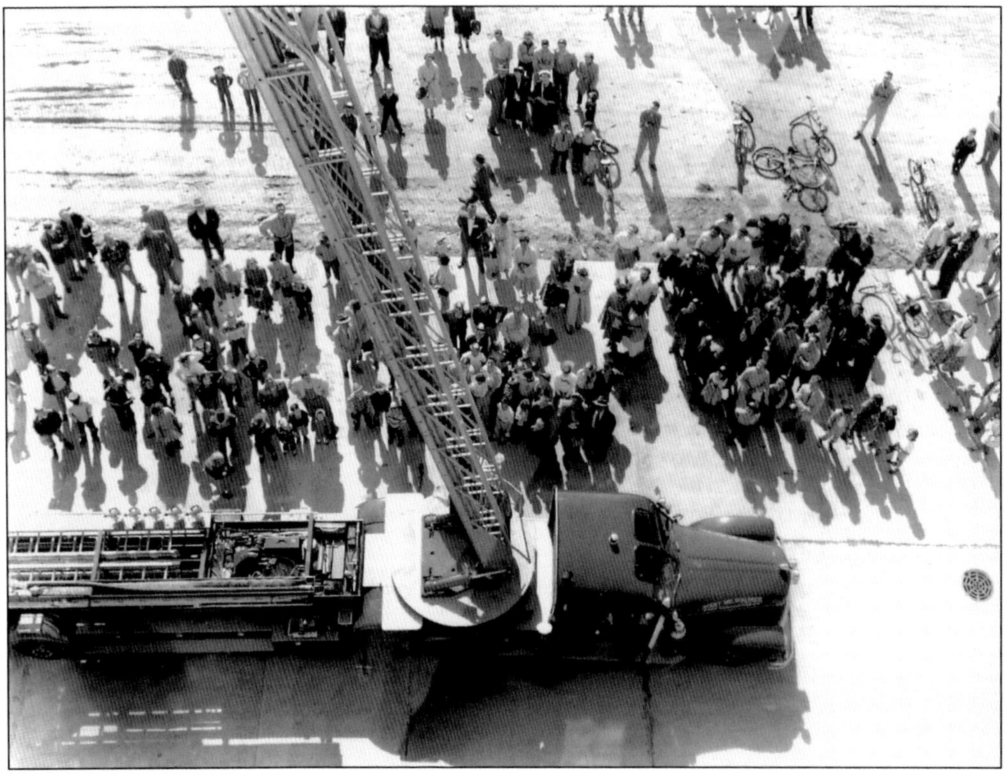

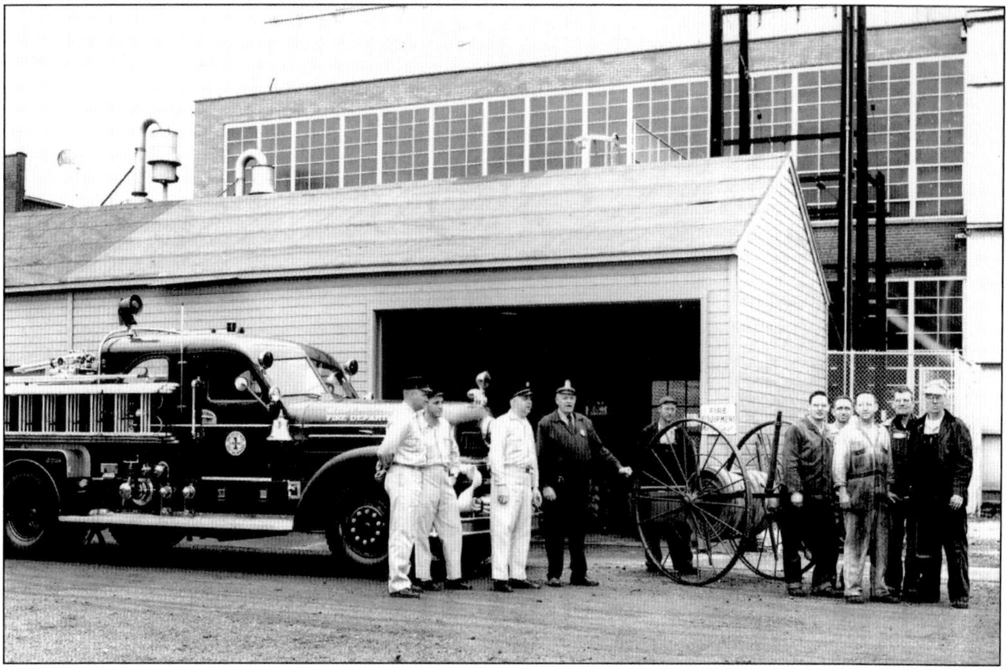

This West Milwaukee industry takes fire safety seriously. Here, workers are pictured with fire department personnel. Note the old fire hose wagon and fire equipment shed. Industries and homes were visited yearly to ensure prevention.

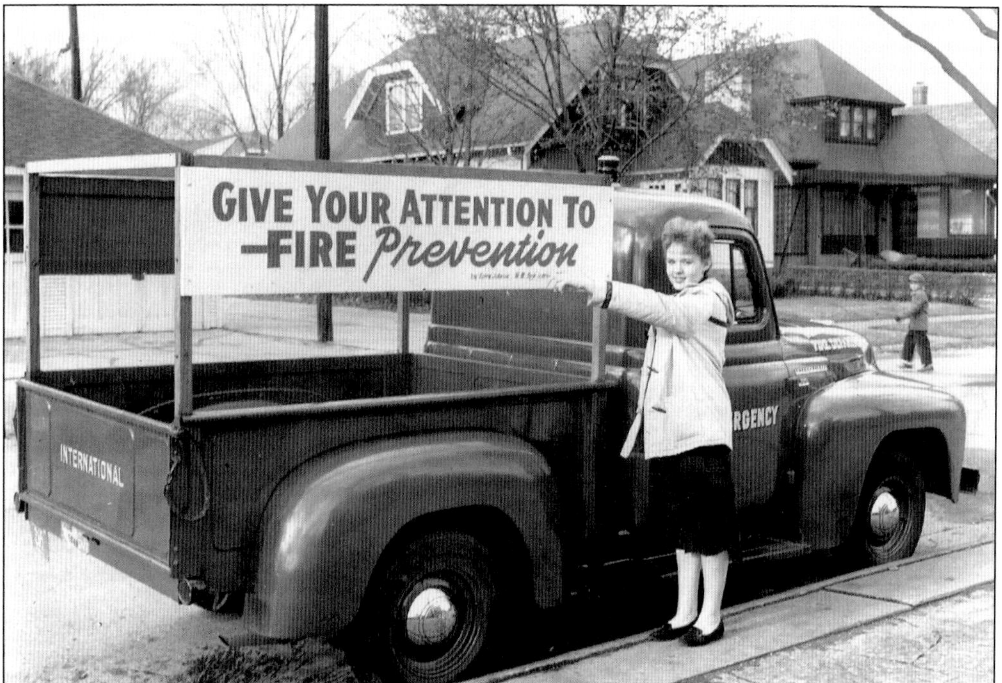

Karen Johnson, a 1959 graduate, points to her winning slogan on the west side of West Milwaukee High School. The fire department encouraged school and community participation in its fire safety campaigns.

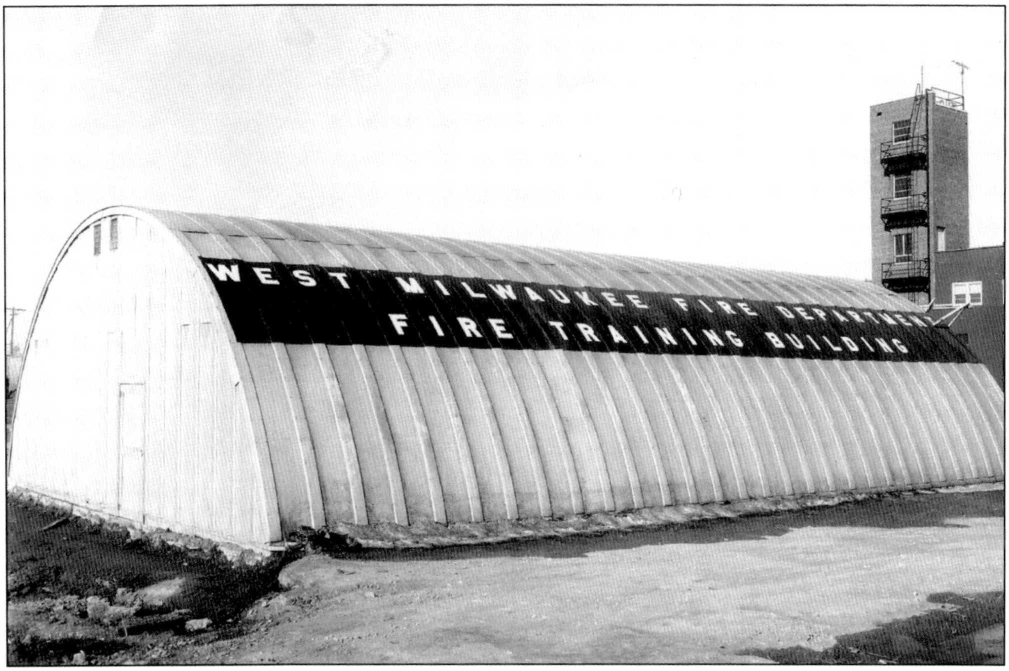

At the fire department training facilities, hoses were hung inside the tower to dry, and firemen trained by rappelling down the outside of the tower.

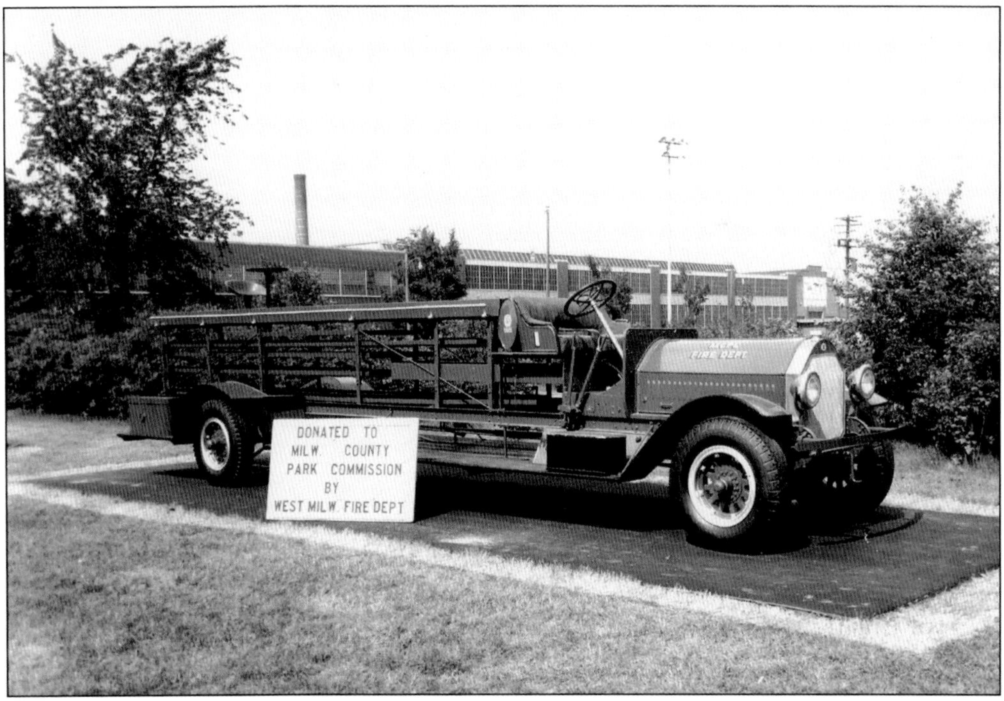

This original fire engine, shown in 1963, was donated to the Milwaukee County Park Commission by the West Milwaukee Fire Department in 1958. After being placed in the park, it became a favorite piece of "playground equipment" for area children. It deteriorated over the years and was finally deemed a safety hazard and removed in 1993.

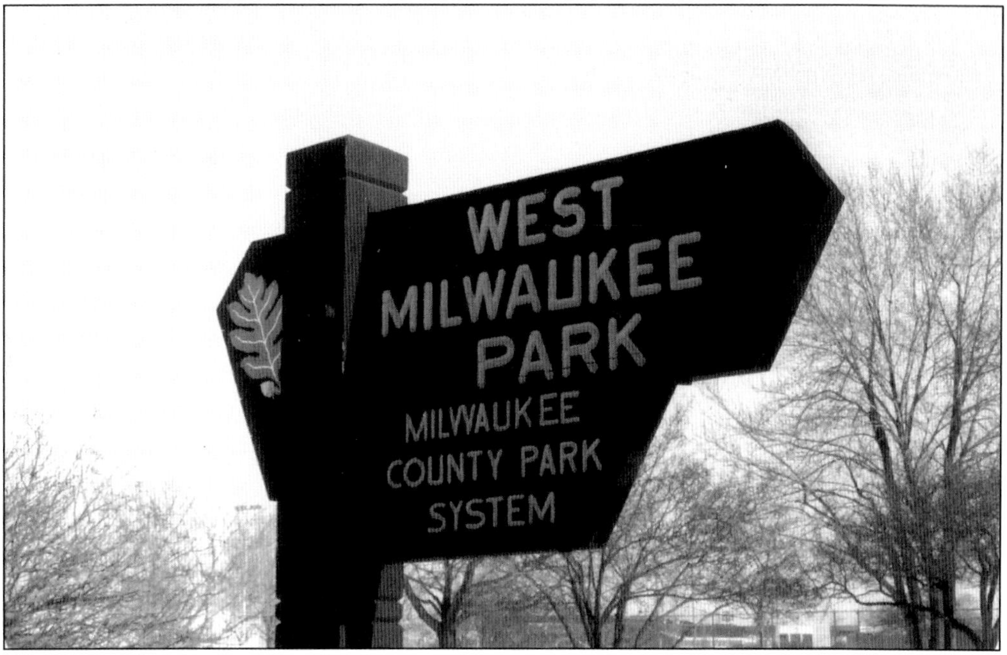

West Milwaukee Park, a part of county park system, is located between Mitchell and Burnham Streets and between Forty-sixth and Fifty-second Streets. It was originally included in the Dickson farm acreage and was well remembered for having a pond where kids skinny dipped and fished. Over the years, the park, minutes from any home in West Milwaukee, has provided recreational space for everything from small family groups to large village events such as Fourth of July celebrations, PRIDE and Labor Day picnics, and the St. Florian's Mass in the Grass. The recreation building, seen below, was used as a changing room during the 1950s when there was an ice-skating rink. The softball fields and play equipment are used daily in season.

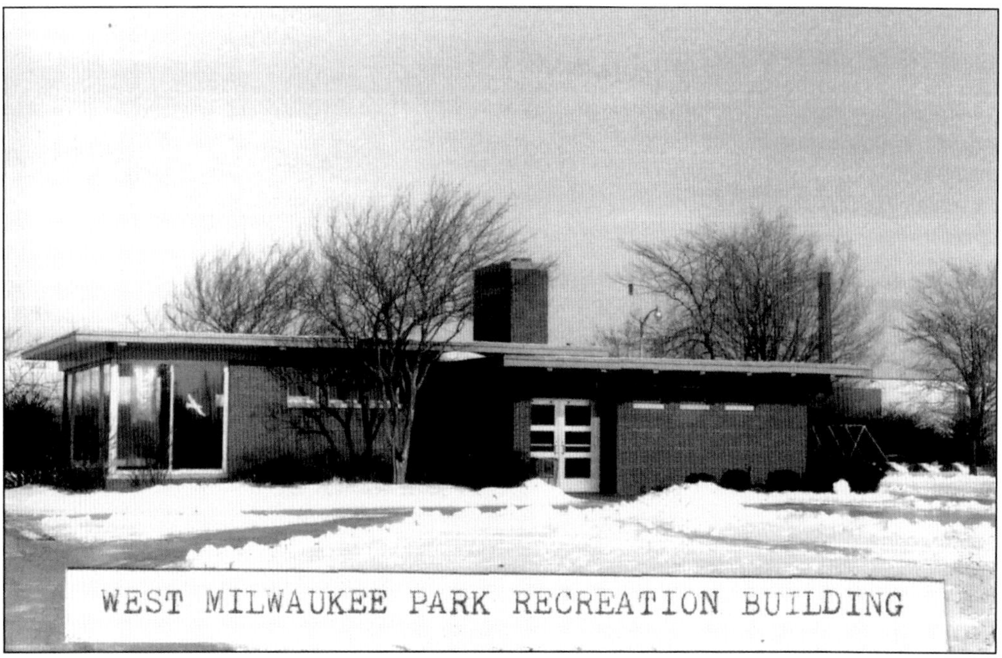

Nurse Frances Lynn Millonig represents a different era when nurses wore starched white uniforms and caps that indicated their nursing school alma mater. Through the years, many capable nurses staffed the village health department, always emphasizing the welfare of children.

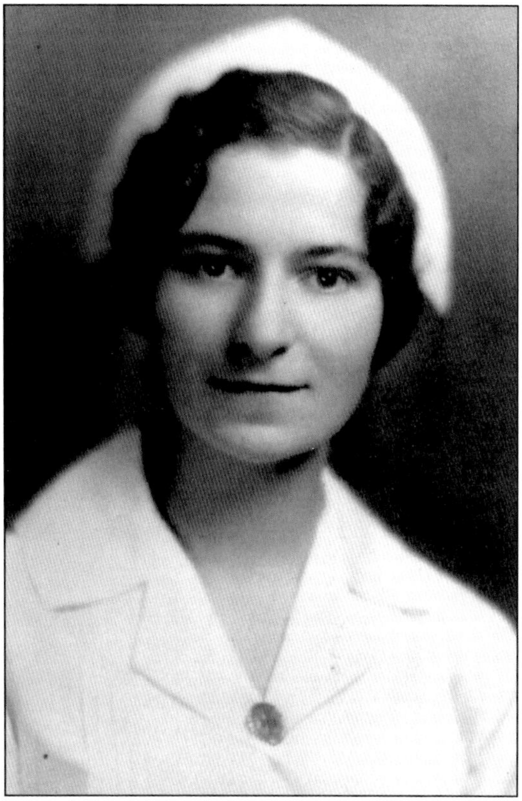

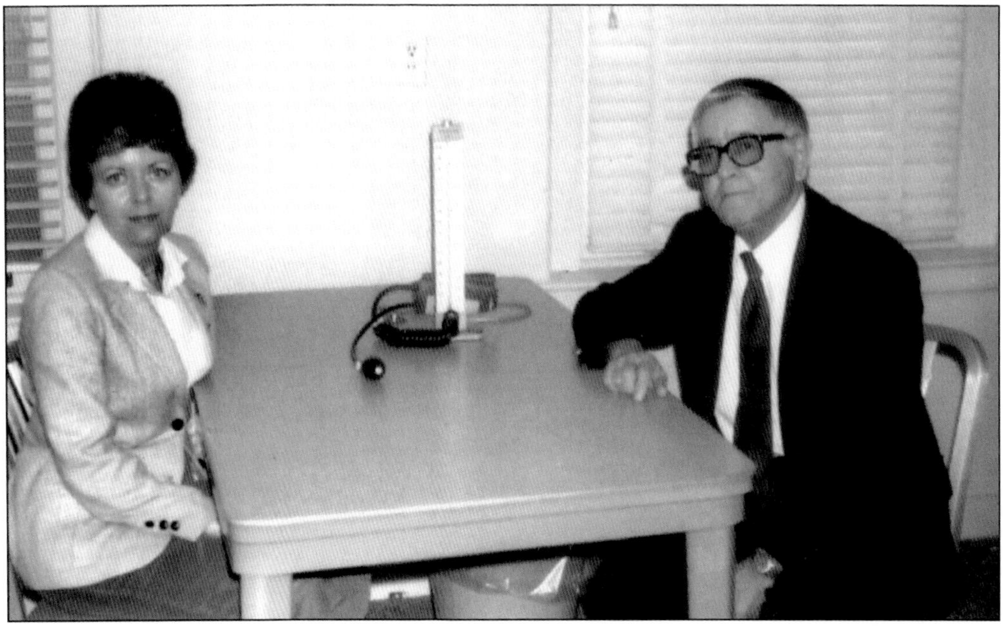

This 1981 image shows longtime medical director Frank X. Schuler and Margaret Sanders, R.N., at their office in the village hall. Programs included physical exams with posture checks, hearing, vision, and dental checks, immunizations, and well child clinics. The West Allis Health Department has provided services for West Milwaukee's residents since 1990.

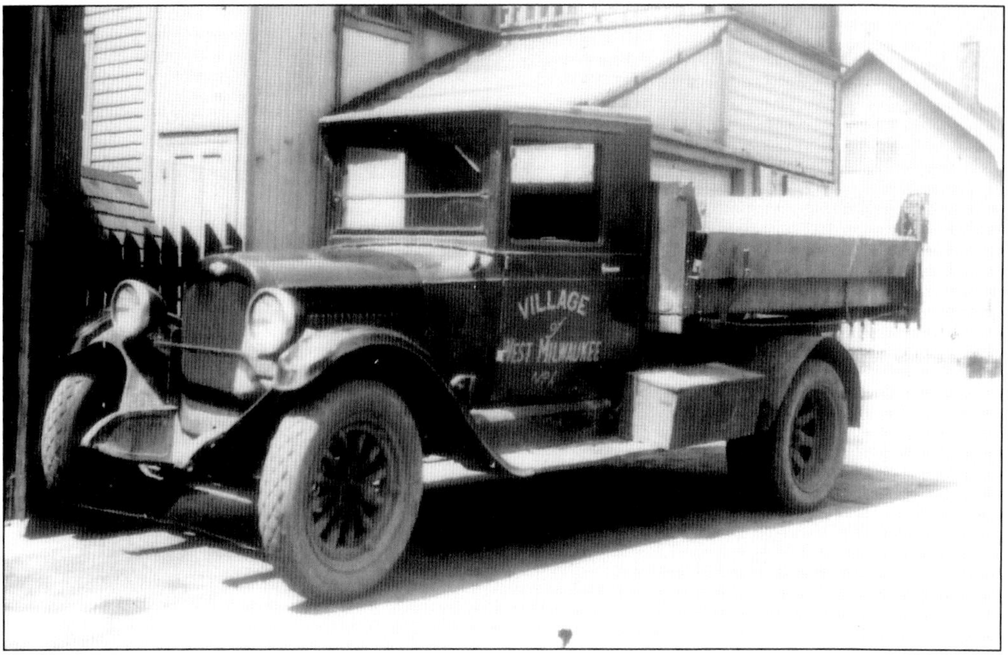

This vintage West Milwaukee truck is pictured in the space between Forty-fourth and Forty-fifth Streets, known by some as "Paradise Alley." The Paradise Alley sign was on Schnabl's garage. Many of West Milwaukee's Austrian families lived along the alley, and their children played there. (Courtesy of Janis Schnabl.)

Burnham street and S. 46th and S. 56th streets were free of roadways. By 1928 the Village streets as they are today were completed and paved.

Ten years later the streets were renamed in accordance with a Village ordinance. The changes, taken from the ordinance, were as follows:

Present Name	Changed to	From	To
Trowbridge av.	S. 38th st.	National av.	Greenfield av.
Thirty-fourth av.	S. 39th st.	S. Pierce st.	National av.
Thirty-fourth av. & Dewey av.	S. 40th st.	North line Sheriff's Sub.	Greenfield av.
Thirty-fifth av.	S. 41st st.	N.L. Sheriff's	Greenfield av.
Thirty-seventh av.	S. 43rd st.	National av.	Burnham st.
Thirty-eighth av. & Arnold av.	S. 44th st.	North Village limits	Burnham st.
Thirty-ninth av.	S. 45th st.	National av.	Greenfield av.
Fortieth av.	S. 46th st.	National av.	Greenfield av.
Forty-first av.	S. 47th st.	National av.	Greenfield av.
Forty-second av.	S. 48th st.	National av.	Beloit rd.
Forty-third av.	S. 49th st.	National av.	Greenfield av.
Forty-fourth av.	S. 50th st.	National av.	Greenfield av.
Bues av.	S. 51st st.	Greenfield av.	Beloit rd.
Hillview av.	S. 52nd st.	National av.	Burnham st.
Daggett av.	S. 53rd st.	National av.	Burnham st.
Forty-fifth av.	S. 54th st.	National av.	Burnham st.
Forty-sixth av.	S. 55th st.	Greenfield av.	Burnham st.

West Milwaukee streets were renamed in 1938.

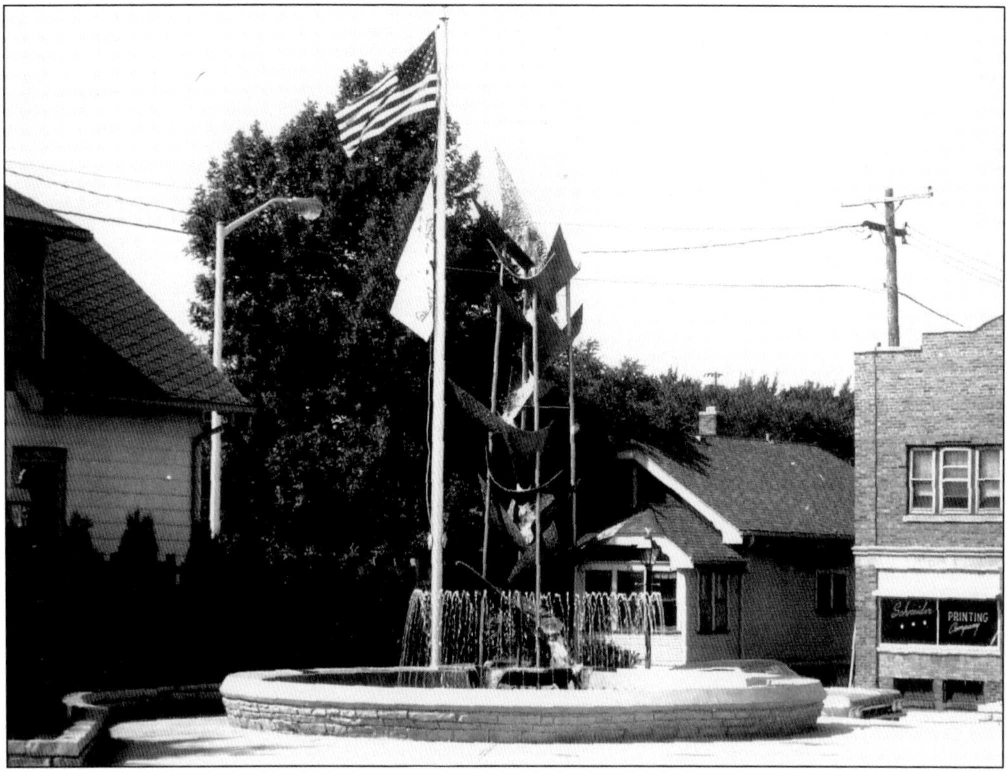

The clock and flower garden where Greenfield Avenue and Beloit Road cross at Forty-ninth Street once contained a metal sculpture surrounded by a water fountain. It was dedicated on August 25, 1968. An embedded plaque reads, "Dedicated to the citizens of West Milwaukee who in the past, through a spirit of independence incorporated as a village, and by dedicated efforts have maintained the Village as a wonderful place in which to live and work."

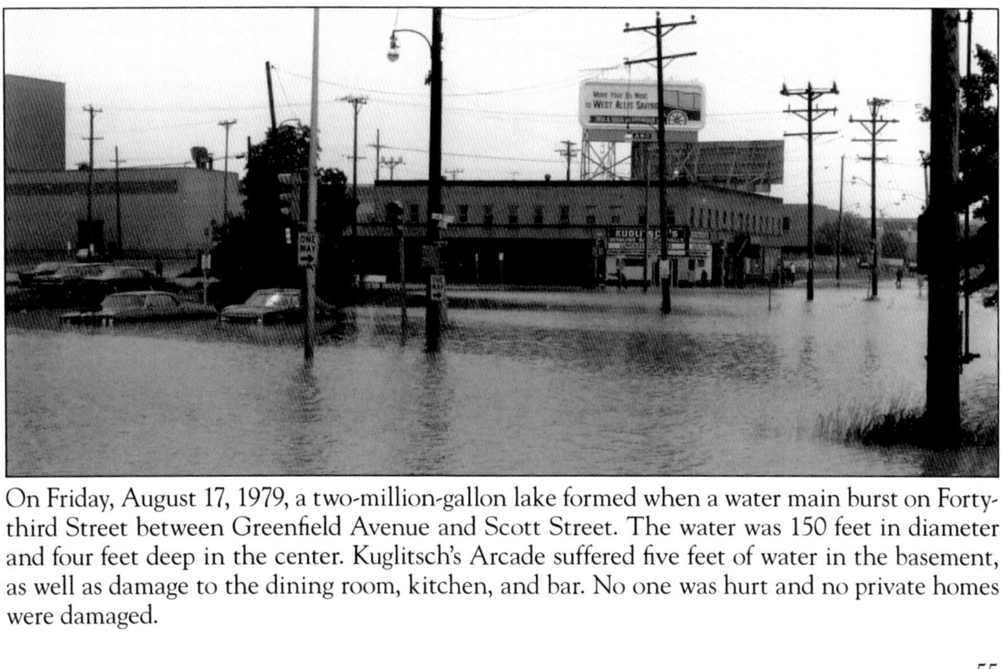

On Friday, August 17, 1979, a two-million-gallon lake formed when a water main burst on Forty-third Street between Greenfield Avenue and Scott Street. The water was 150 feet in diameter and four feet deep in the center. Kuglitsch's Arcade suffered five feet of water in the basement, as well as damage to the dining room, kitchen, and bar. No one was hurt and no private homes were damaged.

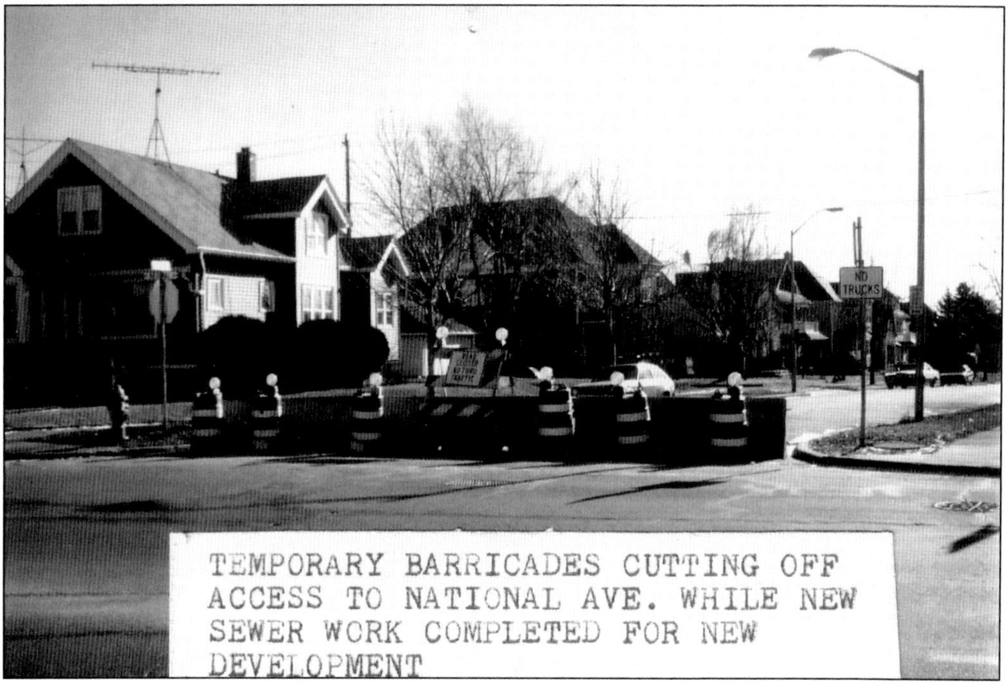

Barricades were placed in 1986, cutting off access to village north-south streets to prevent heavy non-resident traffic while sewer work was completed for new development. The barricades proved unpopular, and everyone was glad when they were removed in 1988.

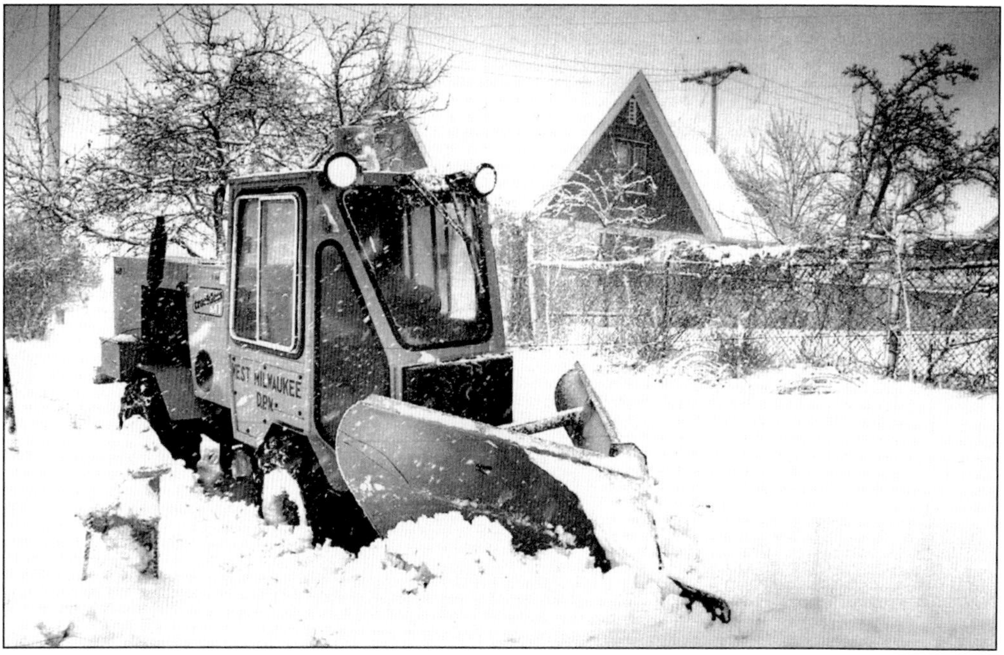

Department of Public Works employee Jerry Sormrude plows a sidewalk in the 4000 block of West Lincoln Avenue on January 26, 1990. Of the neighboring suburbs, only Shorewood also provides this service. Workers plow in West Milwaukee when snow accumulates to more than three inches. (Courtesy of the *Milwaukee Sentinel* © 2004 Journal Sentinel Inc., reproduced with permission.)

Three

SCHOOLS AND CHURCHES

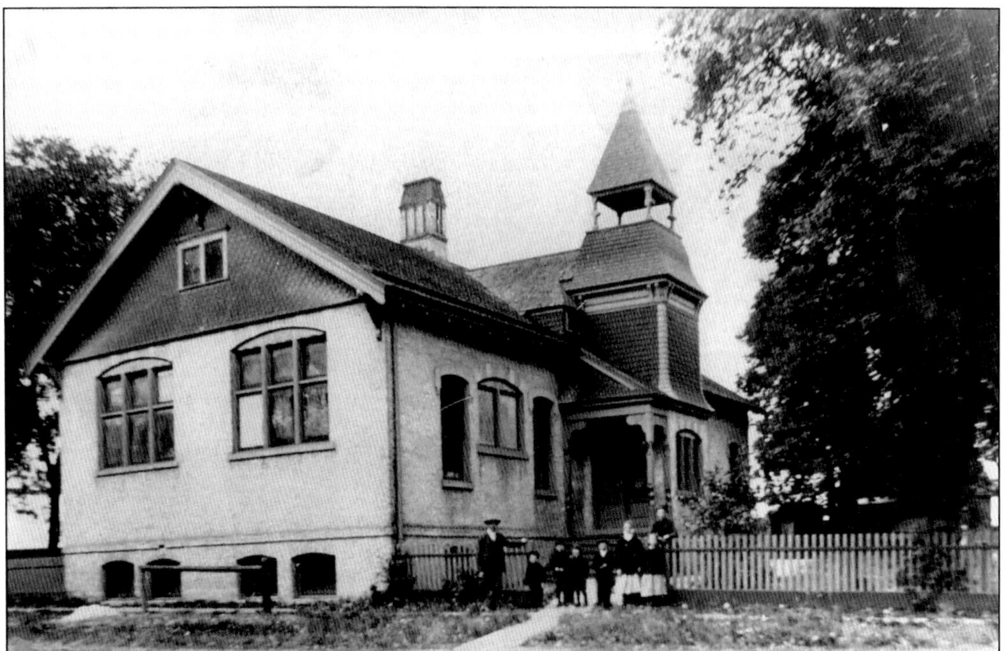

The National Home School, the first serving local children, was situated at what is now South Forty-sixth Street and West Beloit Road. This two-room schoolhouse was organized and functioning as far back as 1879.

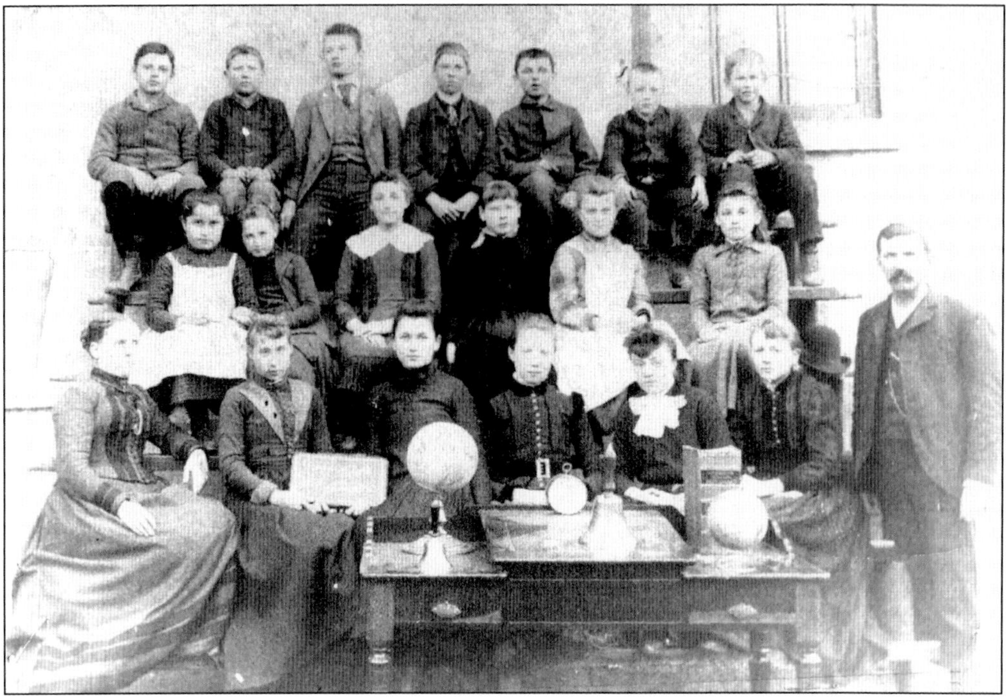

The National Home School class of 1888 gathers for a photograph. Pictured here, from left to right, are the following: (first row) teacher Birdie Trowbridge, Sylvia Davis, Mary Juneau, Lulu Jones, Nancy Hunt, Susan Brew, and Principal Frank Alexander; (second row) Maude Juneau, Elsa Weisel, Elizabeth ?, ? Sweet, Bessie Huny, and Flora Weisel; (third row) Tony Aebli, unidentified, Earl Hinkley, Bob Davis, William Pitts, unidentified, and Andrew Schaefer.

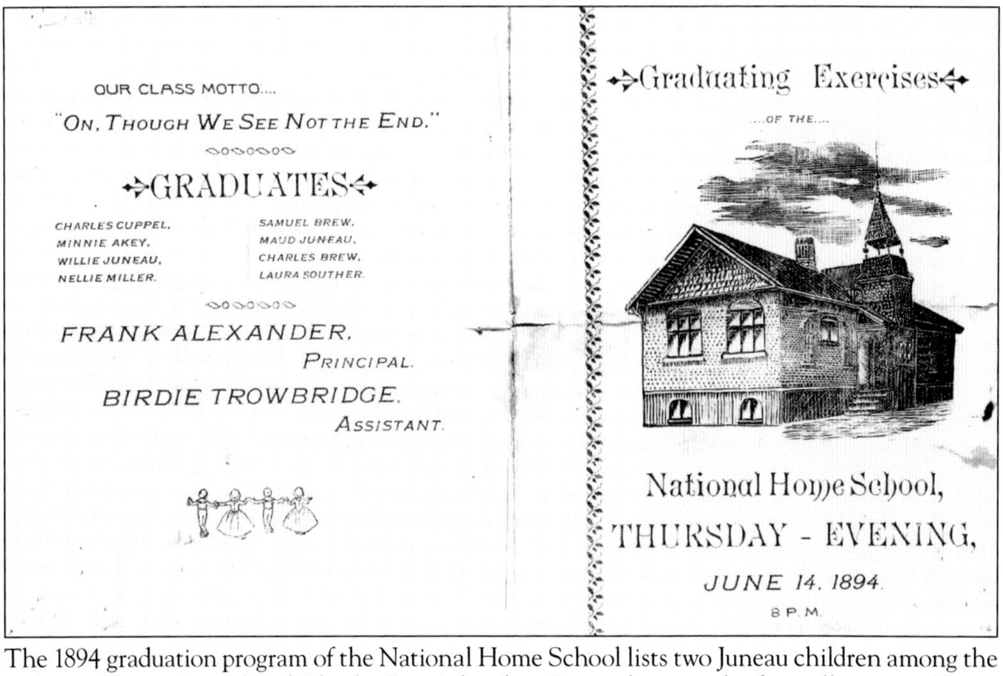

OUR CLASS MOTTO....

"ON, THOUGH WE SEE NOT THE END."

GRADUATES

CHARLES CUPPEL, SAMUEL BREW,
MINNIE AKEY, MAUD JUNEAU,
WILLIE JUNEAU, CHARLES BREW,
NELLIE MILLER. LAURA SOUTHER.

FRANK ALEXANDER,
PRINCIPAL.
BIRDIE TROWBRIDGE,
ASSISTANT.

Graduating Exercises
....OF THE....
National Home School,
THURSDAY - EVENING,
JUNE 14, 1894.
8 P.M.

The 1894 graduation program of the National Home School lists two Juneau children among the eight graduates. Samuel and Charles Brew's brother George became the first village president.

St. Florian's Church, at 1233 South Forty-fifth Street, is the only Catholic parish in West Milwaukee. The first mass was celebrated on Christmas Day 1911. A combination church-school building was dedicated in 1914. The present building started as a basement church in 1924 and was completed in 1939. The school operated until the spring of 2004, when it merged with three West Allis Catholic schools.

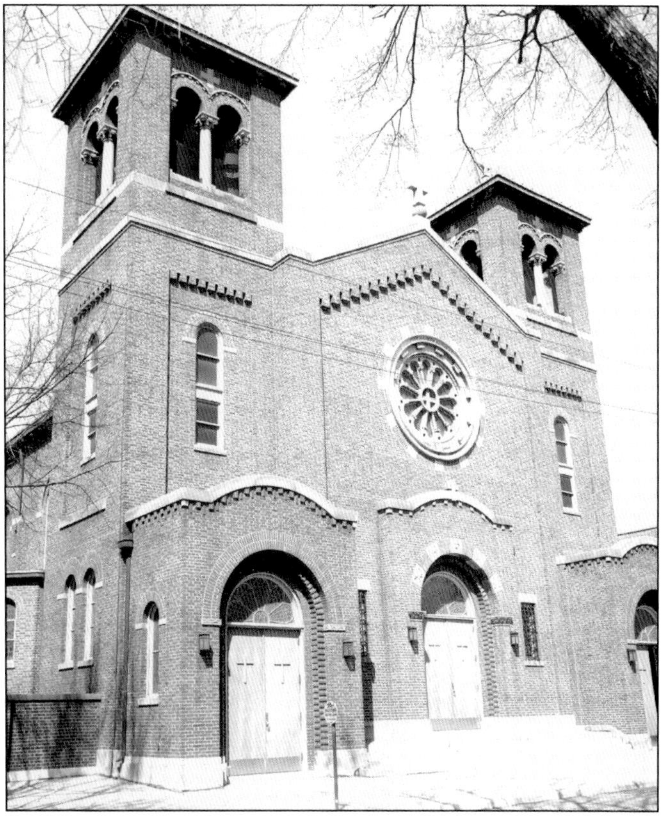

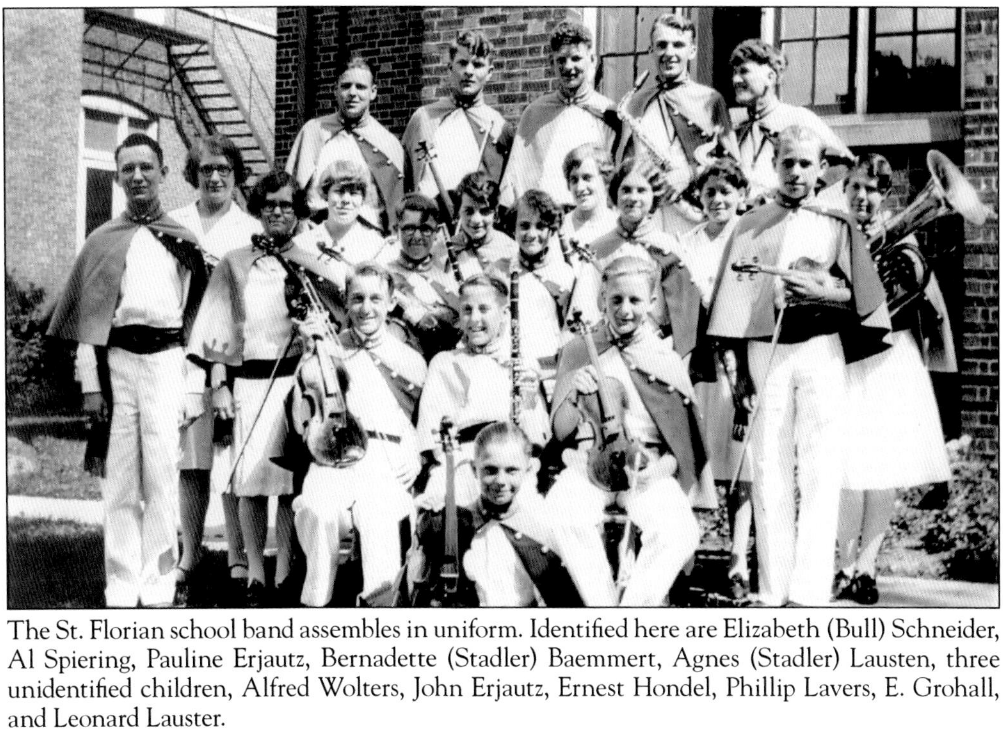

The St. Florian school band assembles in uniform. Identified here are Elizabeth (Bull) Schneider, Al Spiering, Pauline Erjautz, Bernadette (Stadler) Baemmert, Agnes (Stadler) Lausten, three unidentified children, Alfred Wolters, John Erjautz, Ernest Hondel, Phillip Lavers, E. Grohall, and Leonard Lauster.

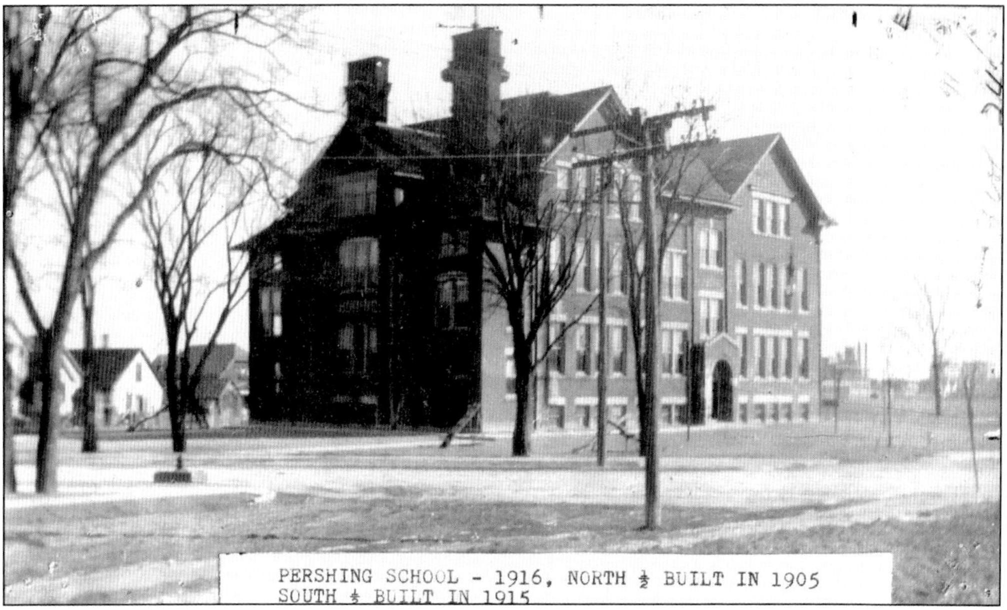

By 1906, the new District 12 School was completed (above), with additions built in 1914 and 1922 (below). In 1919, following World War I, the school was renamed Pershing Elementary in honor of Gen. John J. Pershing, the leader of the American Expeditionary Force in Europe during the war.

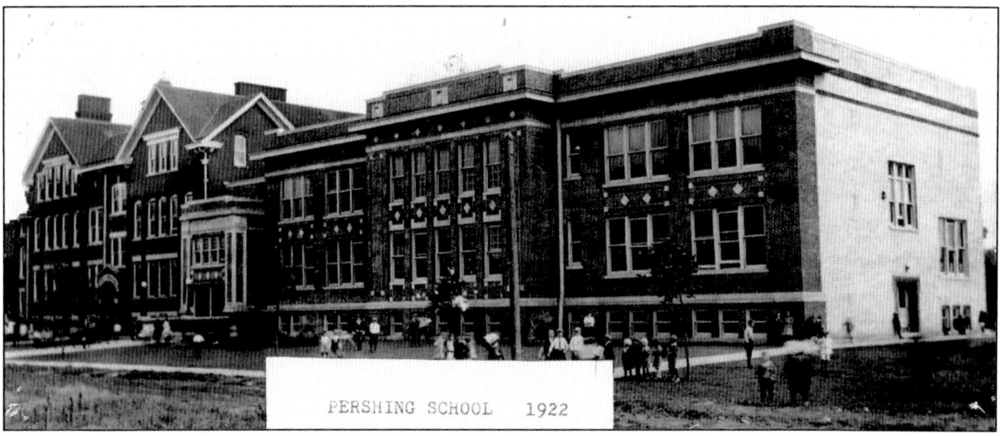

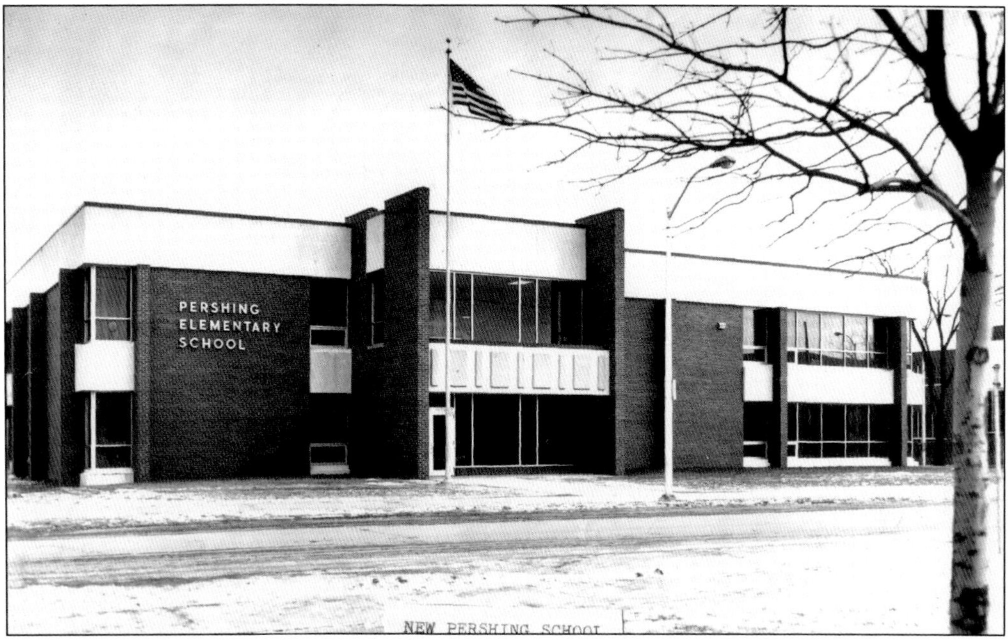

In the early 1970s, the old Pershing Elementary building was torn down and a modern facility constructed, designed without interior walls on the second floor. The open style facilitates the movement of the students to their various skill groupings.

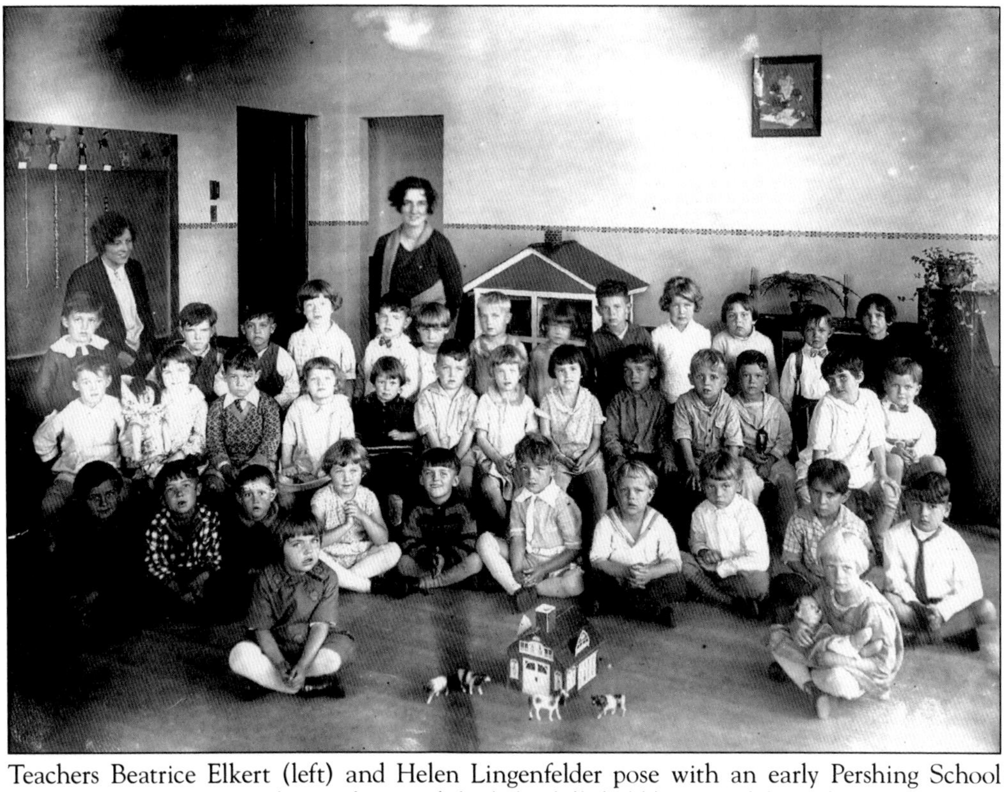

Teachers Beatrice Elkert (left) and Helen Lingenfelder pose with an early Pershing School kindergarten class. Note the toy farm and the baby dolls held by two of the girls.

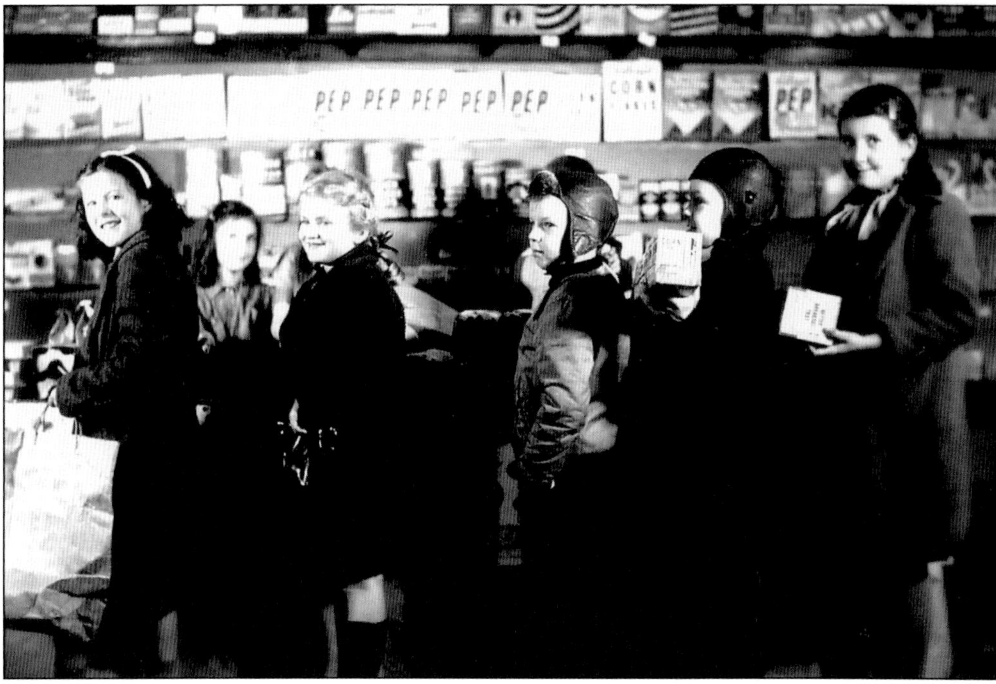

Pershing students buy and sell in a mock grocery store set up to teach economics and mathematics. The children were asked to bring empty cereal boxes and other food containers to stock the "store." (Courtesy of Carol Nawrocki.)

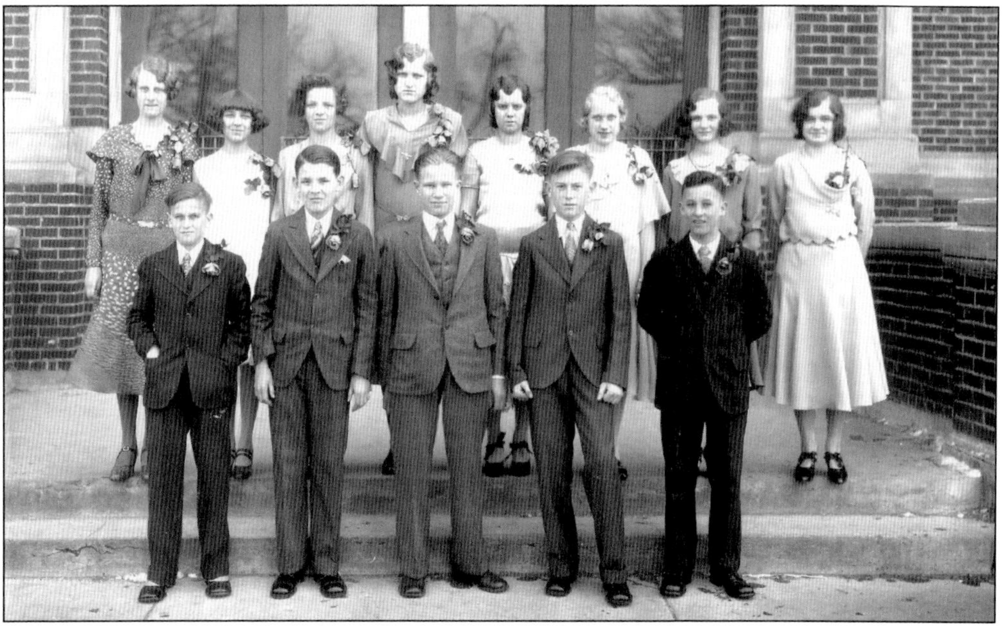

Pershing School's eighth-grade graduation on January 29, 1931, involved the following students, from left to right: (first row) Frank Kuglitsch, Dick Huebner, George Profal, Edward Perko, and Edward Wallner; (second row) two unidentified children, Joetta Stolle, Fannie Kalosh, Leona Klinos, Hilda Konga, Marie ?, and Elsie Wurcherer. Their teacher was Miss Lena Logeman. A curious detail is that the graduates' rose corsages point downward.

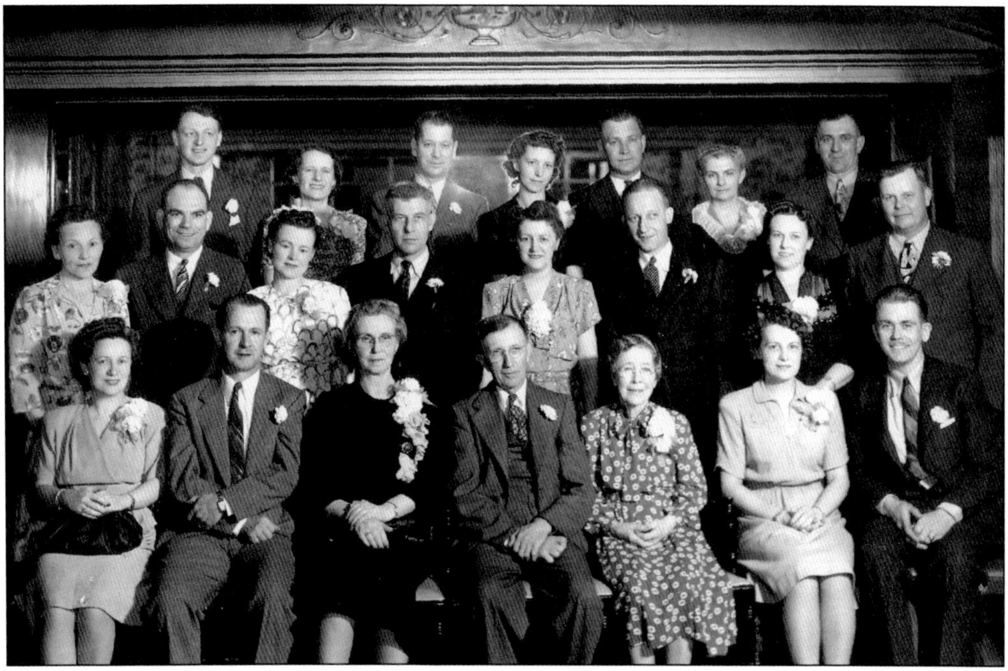

Pershing School graduates from the class of 1920 gather for reunions. The photograph above is from their 25th. Pictured here, from left to right, are the following: (first row) Jessie Ewert, Norbert Flintrop, Elizabeth Flanagan, A. C. Huebner, Margaret McShane, Lillian Thekan, and Clarence Anderson; (second row) Margaret Schuster, Joe Stark, Ruth Heintz, Steve Kuhs, Mary Grafenauer, Mike Schnabl, Ruth Milbrath, and Ted Osmundson; (third row) Walter Funke, Emma Plicta, Paul Kuglitsch, Anna Limpl, Eddie Ott, Alice Lange, and Clarence Bliesner. The photograph below is from their 50th reunion. This was one of the last Pershing classes to use the Ward Theater, situated on the Soldiers' Home grounds, for graduation. The reunions were rather unique in that only classmates and teachers attended.

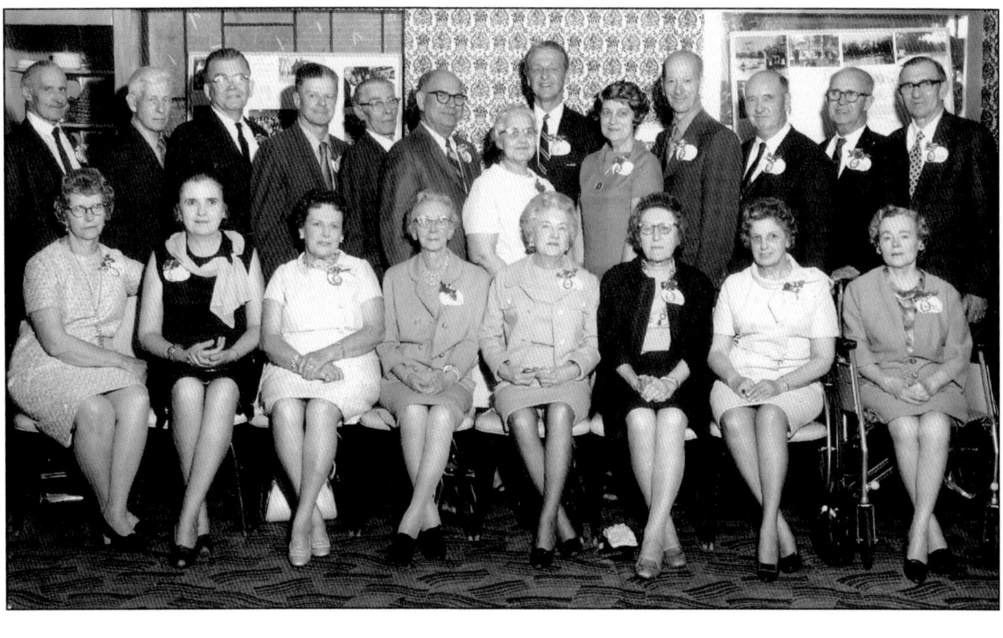

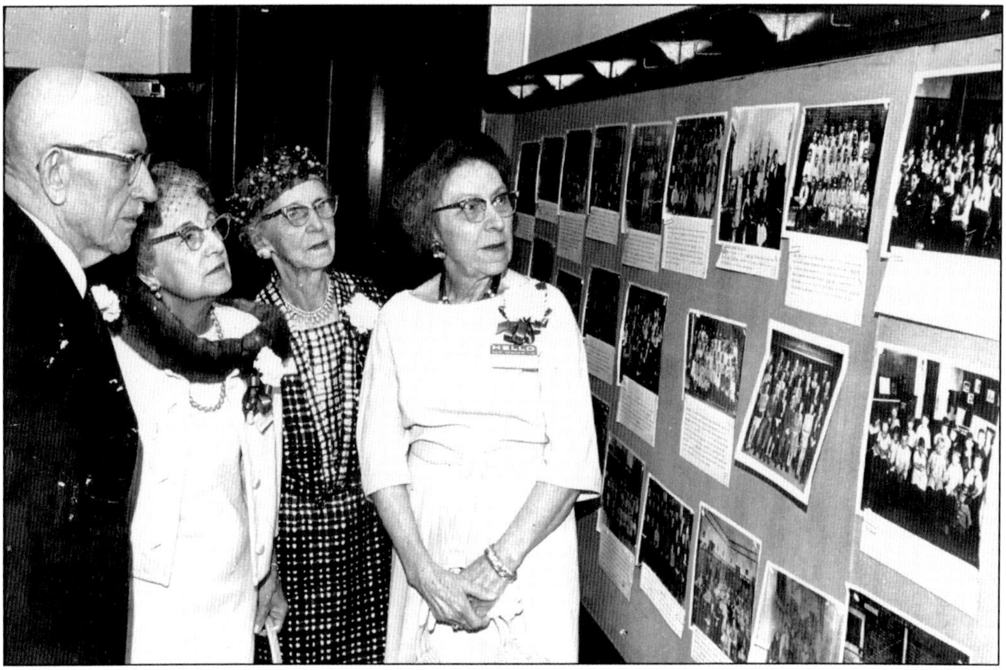

John Kanalz, a janitor at Pershing School from 1914 to 1920, was 92 years old when this photograph was taken at a 1965 reunion. The teachers, from second from left to right, are Mrs. Roethke (formerly Miss Steinhagen), Miss Flanagan, and Miss Neis.

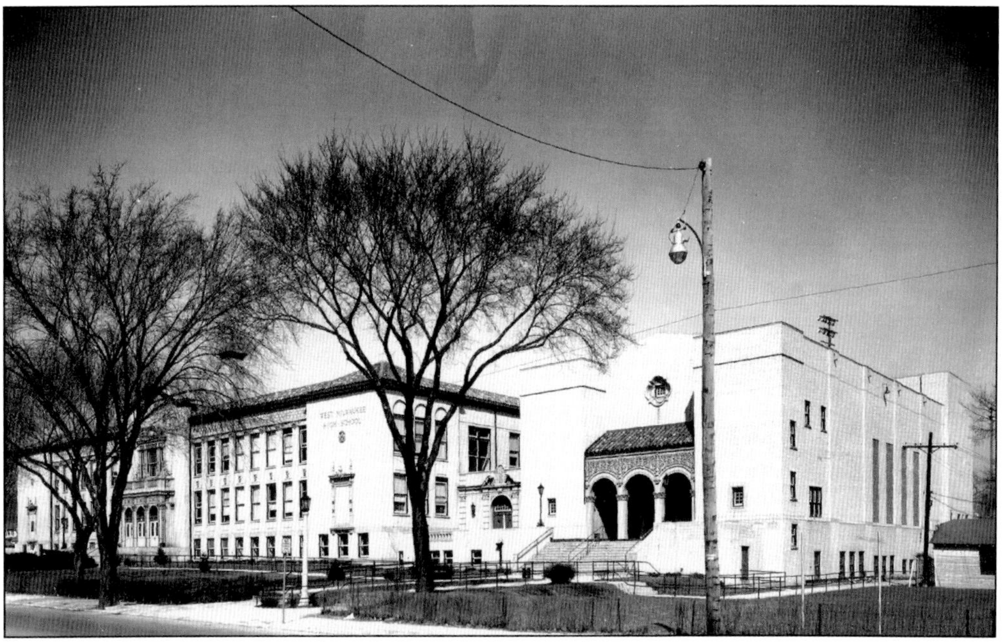

In October 1927, West Milwaukee High School was ready for occupancy. Previously, elementary school graduates who wished to continue their education attended West Allis Central or Bay View High Schools. Prominent West Milwaukee High alumni are Liberace and Paul Poberezny, founder of the Experimental Aircraft Association. The high school was closed in 1992, reopening in 1997 as West Milwaukee Middle School of the West Allis–West Milwaukee School District.

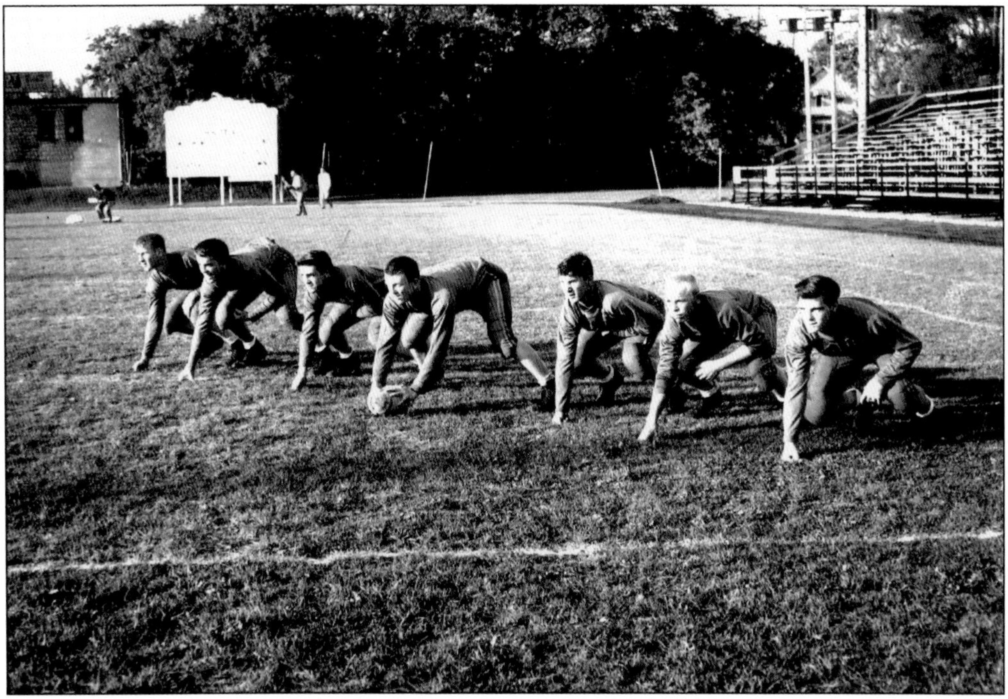

A football team practices on the West Milwaukee High athletic field. The wooden bleachers and scoreboard are now but a memory.

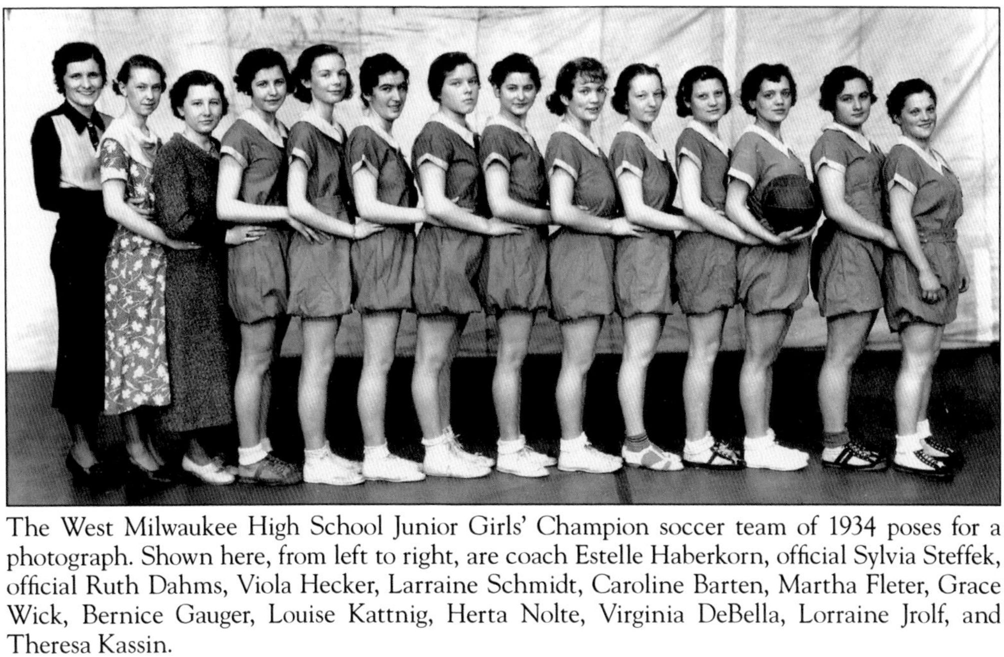

The West Milwaukee High School Junior Girls' Champion soccer team of 1934 poses for a photograph. Shown here, from left to right, are coach Estelle Haberkorn, official Sylvia Steffek, official Ruth Dahms, Viola Hecker, Larraine Schmidt, Caroline Barten, Martha Fleter, Grace Wick, Bernice Gauger, Louise Kattnig, Herta Nolte, Virginia DeBella, Lorraine Jrolf, and Theresa Kassin.

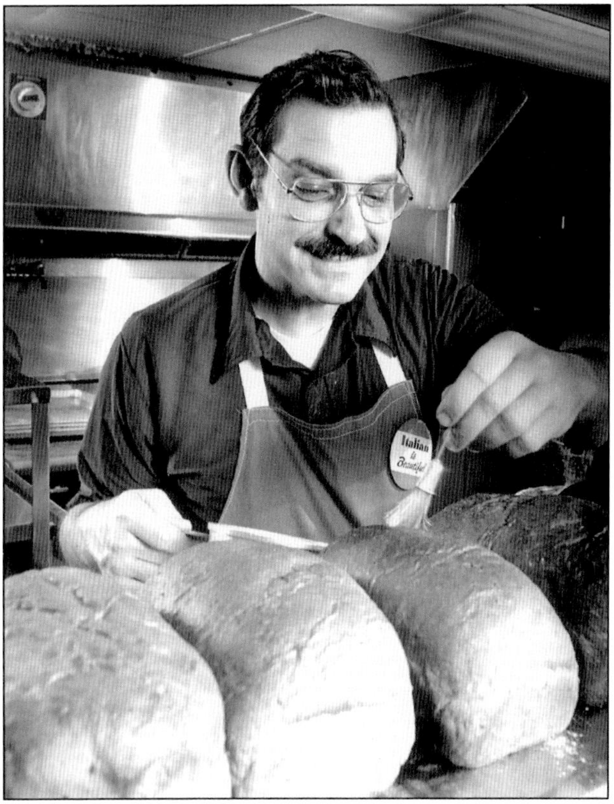

Father Mike Ciullo, one of St. Florian's many beloved pastors, bakes bread for the church's annual festival. Ciullo served the parish from 1981 to 1987. (Courtesy of the *Milwaukee Sentinel* © 2004 Journal Sentinel Inc., reproduced with permission.)

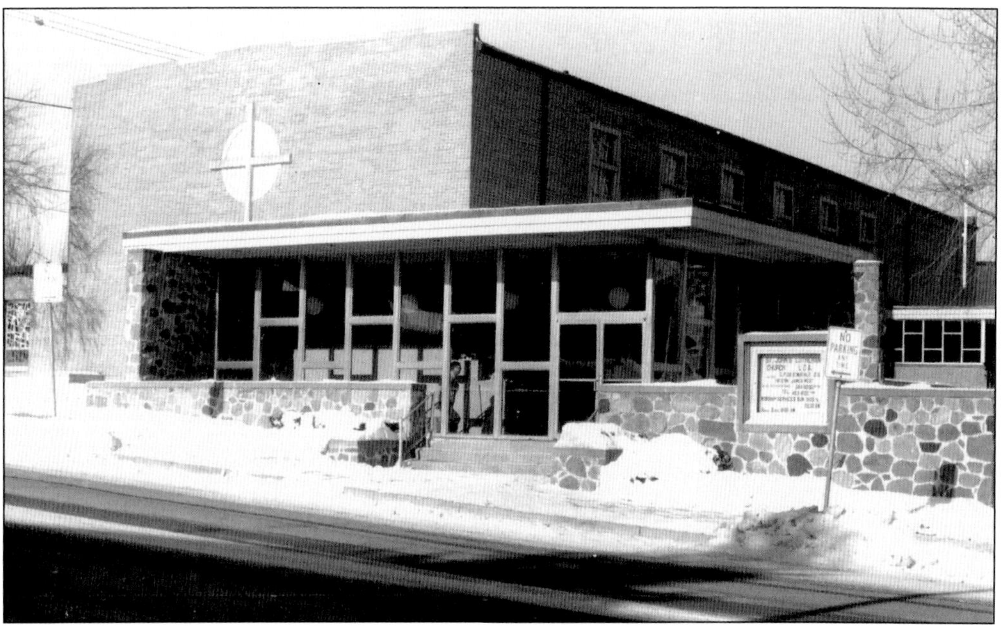

St. John's Evangelical Lutheran Church joined the village in 1960 when its present church was built, replacing the original structure at 1029 South Fifty-eighth Street in West Allis. The church was organized in 1927 and adopted the constitution of the United Lutheran Church of America.

Four

Business and Industry

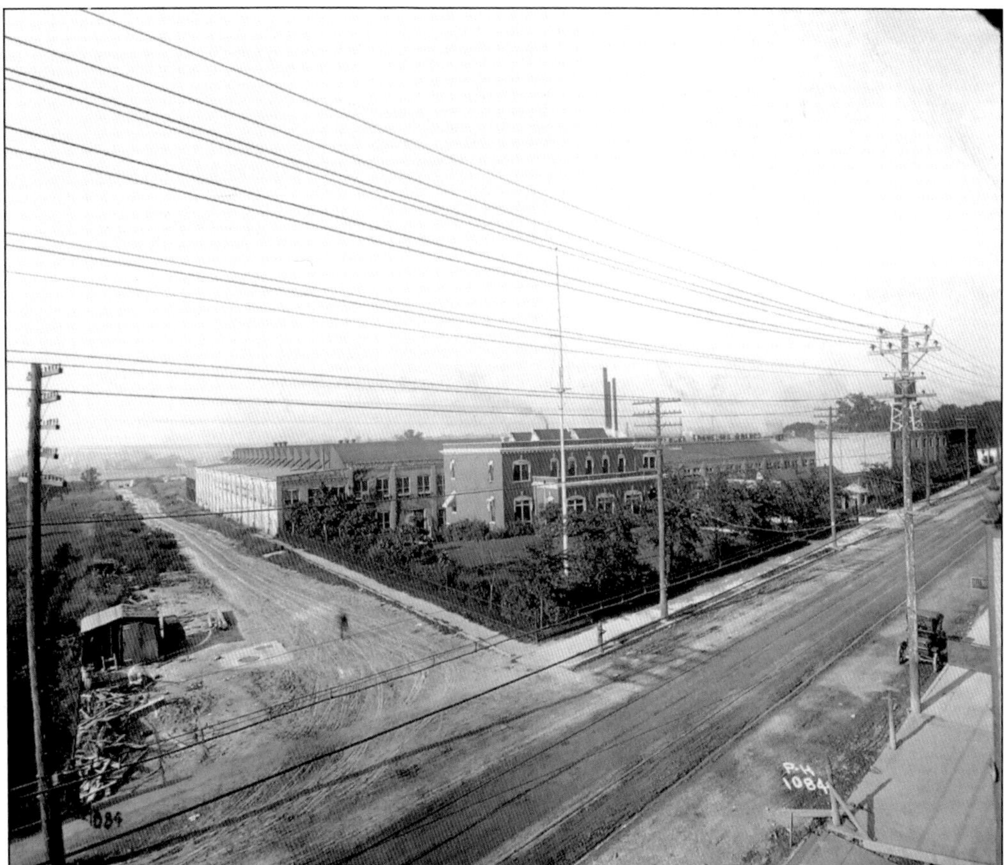

The Harnischfeger Corporation has been located in West Milwaukee since 1903. The company was founded in 1884 as the Pawling and Harnischfeger Machine and Pattern Shop. It specializes in overhead cranes and mining equipment.

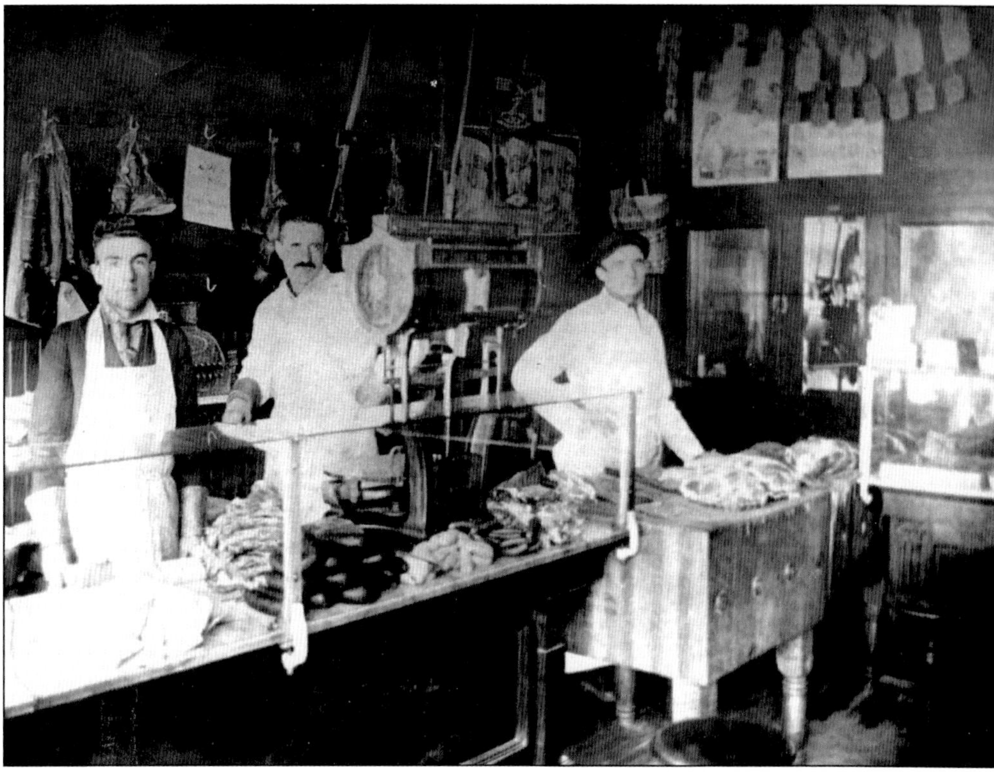

The Sidoff Meat Market stood at 4529 West National Avenue for many years. Pictured behind the counter in 1920, from left to right, are Bill Lazoff, George Sidoff, and Mike Mehelauich.

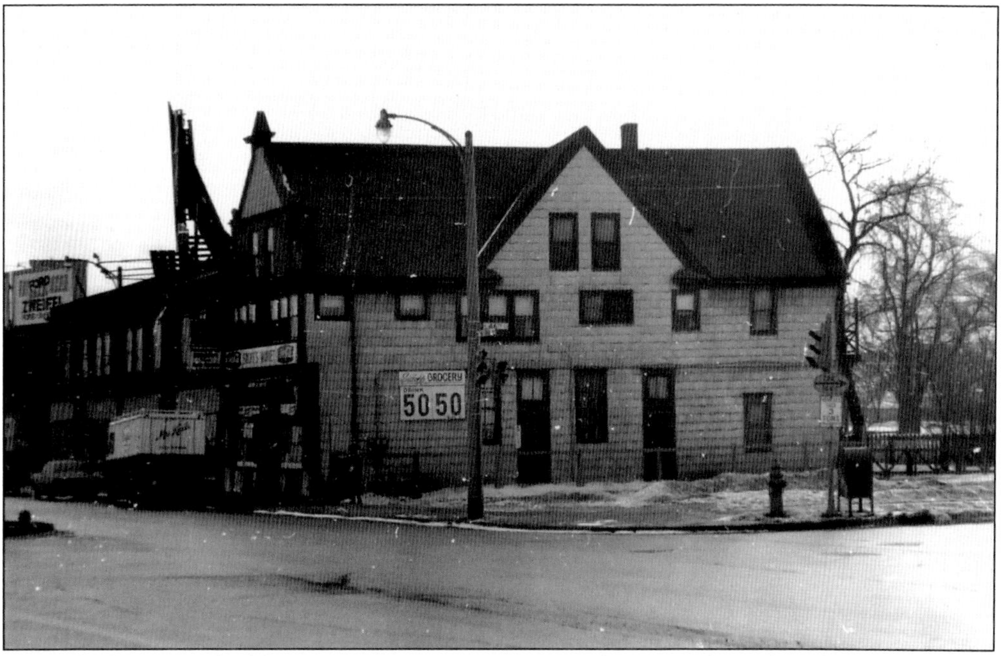

The Sidoff Grocery building appears in January 1972. It has since been demolished and is the present site of Landmark Credit Union.

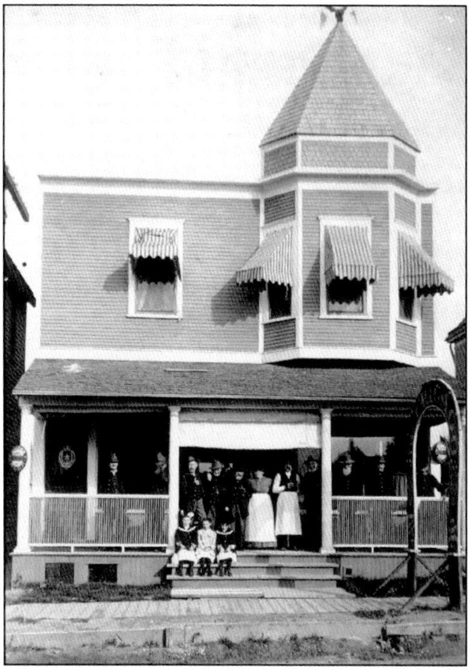

Paul Scheit's Chicago House Saloon stood on the east side of South Forty-fifth Street, a half-block south of National Avenue. Uniformed Civil War veterans can be seen on the porch. The beautiful building was a victim of the freeway corridor. Scheit's daughter, Mrs. Charles Schiller, and her husband and nephew received only $14,800 for the home in 1968.

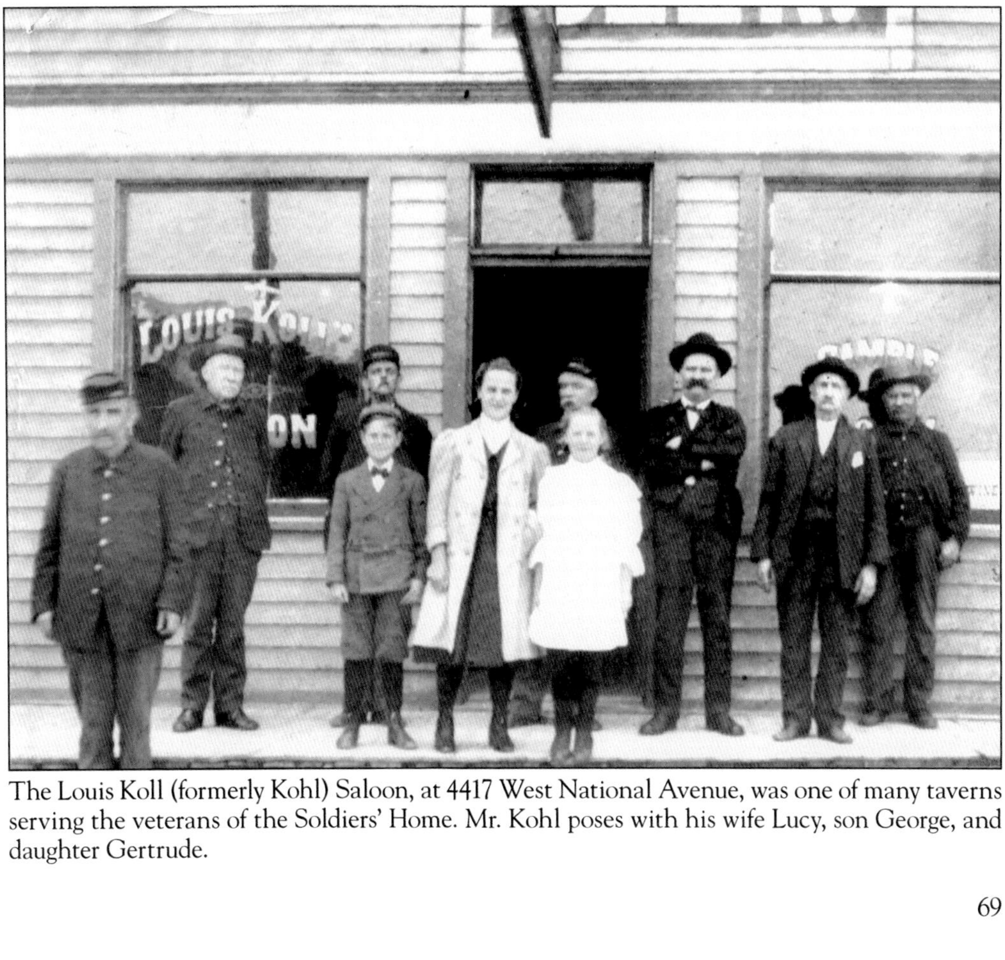

The Louis Koll (formerly Kohl) Saloon, at 4417 West National Avenue, was one of many taverns serving the veterans of the Soldiers' Home. Mr. Kohl poses with his wife Lucy, son George, and daughter Gertrude.

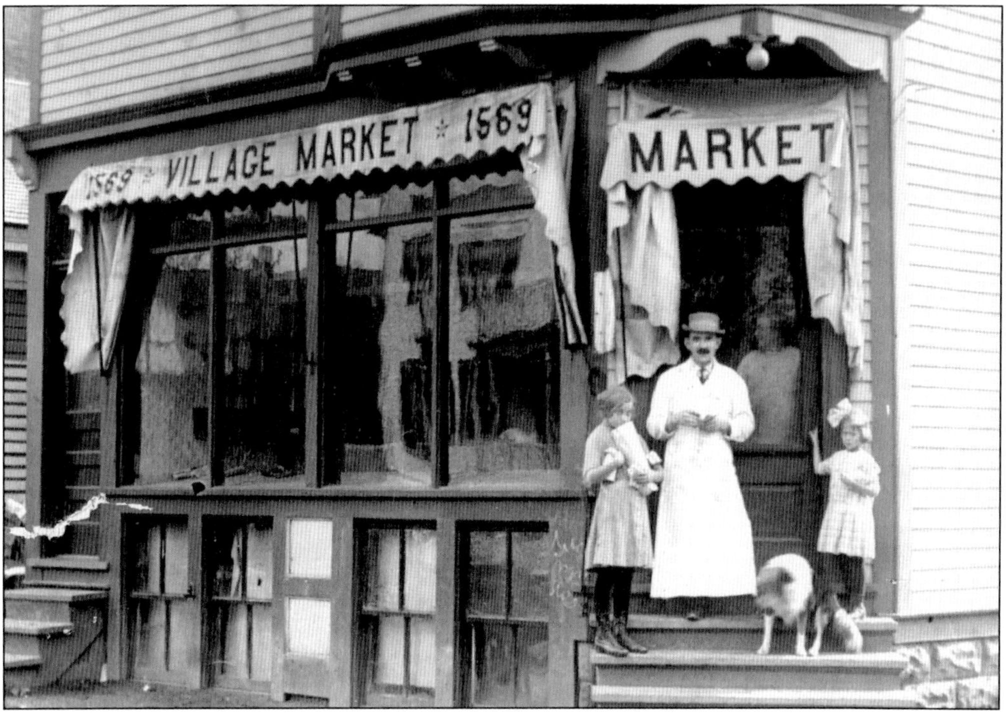

Stocker's Meat Market was located at Scott Street and Beloit Road. The girl at left is Adele Kramer; the others with Mr. Stocker (second from left) are not identified.

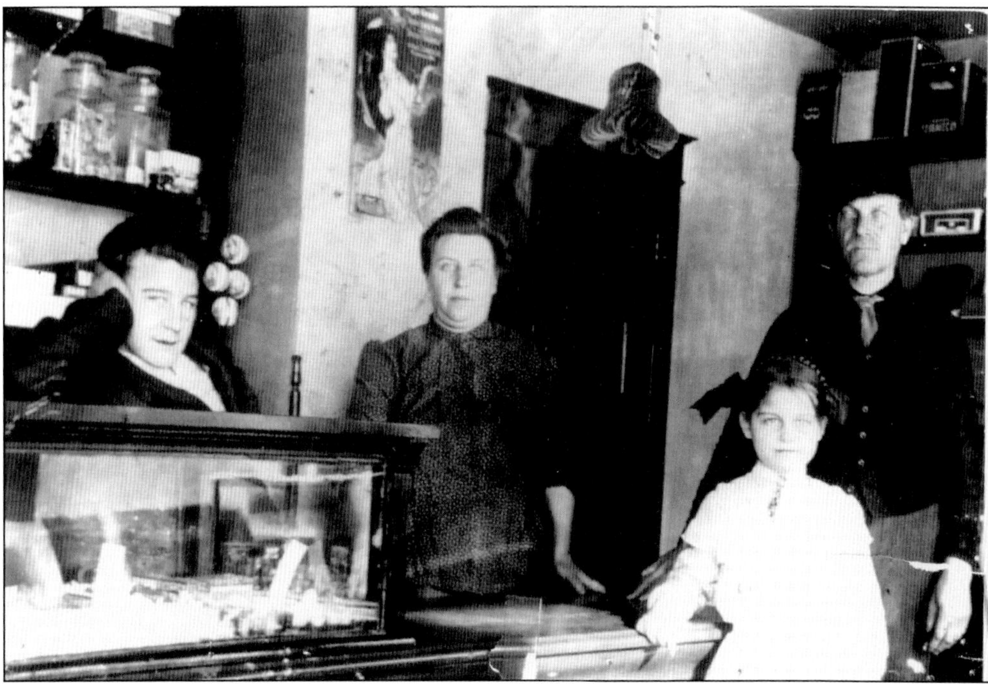

Anton and Mary Kanalz ran a candy and school supply store on South Forty-seventh Street and West Beloit Road, across from the elementary school. From left to right, they are son Joe, Mary, Lucy Fina, who stayed with the family, and Anton.

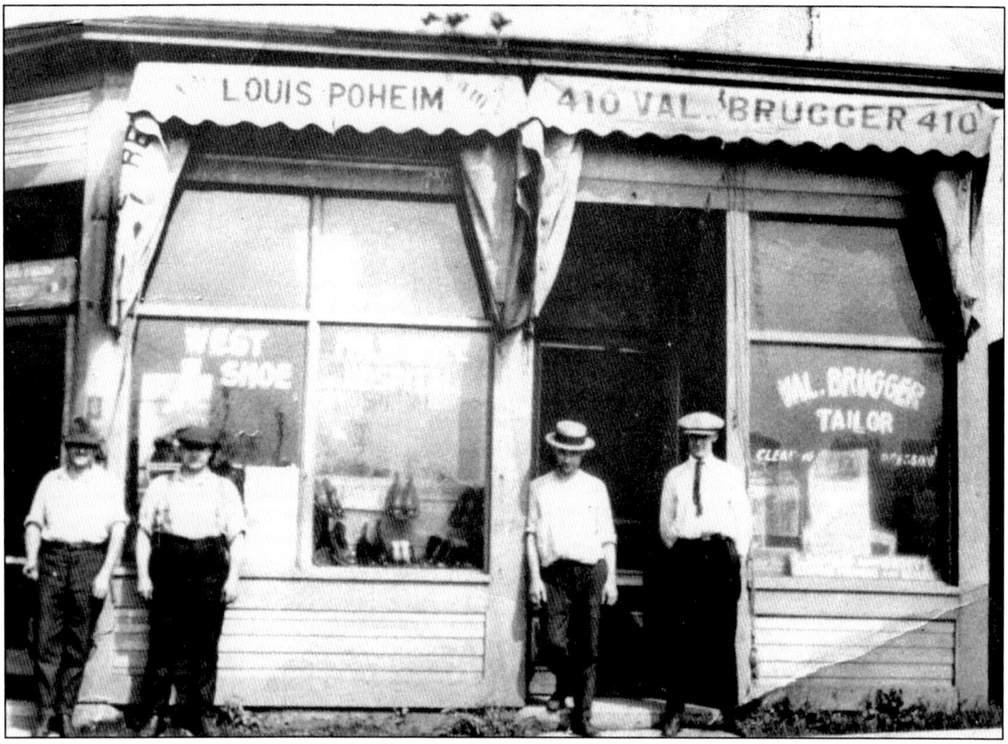

Louis Poheim's shoe store and Val Brugger's tailor shop operated next door to each other on present South Forty-sixth Street. The buildings still stand. (Courtesy of Theresa Sidabras.)

We Cannot Save Souls — But We Can Fix Them

Guaranteed Work at a Fair Price

OTTO DIEDRICH

410 40th Ave.

You Will Wear Out Your Shoes

Hunting for a Better Place to Repair Them

West Milwaukee **Wisconsin**

The Otto Diedrich shoe store (same location as Louis Poheim, above) was advertised in the 1928 Village Directory.

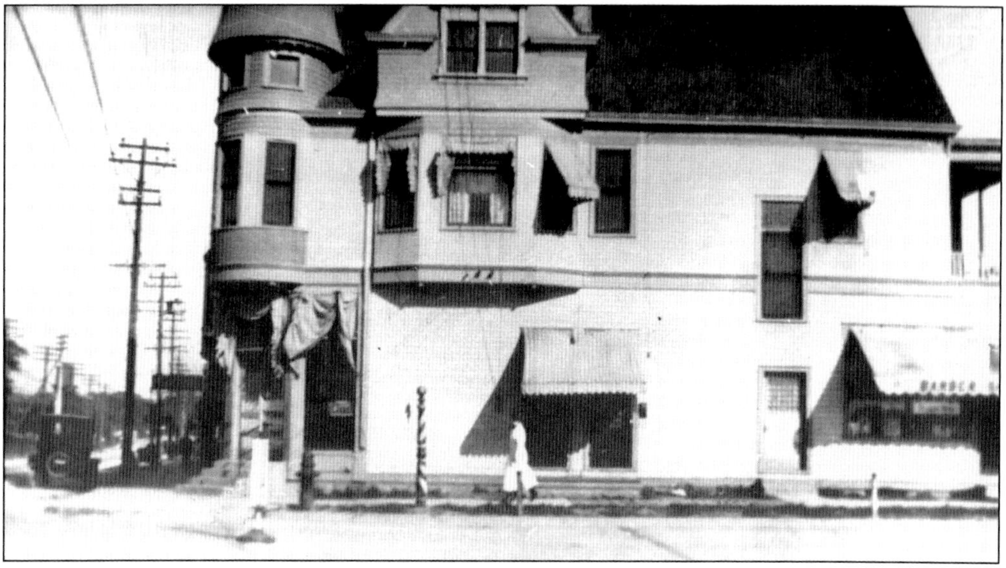

This early-20th-century view shows the Peoples Drug Store on the corner of Forty-sixth and National. The striped pole advertises the barber shop on the side of the building.

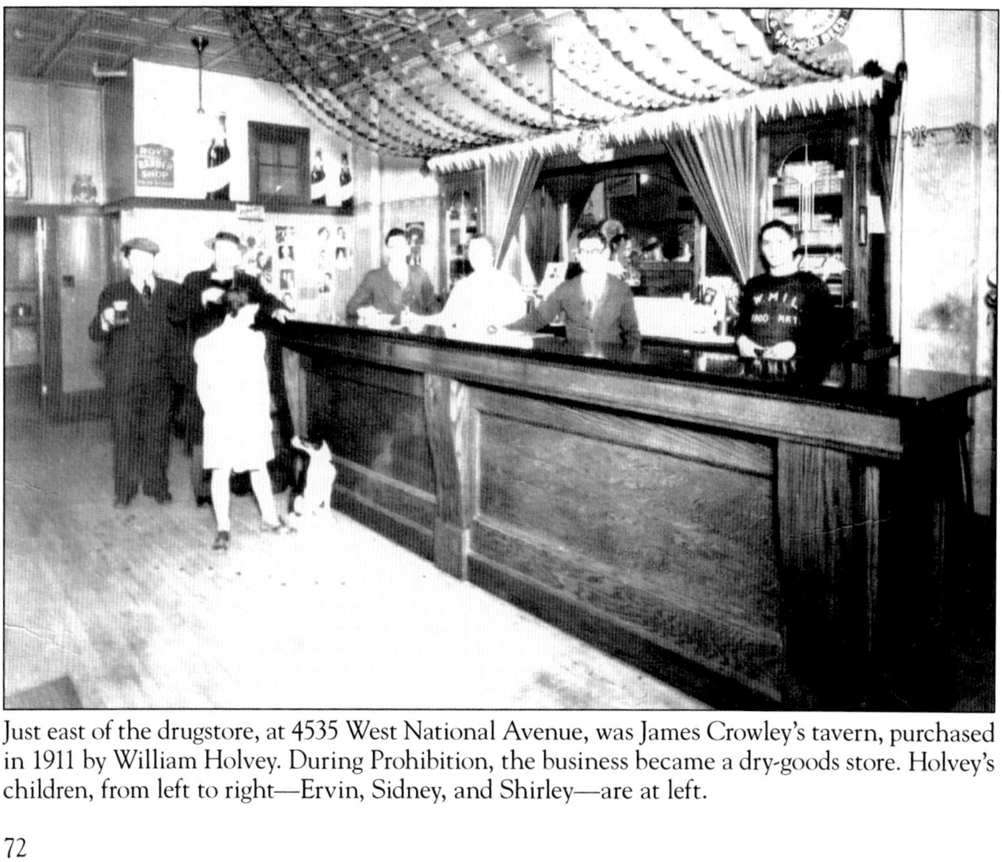

Just east of the drugstore, at 4535 West National Avenue, was James Crowley's tavern, purchased in 1911 by William Holvey. During Prohibition, the business became a dry-goods store. Holvey's children, from left to right—Ervin, Sidney, and Shirley—are at left.

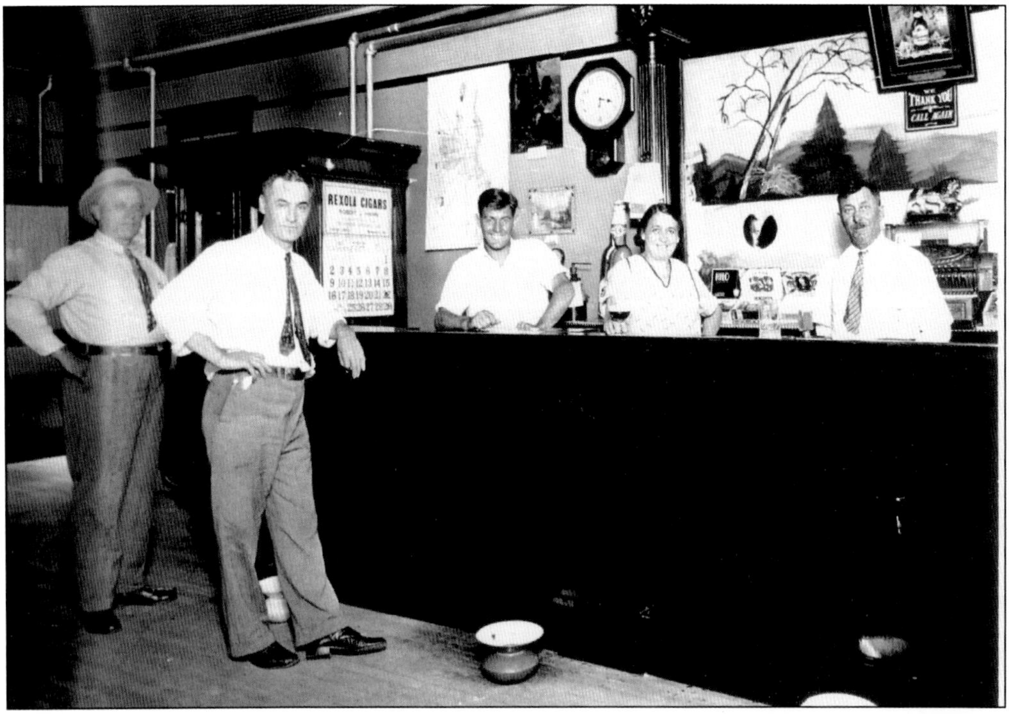

Seen here, at the National Avenue tavern, from left to right, are Frank Kassin Sr., Val Brugger, Frank Grafenauer, Theresa Grafenauer, and John Grafenauer.

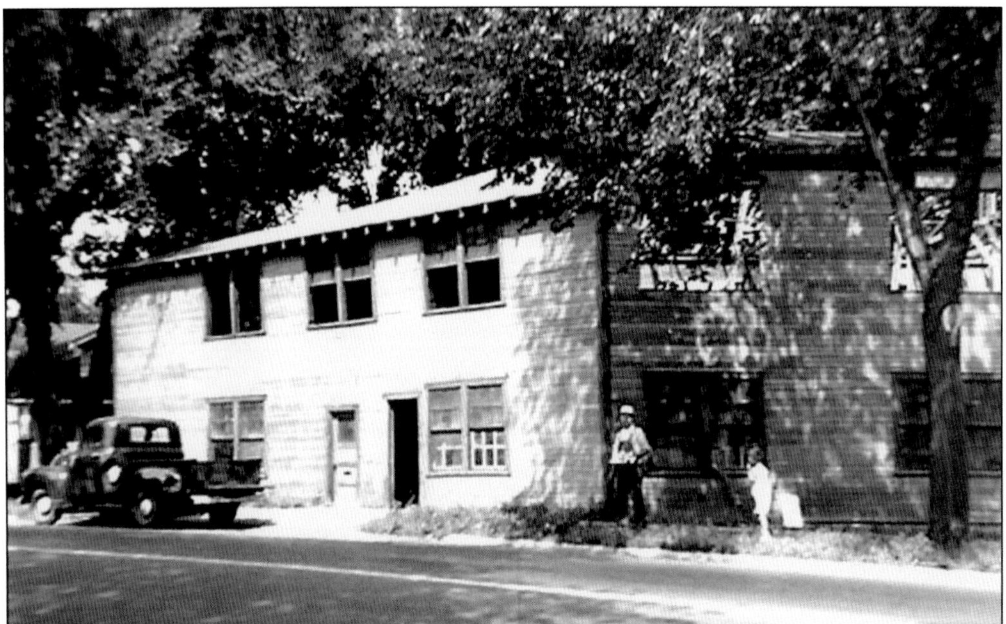

Val Mitsche's woodworking shop, at South Fifty-fifth and Beloit Road, is seen in 1959. Mitsche was originally a home builder who later specialized in cabinetry and wooden crates for area factories. The site became a gas station, and the property has recently been sold. (Courtesy of Joyce Maher.)

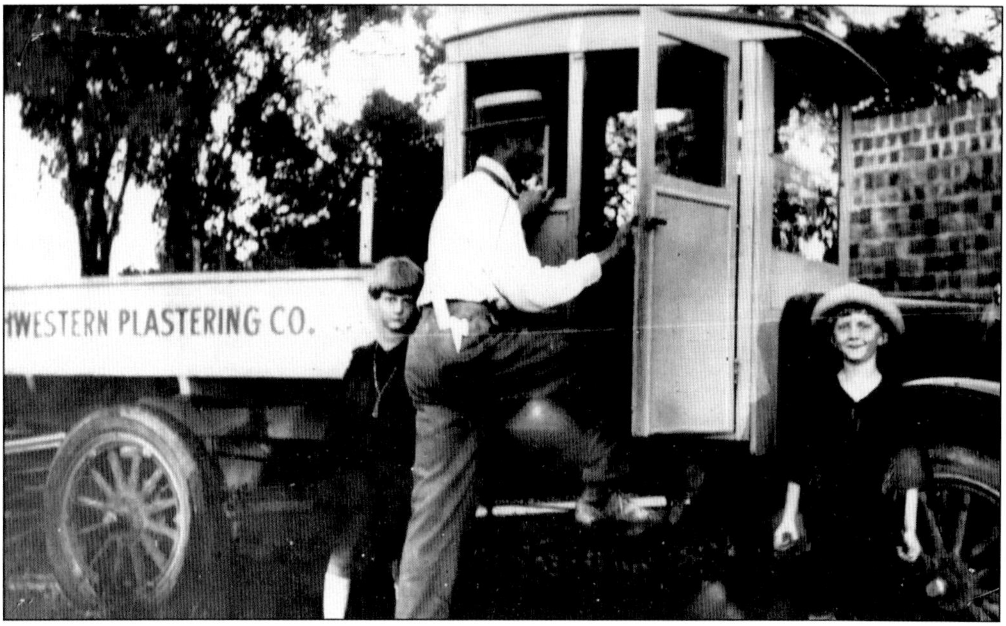

Louis Moosbrugger, founder of the Northwestern Plastic Art Company, is pictured with his daughter June and son Robert in 1923. The company specialized in exterior veneers, plastering, and lathing. Many Nu-Stone—an exterior veneer resembling lannon stone—buildings can be seen in the village today.

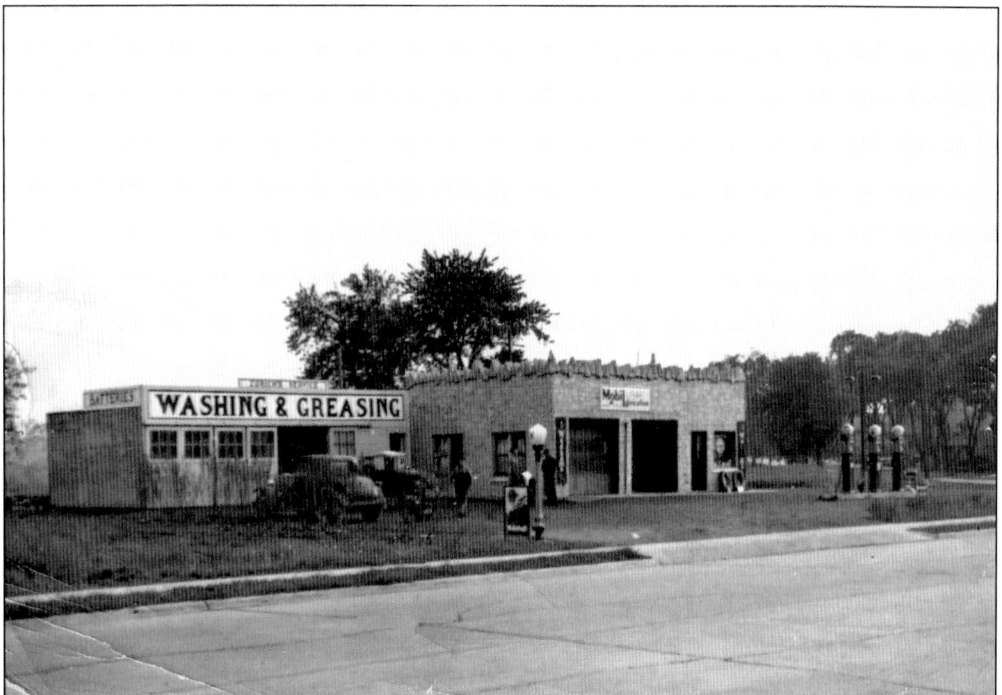

The Zurich Service Station was situated at 4829 West Greenfield Avenue, now part of the Rexnord parking lot. The lower portion of the building was constructed of Moosbrugger's Nu-Stone and the garage top of unusually placed lannon stone.

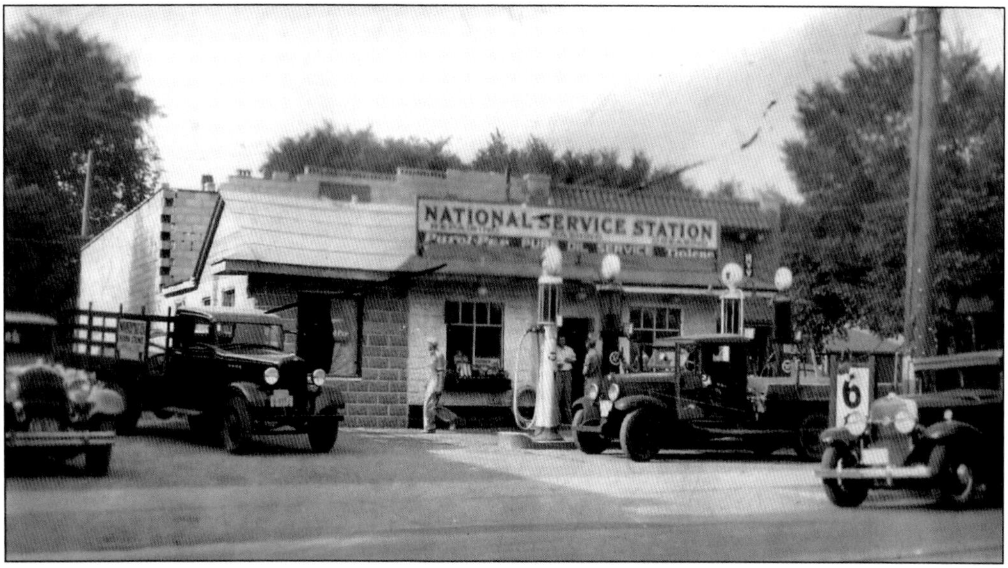

The National Service Station, pictured above, stood on the southeast corner of Forty-ninth and National, across the street from the lilac-tree-lined Soldiers' Home to the north and the Liberace home to the west. Dewey Slocum was the proprietor. Charlie Smead, seen below, worked at the station from 1929 to 1939, starting while still in high school and taking over for Slocum in his absence. Smead, a longtime member of the West Milwaukee Lions Club, then worked at Harnischfeger until retirement. The present owner of the business, now called Schaumann Auto Electric, is Ted Schaumann, who formerly ran the business with his father.

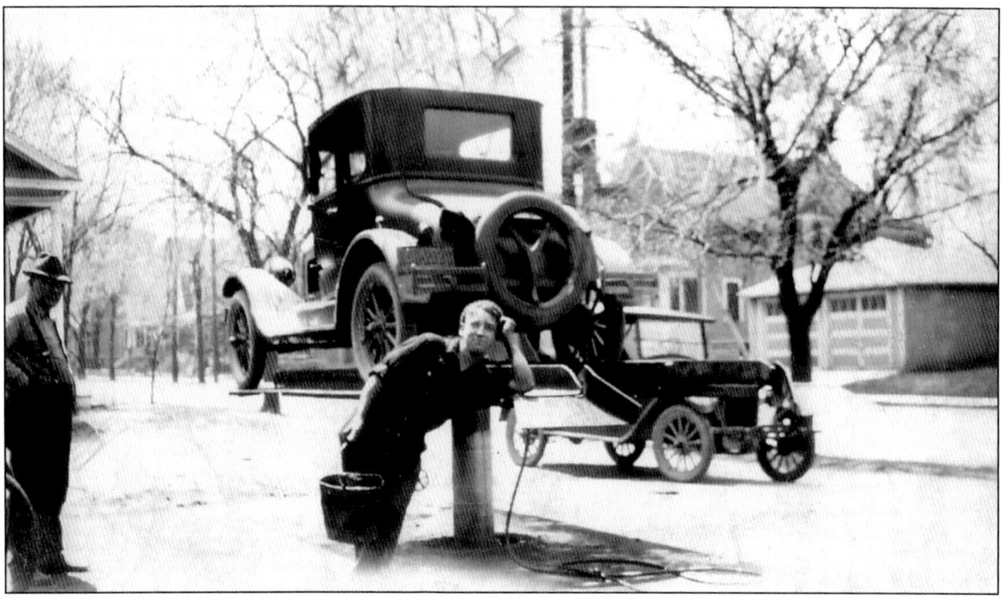

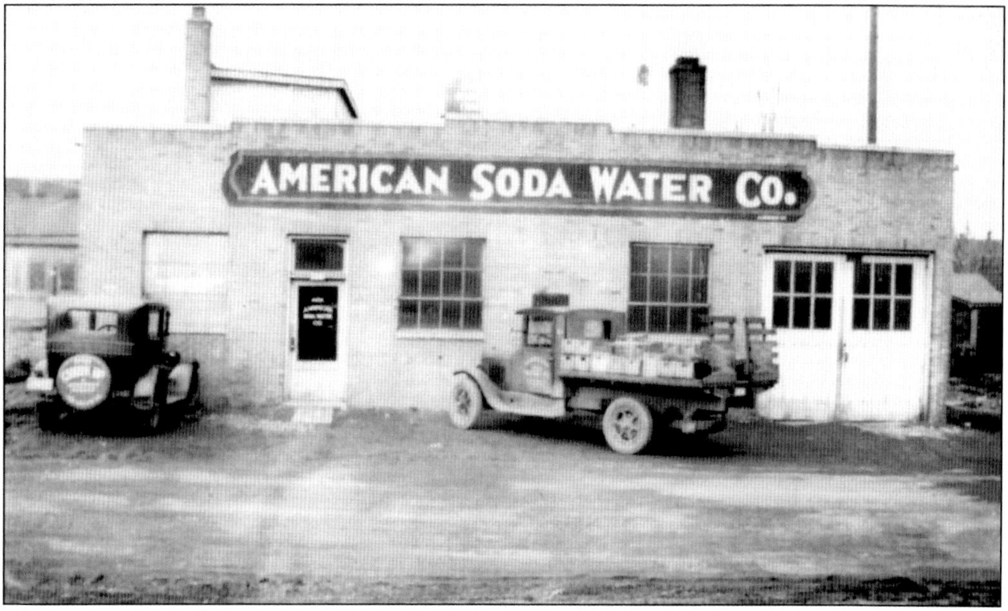

The American Soda Water Company was founded by Joseph Schauz Jr. in 1929. Its first location was at South Seventh Street and National Avenue in Milwaukee. In 1931, the company moved to South Forty-fourth Street and Mitchell, which was a dirt road. Schauz later petitioned for the paving of Mitchell Street. (Courtesy of Joseph F. Schauz.)

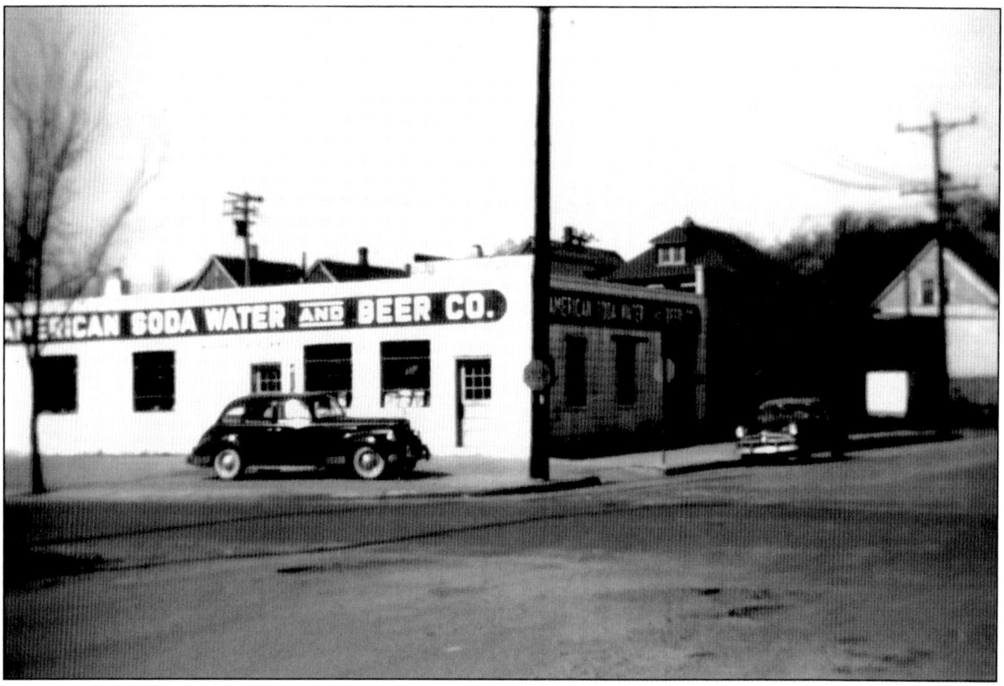

In 1949, American Soda Water built a manufacturing and retail facility (above) at South Forty-third and West Mitchell Streets. In 1972, the company moved its operations to 4040 West Loomis Road until the corporation was terminated on July 4, 1992. Schauz's son Joseph F. still lives in the family home on South Fifty-third Street. (Courtesy of Joseph F. Schauz.)

Tillie Plansky stands in the doorway of Tillie's Village Restaurant, 4409 West National Avenue.

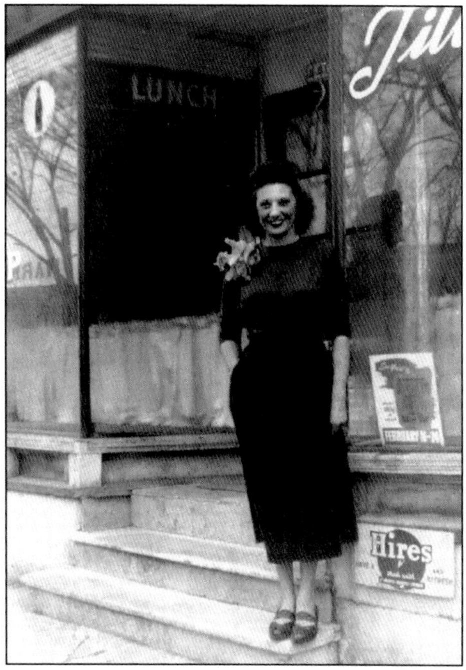

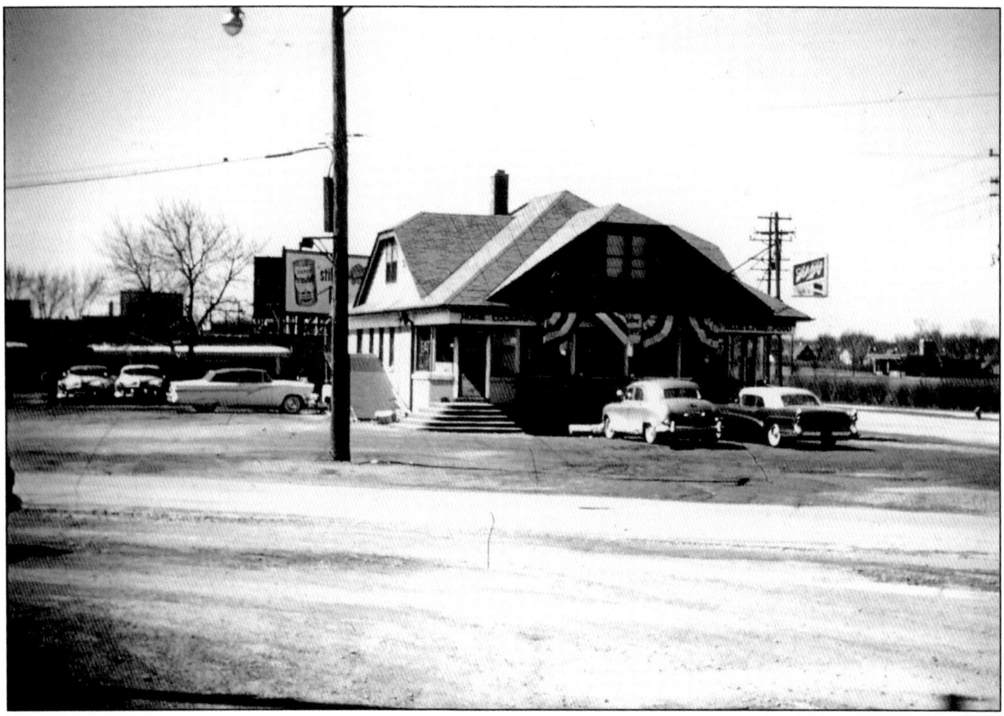

Tillie's Triangle, Tillie Plansky's tavern and restaurant, was located at the intersection of South Forty-sixth Street, Burnham Street, and Electric Avenue from 1956 to 1975. The site is currently occupied by the Two Brothers Restaurant. Plansky also ran Tillie's Village Restaurant on National Avenue, across from the Harnischfeger Corporation, from 1950 to 1972. She sponsored teams for various sports, including bowling, darts, children's softball, and soapbox car racing.

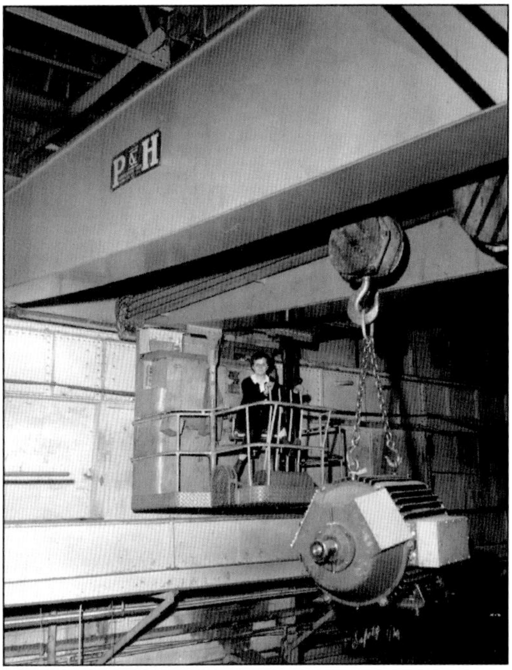

West Milwaukee's own "Rosie the Riveter," Rose Kaminski was a crane operator at the Harnischfeger Corporation for 32 years, beginning during World War II. Rose is still very active in the village.

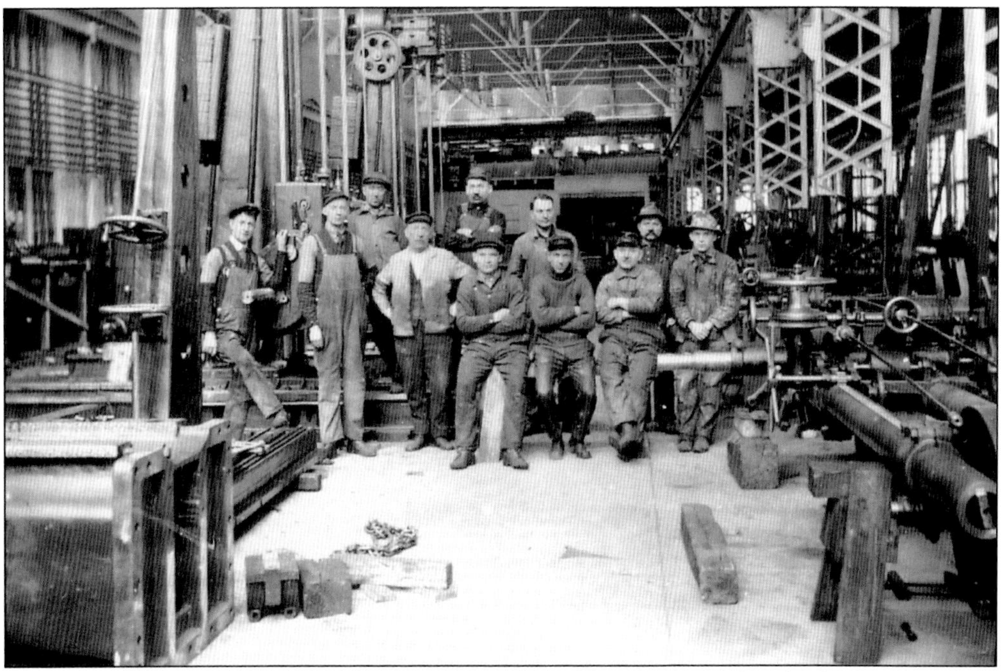

Harnischfeger workers pause for the camera in this undated photograph. The firm is one of the village's oldest in continuous operation.

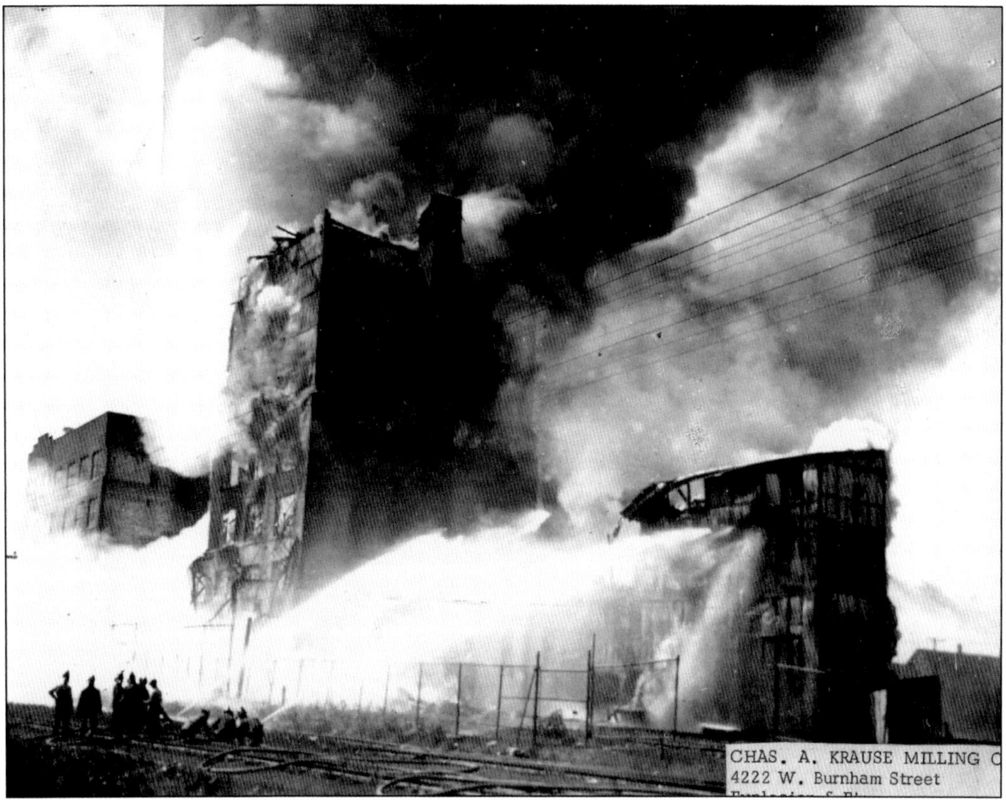

The Charles A. Krause Milling Company suffered two major explosions and fires. The first, pictured here, occurred on September 2, 1924, followed by an April 10, 1937, blast that killed three and injured 29. Krause Milling processed dry corn products for food and industrial use.

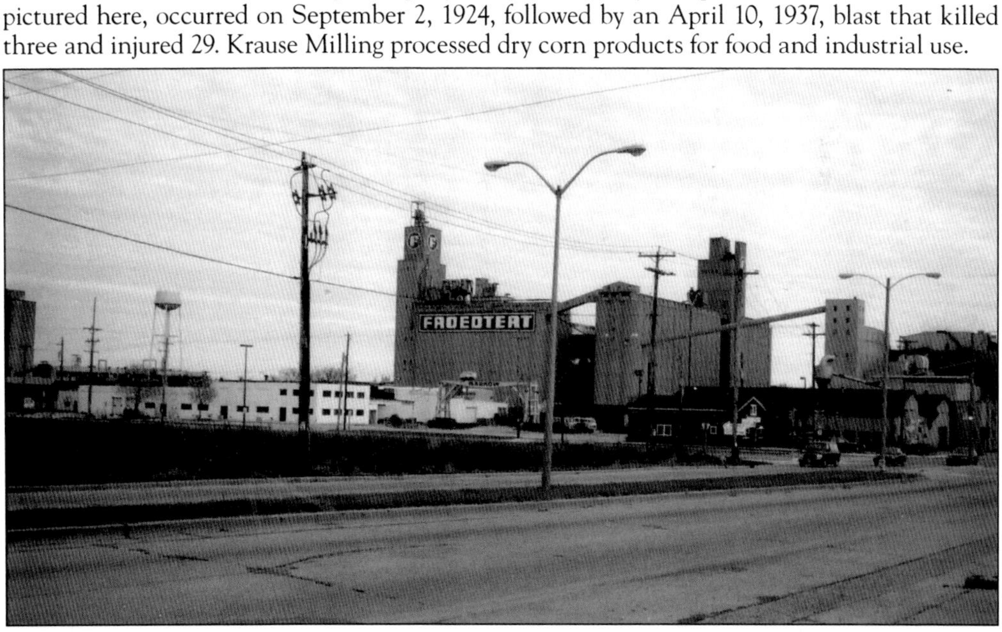

The Froedtert Malt Corporation joined West Milwaukee following the 1951 annexation from the town of Greenfield. It is one of the world's largest commercial malting firms, supplying brewers, distillers, and the food industry.

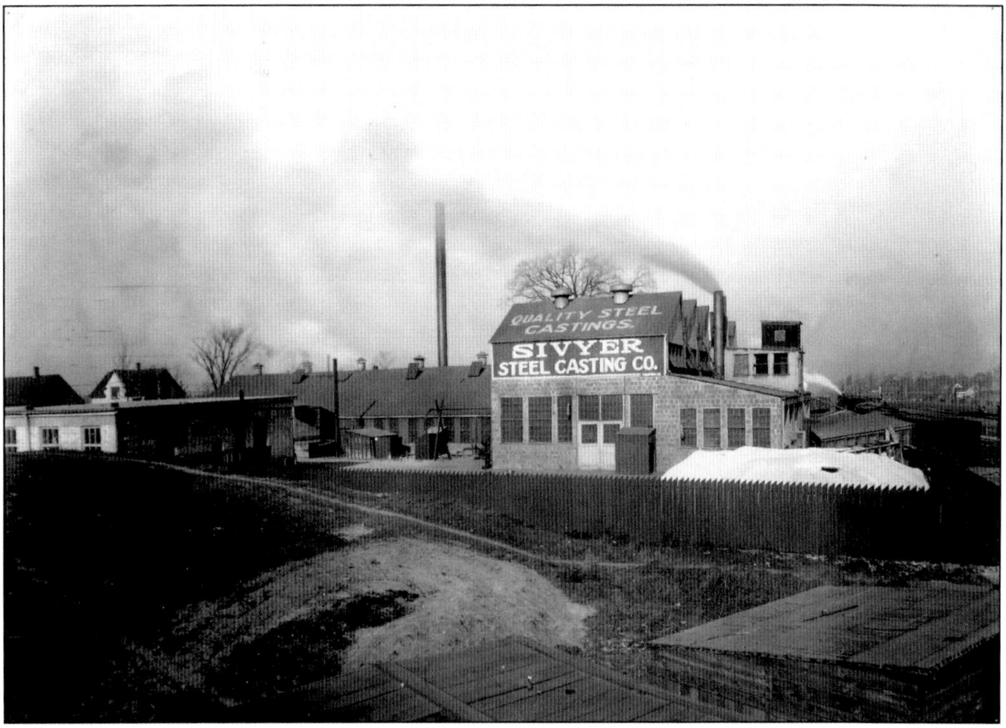

The Sivyer Steel Casting Company, seen above, began operation in 1909. The foundry made castings of carbon, alloy, and stainless steel. Located on South Forty-third Street near Mitchell, Sivyer was razed for the freeway. The undated photograph below, showing a military ceremony of some sort, was taken from the office building of Sivyer Steel.

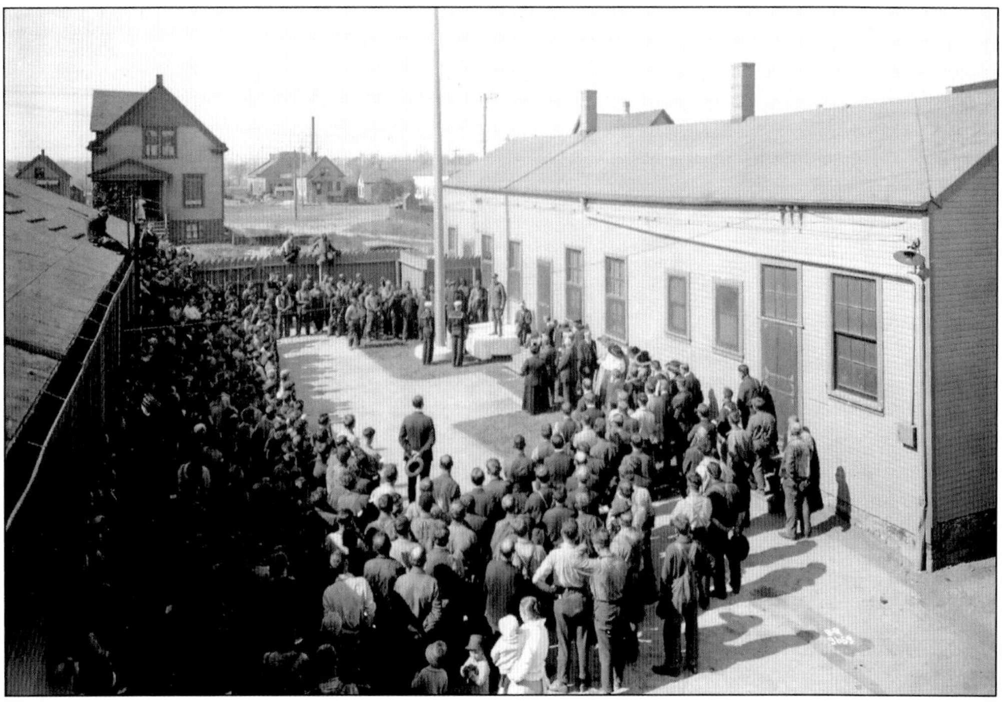

The Rex Chain Belt factory, shown here in 1940, was created in 1892 to produce a detachable chain invented by Christopher Levalley. In 1908, Levalley designed a concrete mixer with a chain belt drive, and the "Rex" brand mark first appeared on it.

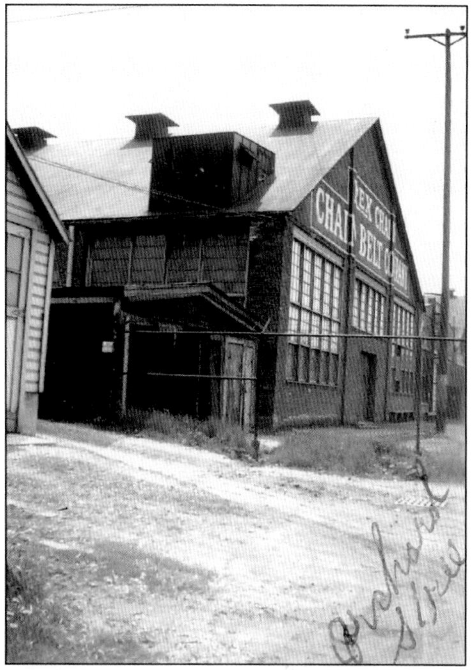

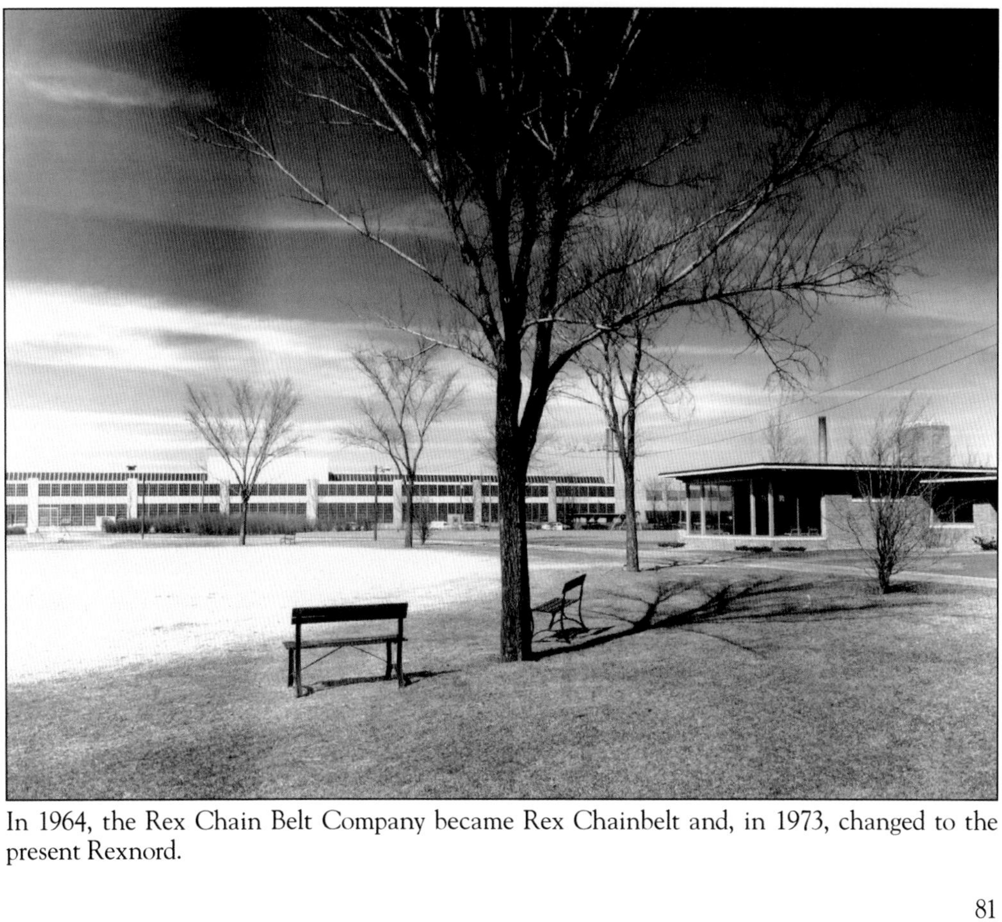

In 1964, the Rex Chain Belt Company became Rex Chainbelt and, in 1973, changed to the present Rexnord.

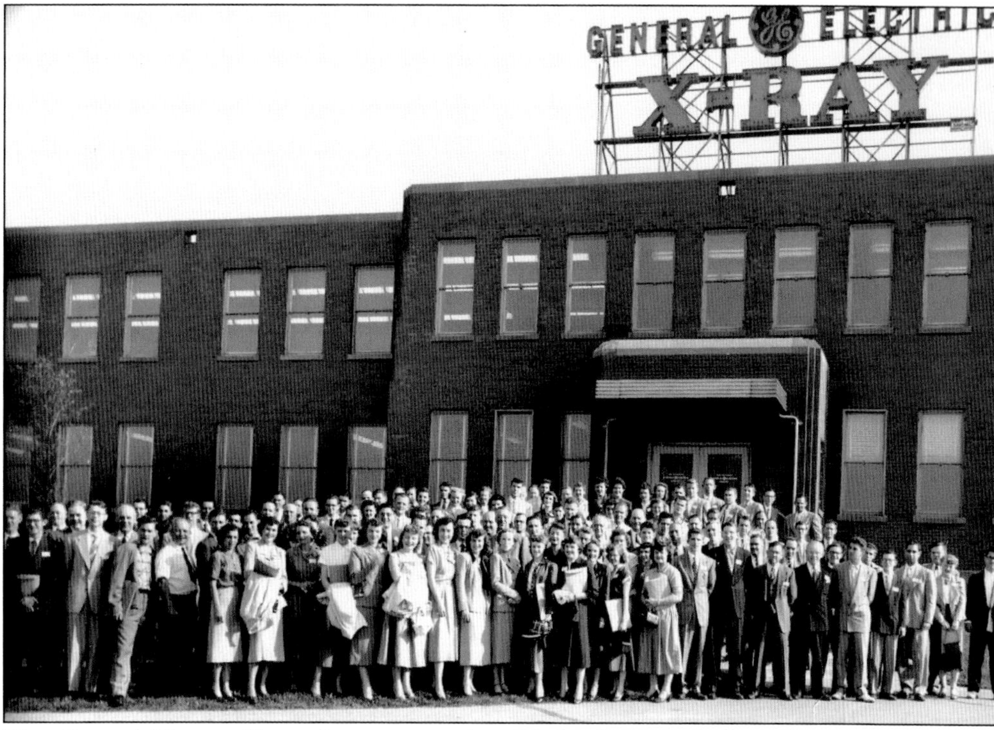

The General Electric X-ray plant, pictured in 1948, also joined the village with the 1951 annexation. Known today as GE Medical, it continues to manufacture X-ray and medical diagnostic equipment. (Courtesy of GE Medical.)

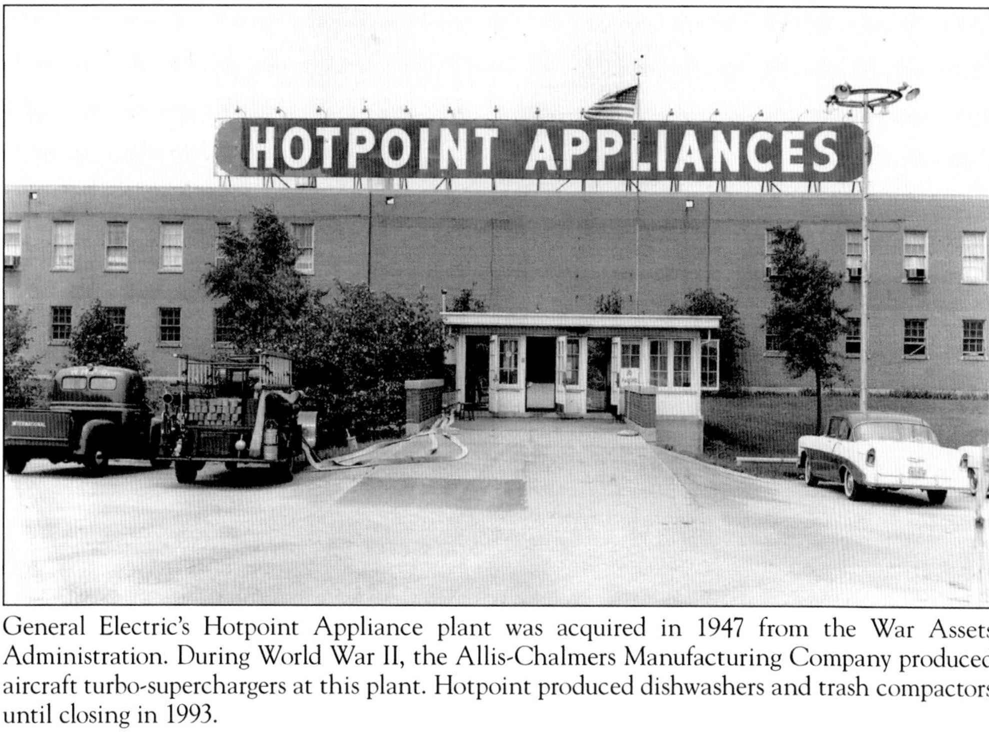

General Electric's Hotpoint Appliance plant was acquired in 1947 from the War Assets Administration. During World War II, the Allis-Chalmers Manufacturing Company produced aircraft turbo-superchargers at this plant. Hotpoint produced dishwashers and trash compactors until closing in 1993.

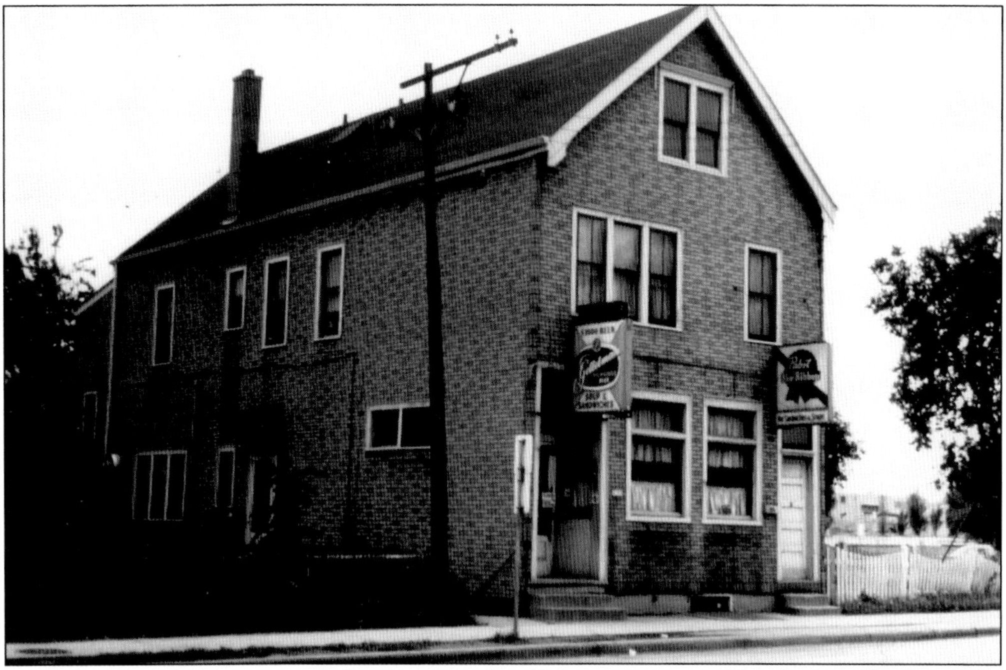

The John Kastelic Tavern, at 4309 West Burnham Street, was owned by the Kastelic family for almost 50 years. The building was demolished, as were so many others, for the Stadium freeway that was never built. (Courtesy of Ed Kastelic.)

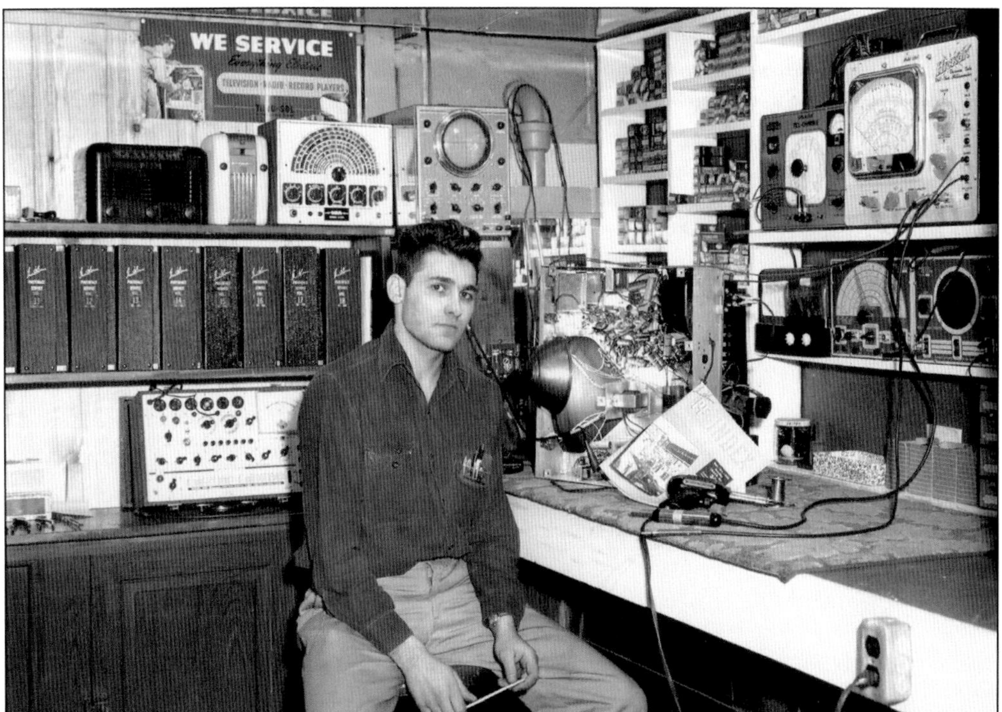

John Lukich is seen in his basement workshop at 1216 South Forty-eighth Street in 1953. In the mid-1950s, he opened Lukich TV, a repair shop at 4416 West Greenfield Avenue.

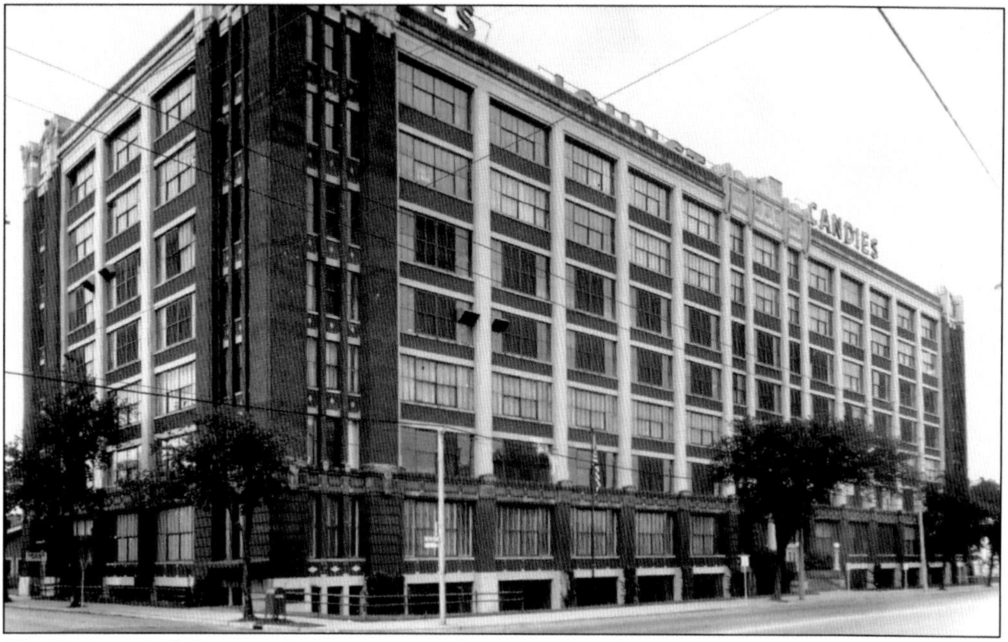

The Robert A. Johnston Company, manufacturer of cookies, crackers, candy, and chocolate products, built a plant between June 1919 and June 1920 at 4023 West National Avenue. It was a family-run business from 1848 to 1980, when it was sold to the Masterson Company. Masterson produces ice-cream toppings and other food industry products. People from all over the Milwaukee area remember buying large bags of broken Johnston cookies for 50¢. (Courtesy of the Masterson Company.)

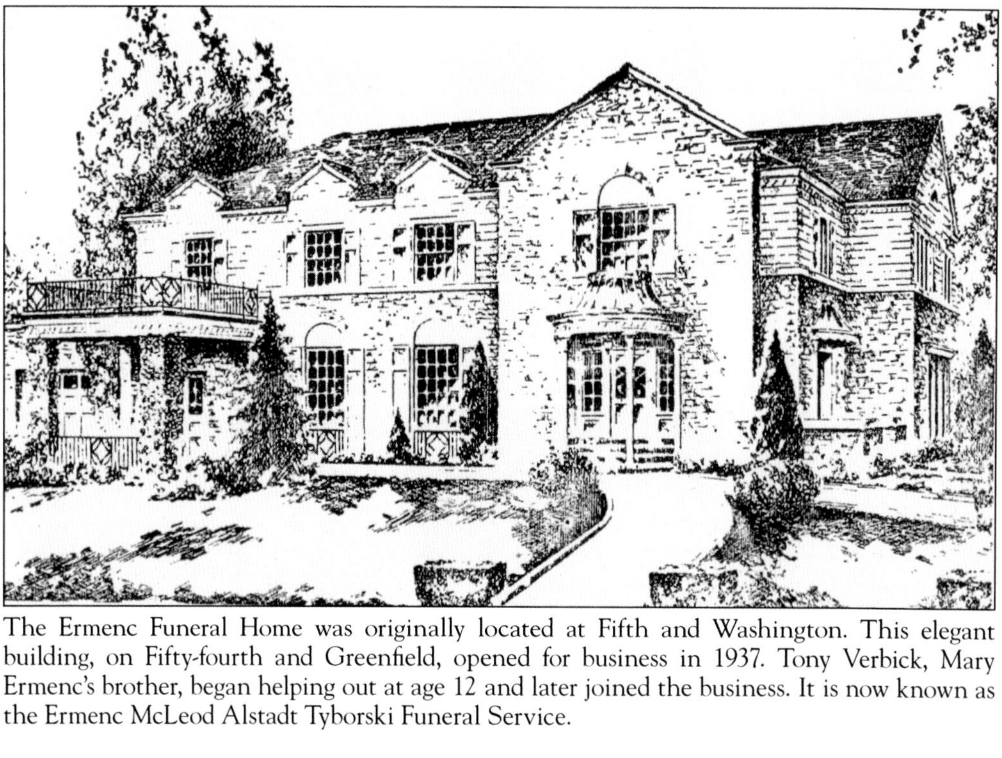

The Ermenc Funeral Home was originally located at Fifth and Washington. This elegant building, on Fifty-fourth and Greenfield, opened for business in 1937. Tony Verbick, Mary Ermenc's brother, began helping out at age 12 and later joined the business. It is now known as the Ermenc McLeod Alstadt Tyborski Funeral Service.

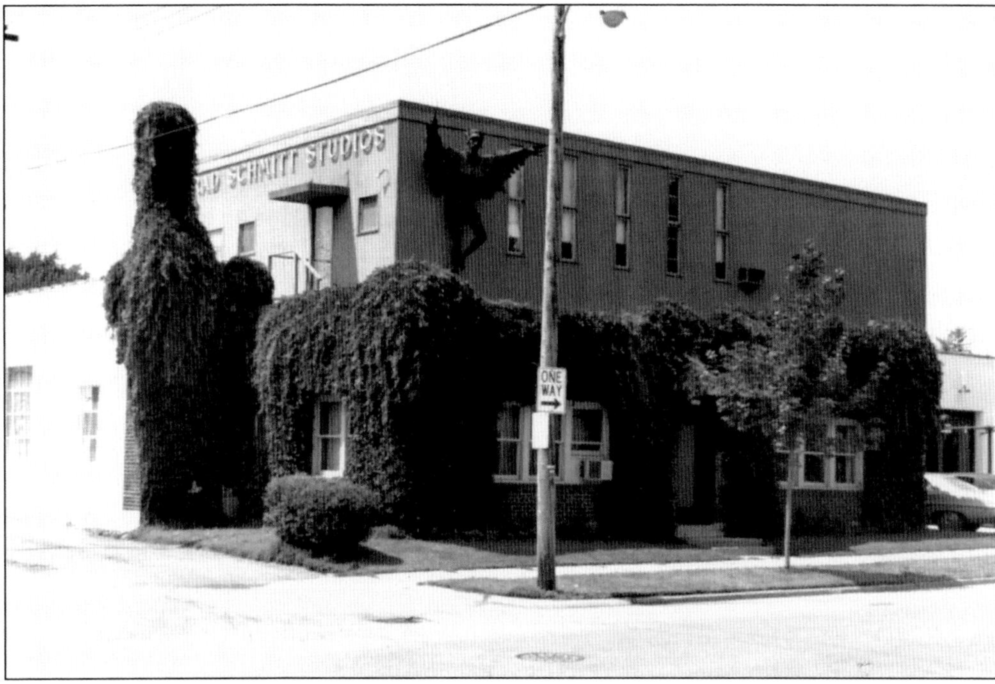

Founded in 1889, the internationally recognized Conrad Schmitt Studios creates and restores timeless interiors and fine works of art for buildings of architectural, historic, and religious significance. Also one of the oldest and largest glass studios in the country, it is known for outstanding craftsmanship in the creation, conservation, and restoration of stained glass. Shown here in July 1969 is the South Forty-third Street building. Conrad Schmitt was located here from 1946 to 1973, when the studio moved to its current location in New Berlin. (Courtesy of Conrad Schmitt Studios.)

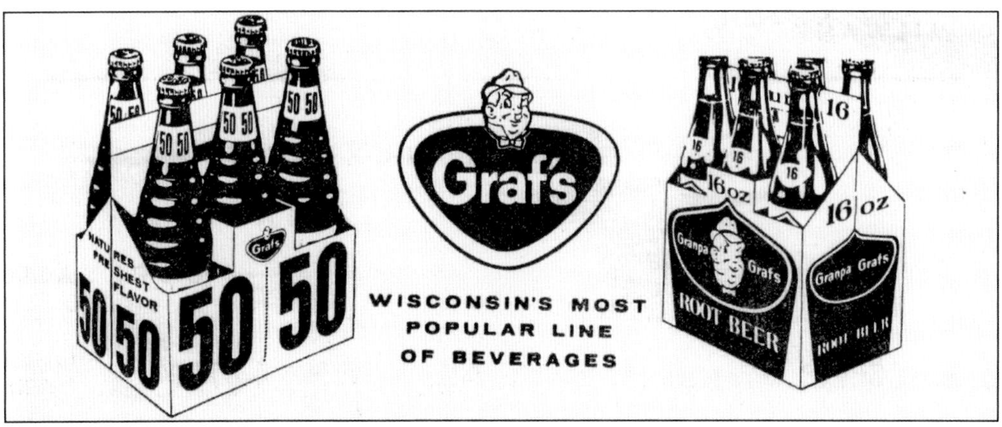

Graf's Beverages, founded in Milwaukee in 1873, moved to 4040 West Greenfield Avenue in 1937. In 1968, Graf's was purchased by the Univest Corporation, which then sold it to the Canada Dry Company in 1979. In 1984, the facility closed, with the Canfield Company of Chicago purchasing the Graf name. In 1988, the remodeled building became a Sentry food store, which itself recently closed.

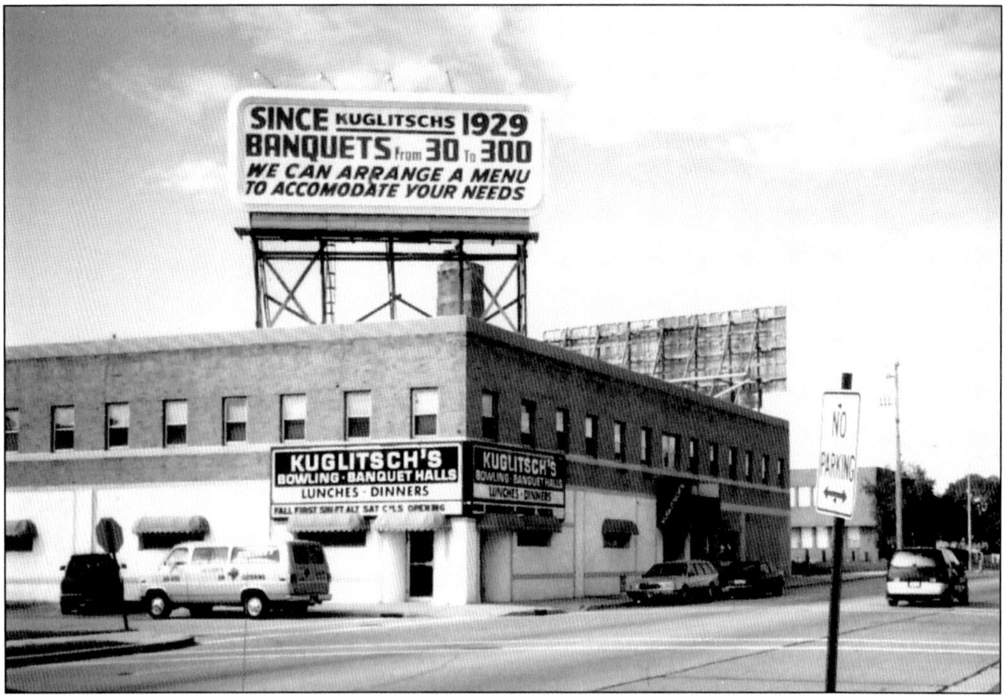

In 1929, Paul Kuglitsch Sr. and his wife, Frances, built Kuglitsch's at Forty-fourth and Greenfield as a bowling alley, bar, and lounge. An addition in 1957 added eight more lanes (for a total of 16) and a large banquet facility with catering. Kuglitsch's was one of the first Midwest bowling centers to switch from pin boys to automatic pin-setting machines. Initially, the nine second-floor apartments housed first- and second-generation Kuglitsch families. The business's operation continued in the family until the building's demolition in 2001.

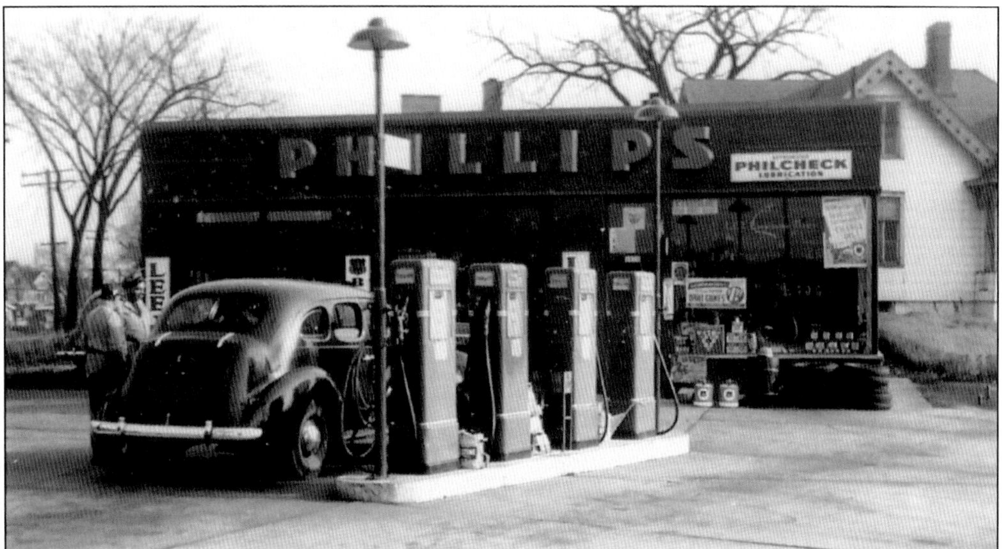

This Phillips 66 service station at West Greenfield and West Beloit Road was operated by the Bliesner brothers, Clarence and Hilbert "Hip" Bliesner, from the 1930s until Hip's death in the mid-1960s. The Dickson home is seen in the background. (Courtesy of Sally Burke.)

Five

Village Life

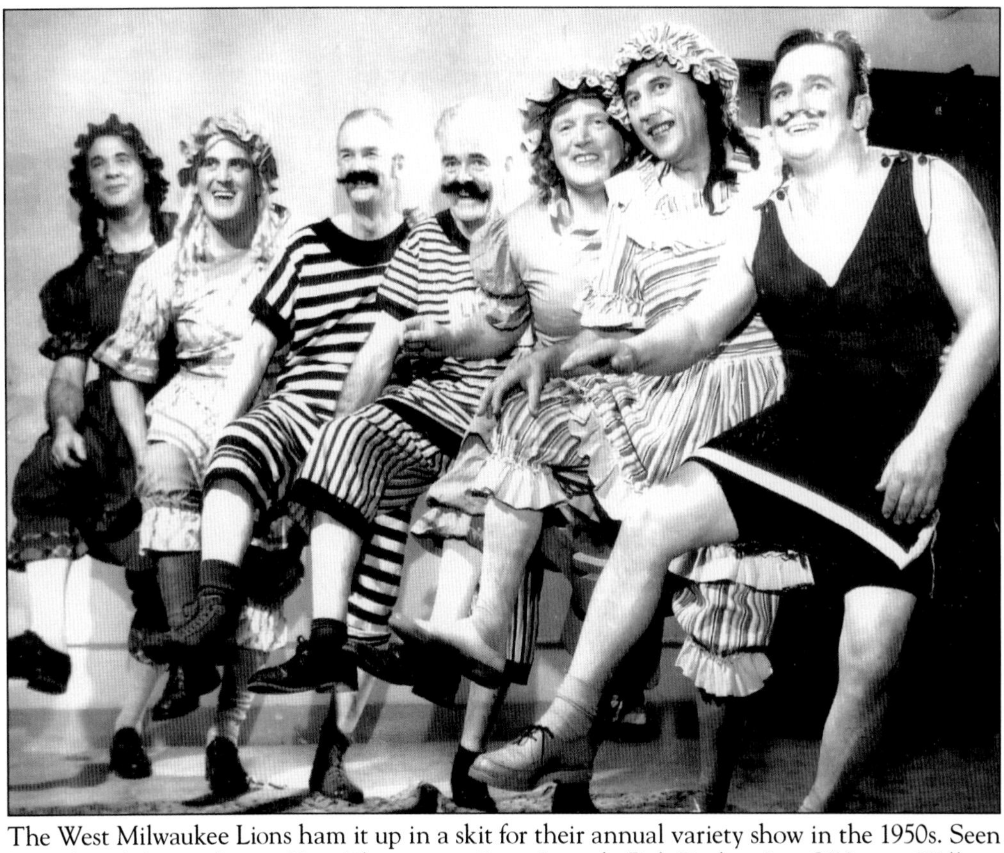

The West Milwaukee Lions ham it up in a skit for their annual variety show in the 1950s. Seen here, from left to right, are Dan Thompson, Gene Strandt, Bob Durbin, Les O'Herrin, William "Red" Testdorf, Steve Goran, and Clarence Baker.

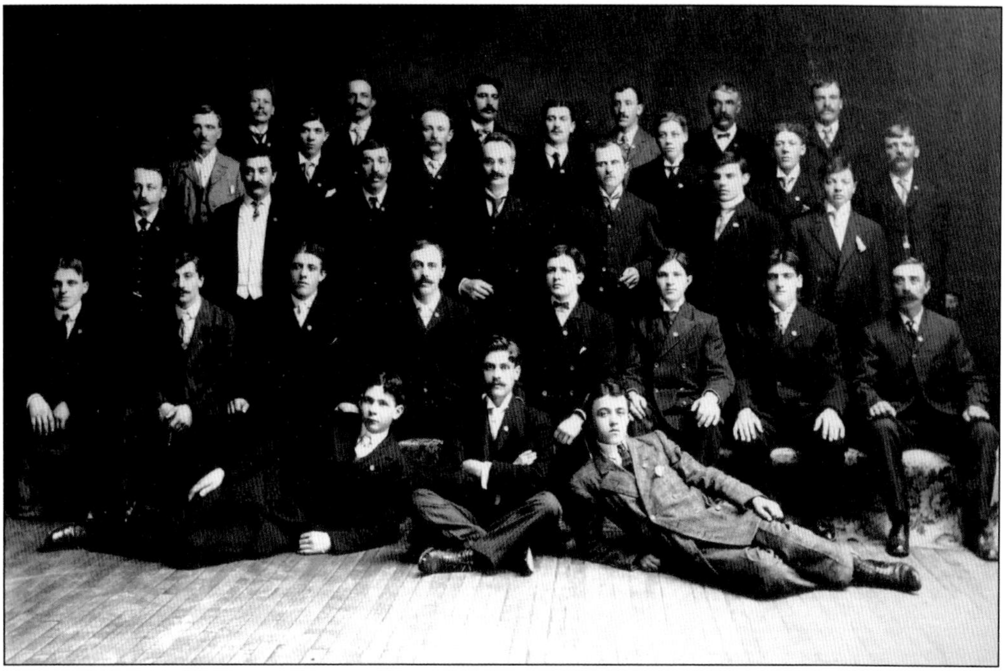

Several West Milwaukee residents were members of the Edelweiss Mannerchor (Men's Choir), shown in this 1906 photograph. Some familiar names listed as members are Thekan, Schnabl, Kuglitsch, Abuja, and Fina.

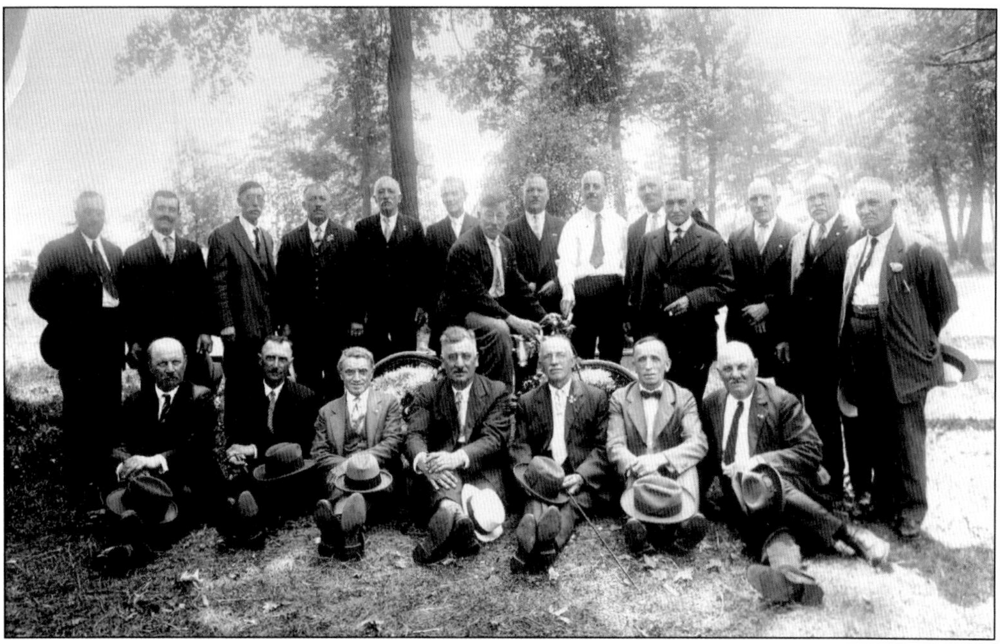

This men's group called itself the Edelweiss Bicycle Society, although nothing is known about its activities. Identified in the first row are Joe Lewein (left), Mr. Druml (second from left), Mr. Thekan (fifth from left), and Vincent Lewein (seventh from left). Those named in the second row are Martin Tabushing (left), Mike Schnabl (fifth from left), and Paul Brenner (10th from left).

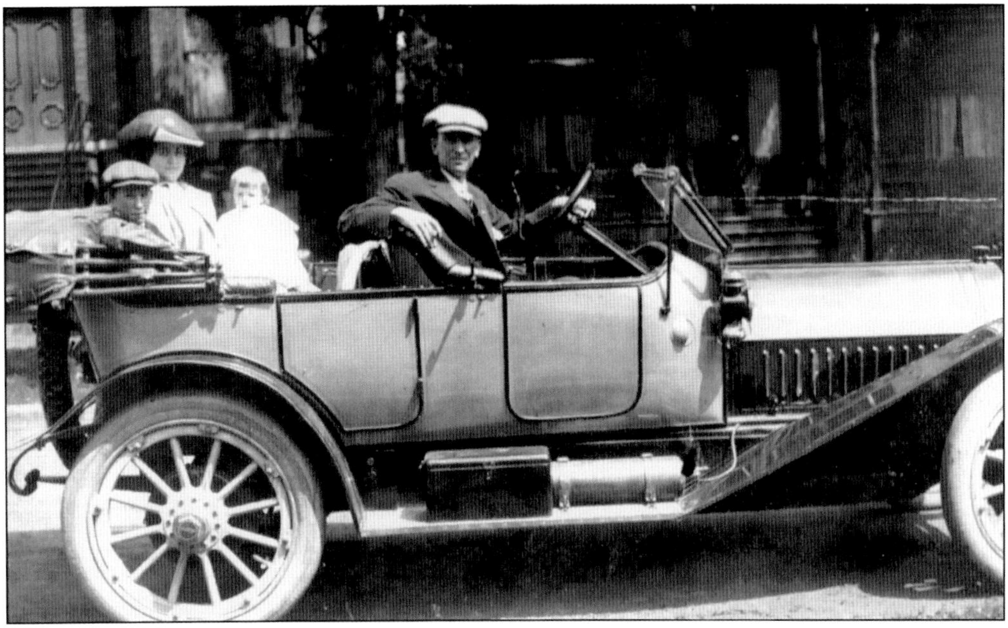

The Sheriff family enjoys an outing in the roadster. George is pictured with his wife Edna, son Emmet, and daughter Christina.

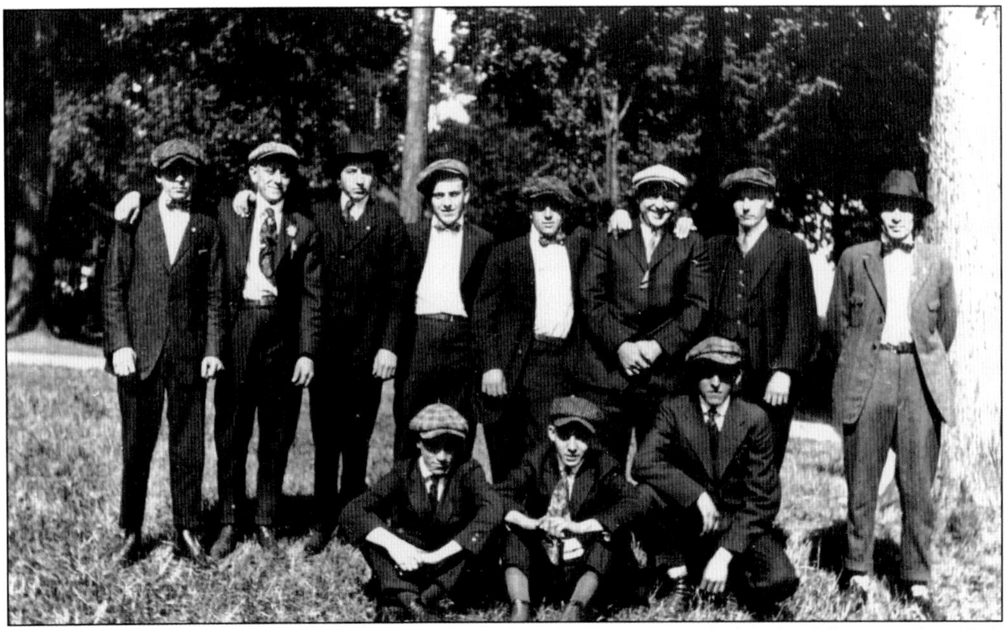

This group, identified only as the "1920 West Milwaukee Gang," includes the following, from left to right: (first row) Jim Crowley, Oscar Kramer, and Erwin Buth; (second row) Erwin Kramer, Frank Wagner, Frank Gross, Fred Schuster, Frank Grafwallner, John Wagner, Frank Zastrow, and Jack Kramer.

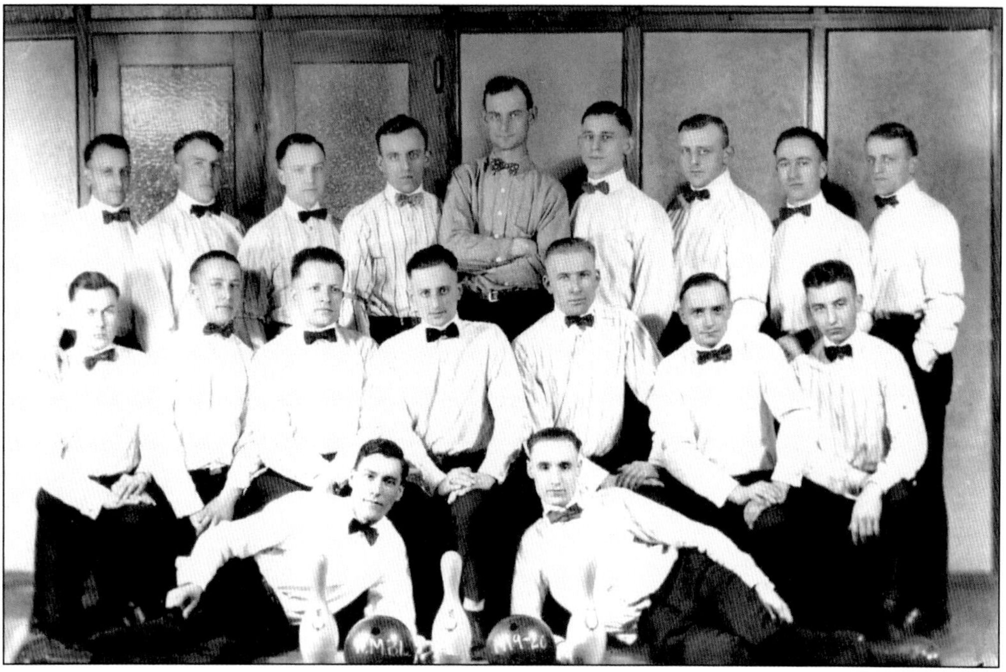

The first bowling league in the village formed for the 1919–1920 season. Team members were as follows, from left to right: (first row) Tom Pipp and Mike Brugger; (second row) Frank Zastrow, John Schmidt, Max Thekan, Charles Thekan, Leo Hintz, Joe Schuller, and Frank Gross; (third row) Charles Heipel, Frank Grafwallner, John Bartalotis, ? Buth, Al Zunker, Joe Hanseder, John Wagner, Lawrence Andrits, and Anton Thekan.

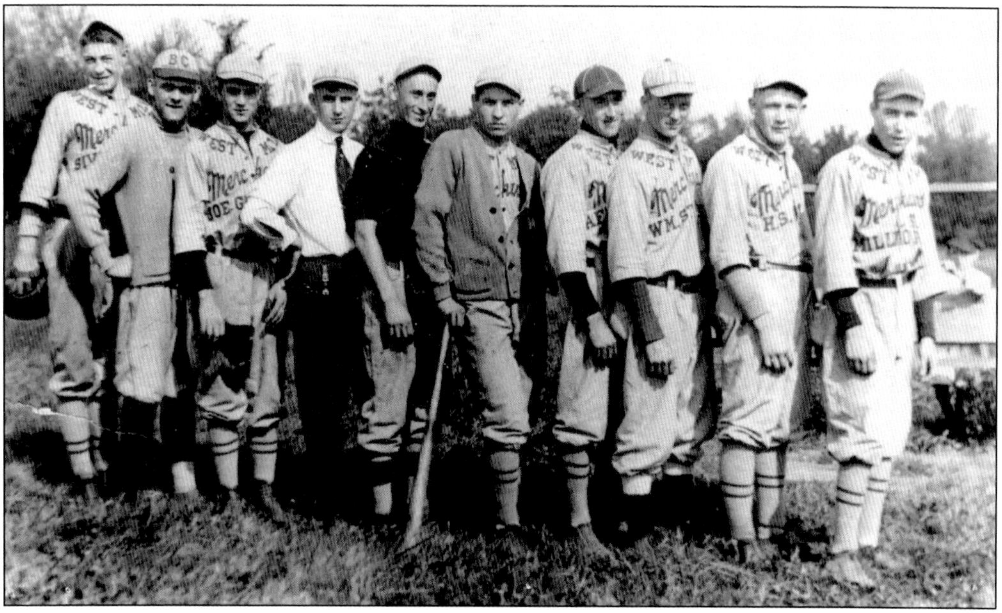

An early West Milwaukee Merchants baseball team lines up in this undated photograph. Pictured from left to right are Bob Shaud, Dave Milbrath, Ben Milan, Ed Zunker, ? Drews, "Rags" Reckowski (who played for Detroit as Joe Rick), Buck Hielman, ? Phillips, Tim Ryan, and ? Dooley.

Residents took pride in their beautiful homes, many of which have unfortunately been lost to the failed freeway plan. Mrs. F. Schuster stands in front of her home at 4420 West Scott Street in 1920. She wears a dusting cap to help keep her hair clean while doing household chores.

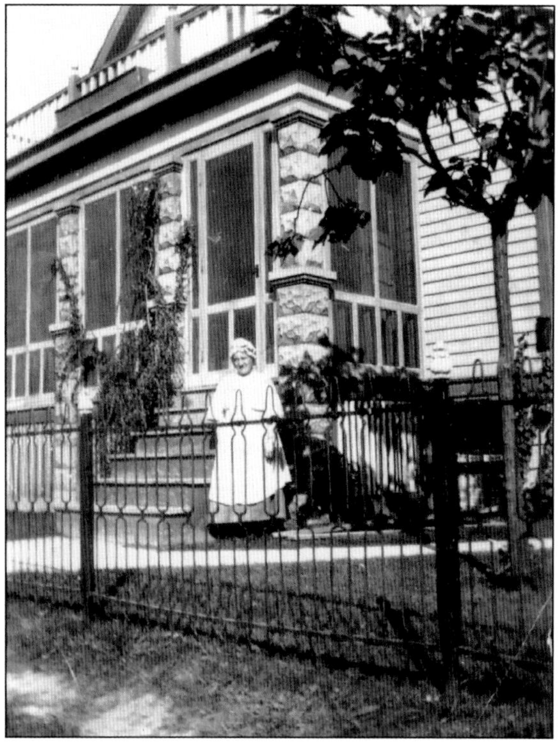

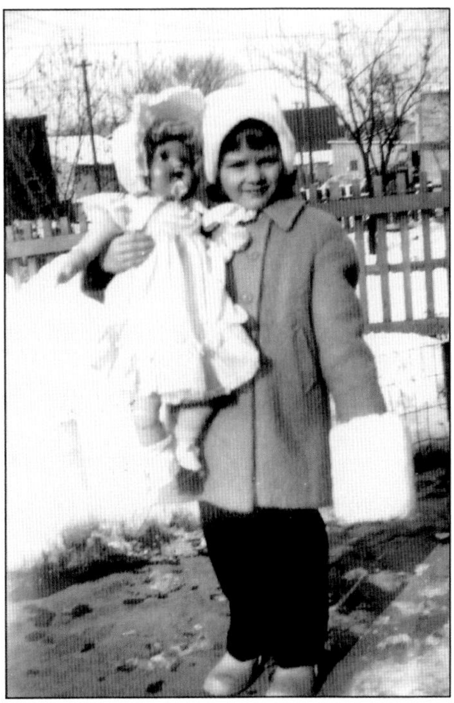

Rosie Nikolaus plays with her doll outside her South Forty-third Street home. These happy times are only memories for those who lived in the freeway corridor. (Courtesy of Rose Nikolaus.)

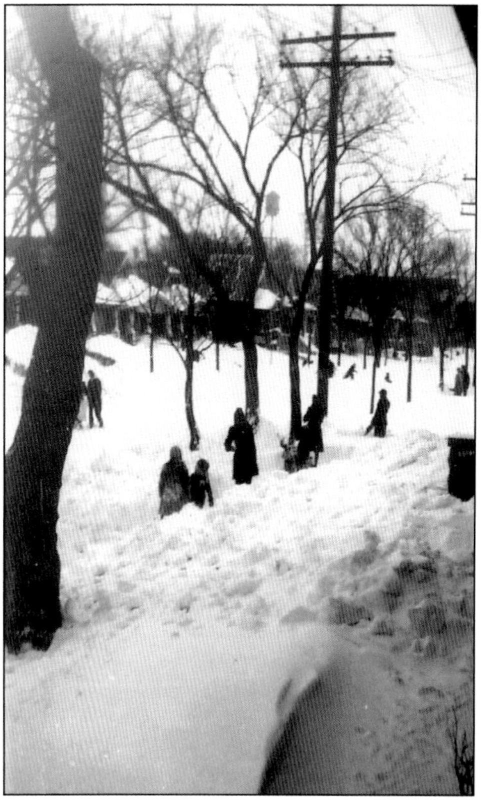

Residents dig out following the record snowfall during the blizzard of 1947. Between January 28 and 31 of that year, up to 18 inches of snow fell, with high winds causing drifts of up to 17 feet.

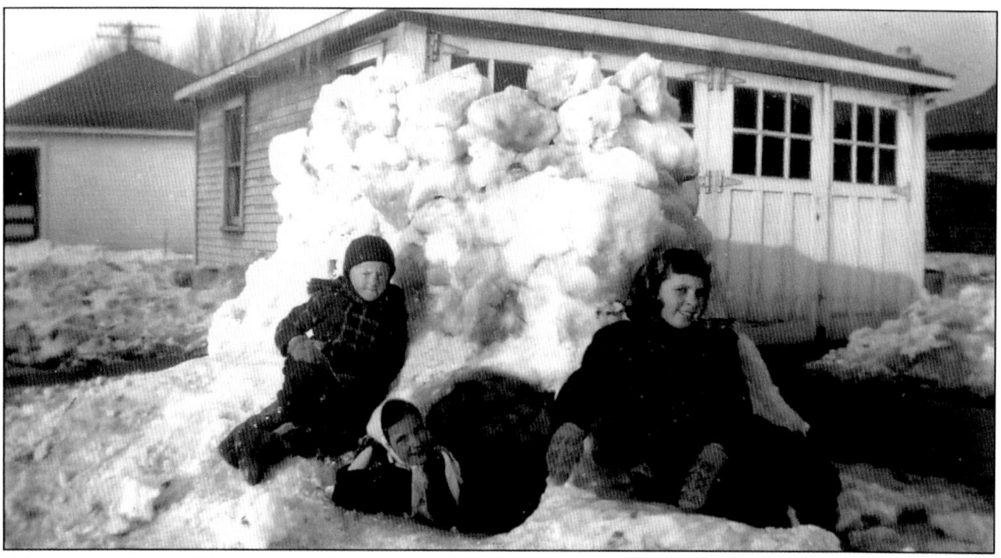

Winter fun for children is timeless; snow forts have always been fun to build. In front of the Nawrocki garage are Paul Nawrocki (left), Carol Nawrocki (center), and Mary Schauz. (Courtesy of Carol Nawrocki.)

The Soldiers' Home, bordering West Milwaukee to the north, provided a great recreation area for villagers. Concerts and picnics were popular for many Milwaukee residents, since the National Avenue streetcar line extended this far west. Here, Walter Funke stands on a ski jump on the eastern end of what is now the Clement J. Zablocki V.A. Medical Center.

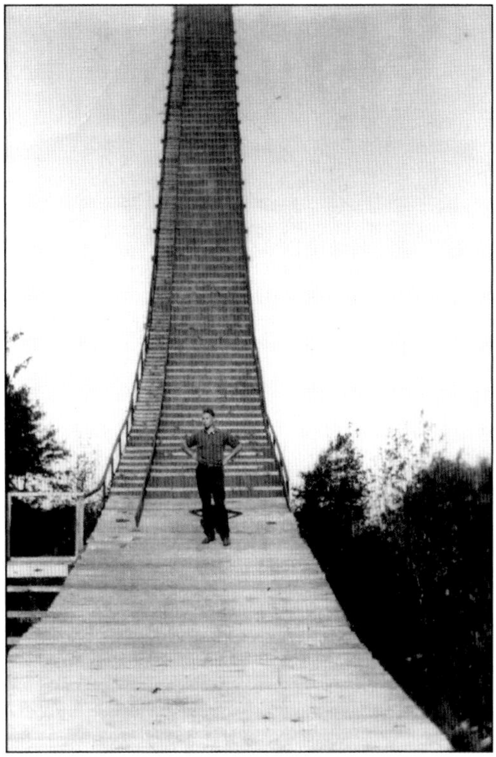

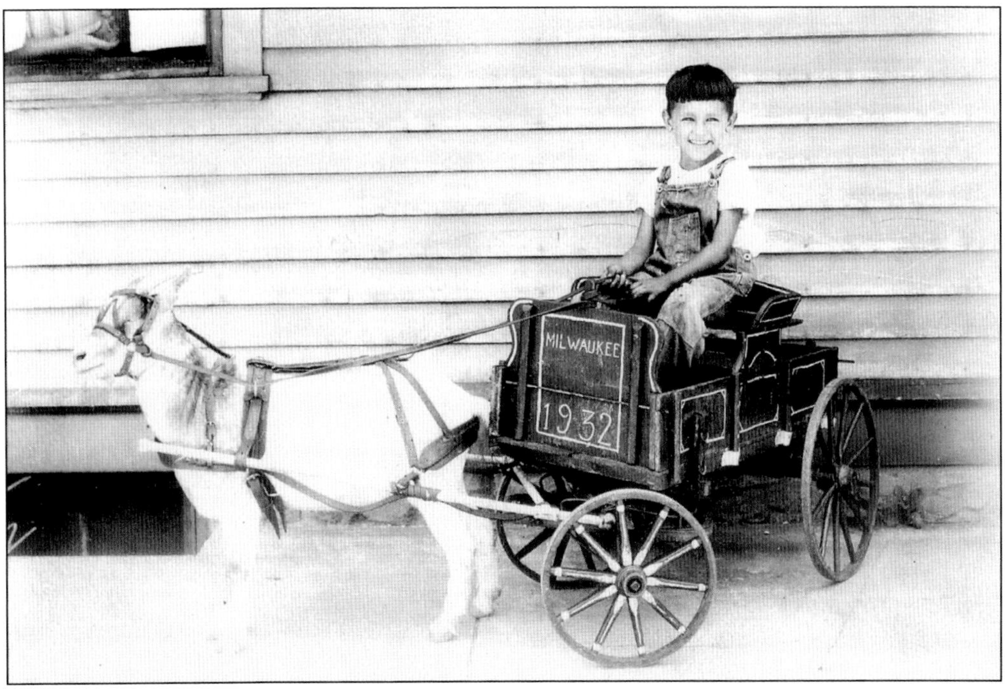

Little John Lukich drives a goat cart in 1932. He later grew up to become the owner and operator of Lukich TV.

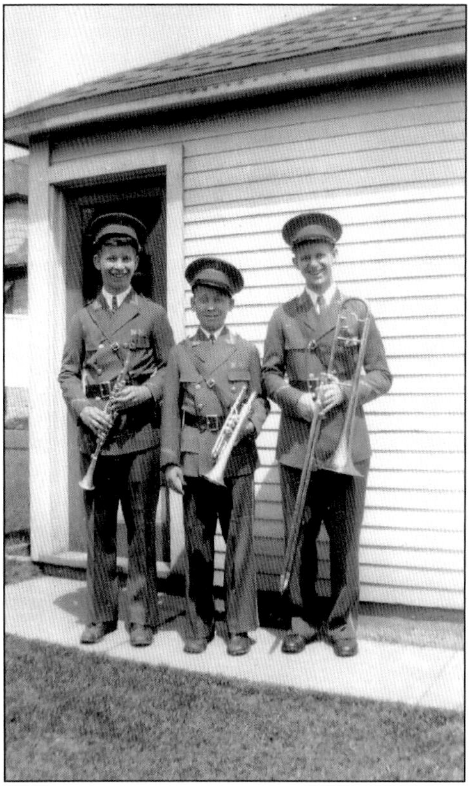

George (left), Jack (middle), and Joseph Schauz toot their horns for the school band in 1943. (Courtesy of Joseph F. Schauz.)

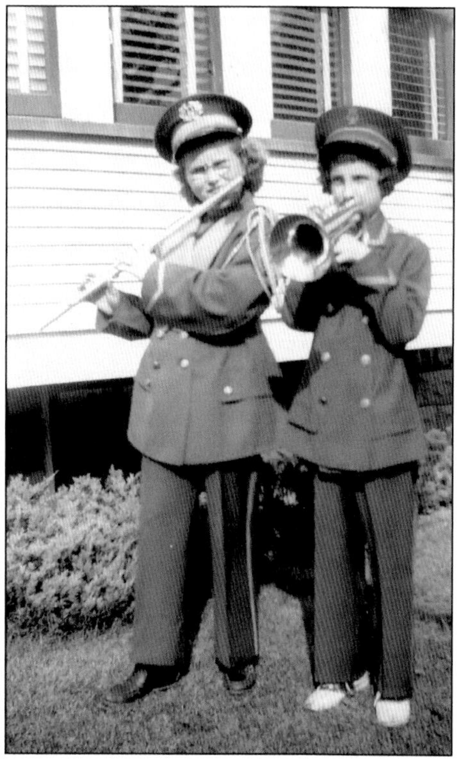

Lois Eichhorst (left) and Carol Nawrocki were musicians and also drum majorettes for the high school marching band. The 1956 graduates appear here outside the Nawrocki home. (Courtesy of Carol Nawrocki.)

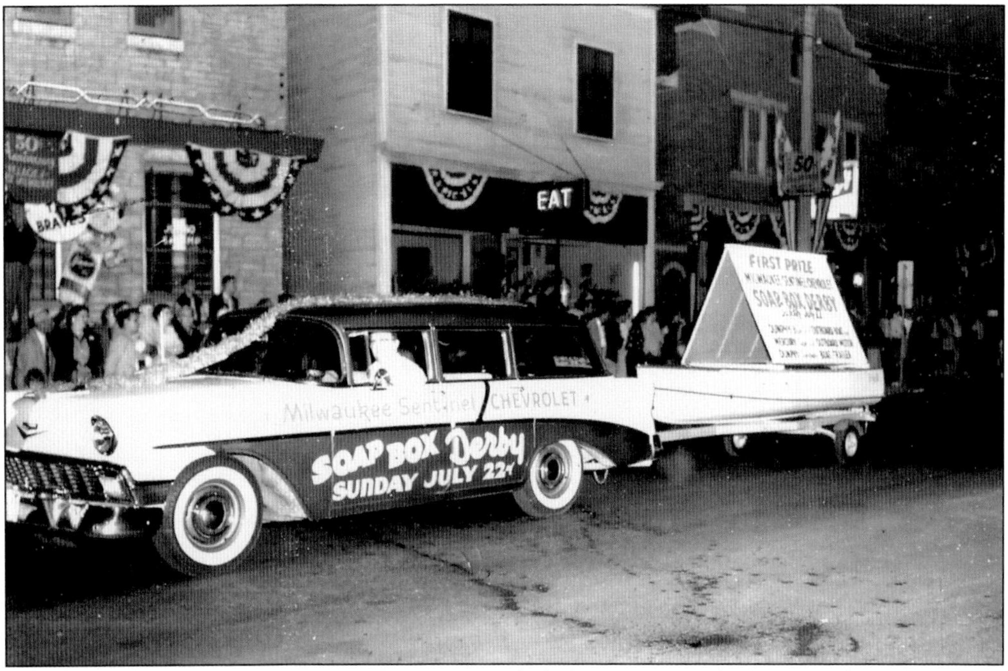

The village's 50th anniversary parade in 1956 included a promotion for an annual soapbox derby co-sponsored by the *Milwaukee Sentinel* newspaper and Milwaukee County Chevrolet dealers, along with the West Milwaukee Fire Department.

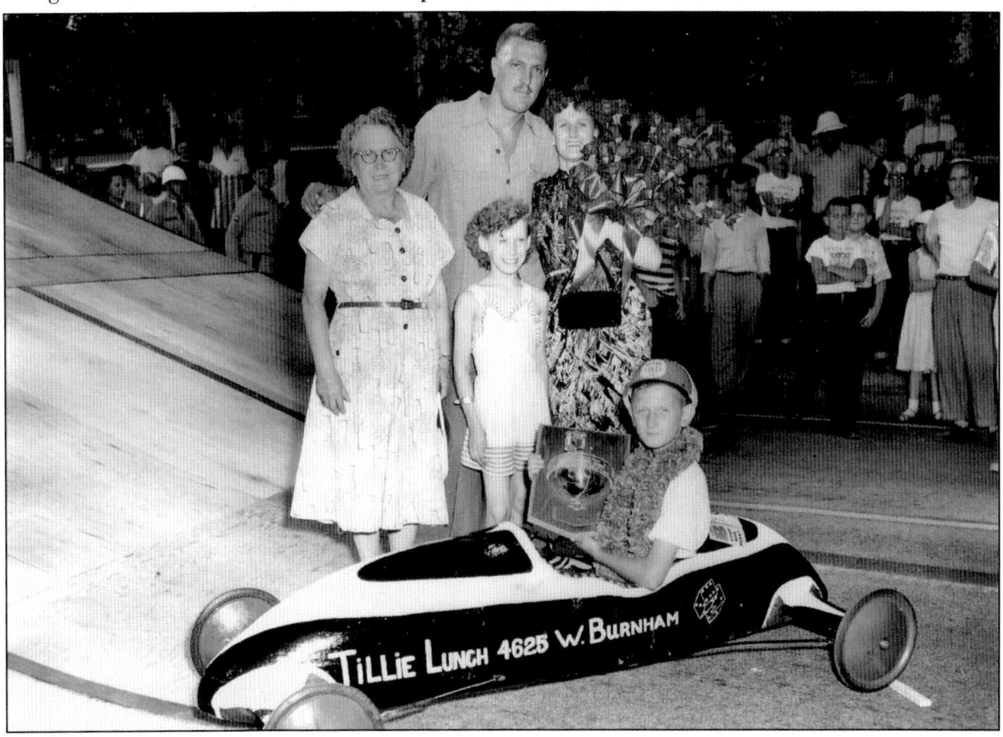

A soapbox derby winner, in a car sponsored by Tillie's Lunch, shows off his prize as his family proudly looks on in the 1950s.

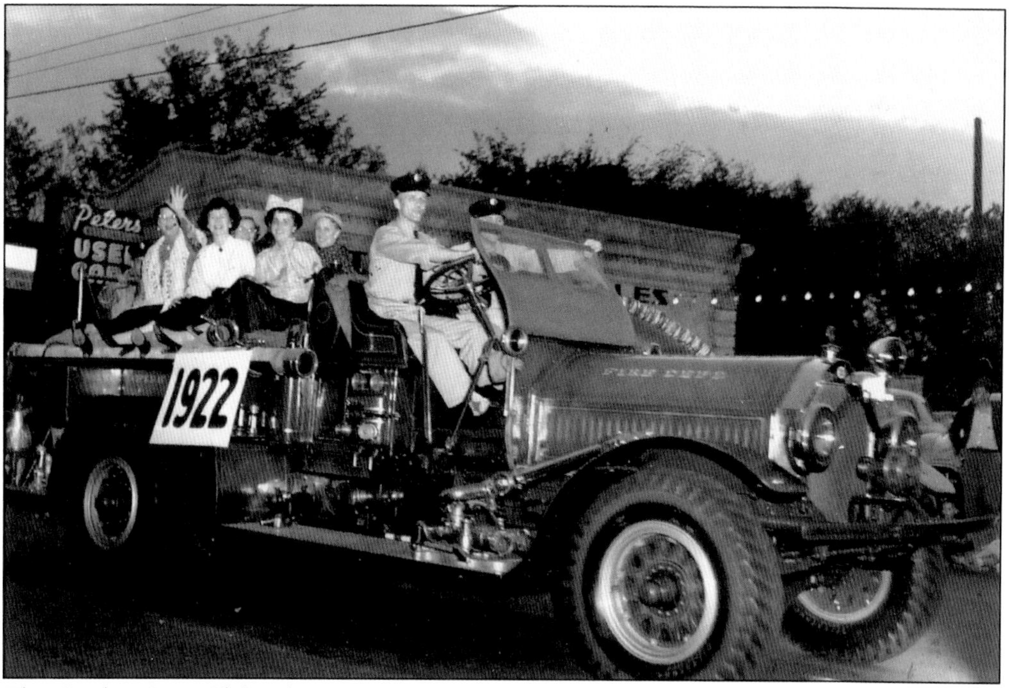

The Garden Gate Club rides atop an old fire truck for the village's 50th anniversary parade on May 26, 1956. According to the club's charter, its purpose "shall be to work together as gardeners and neighbors in the exchanging of garden knowledge for our own benefit and that of our community and to promote educational and artistic projects pertaining to gardening." Its members still meet informally.

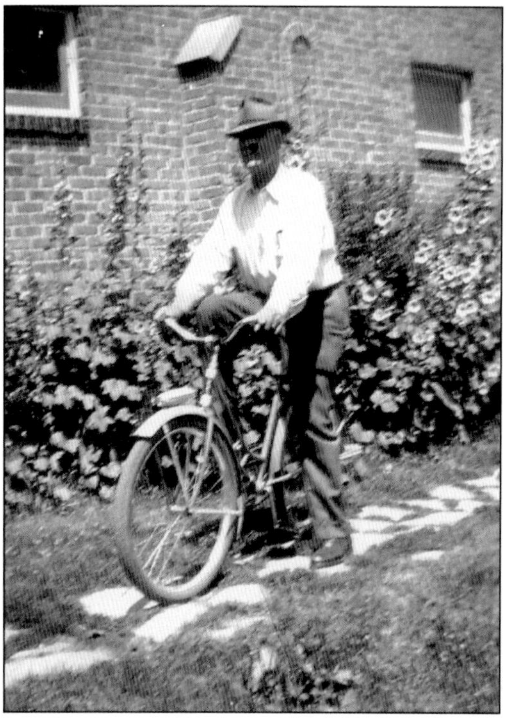

John Bensene rides his bicycle alongside his house at the corner of South Fifty-second and Mitchell Streets. At the time, Mitchell Street was unpaved west of Forty-third. (Courtesy of Jean Cefalu.)

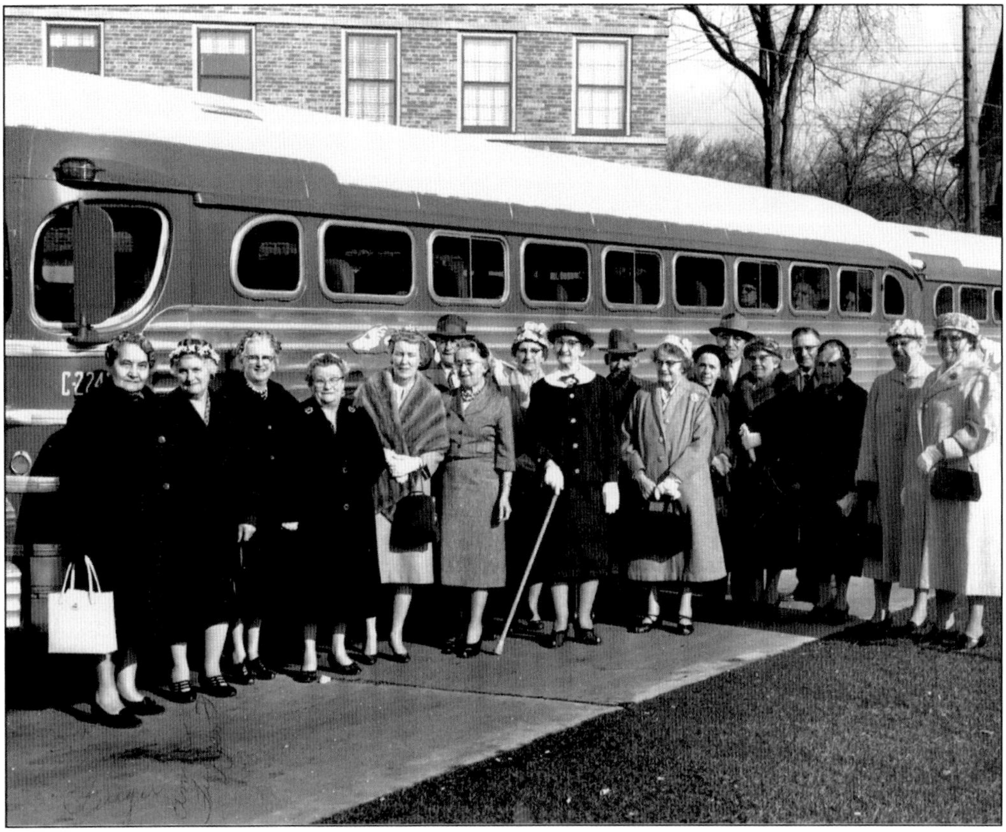

The West Milwaukee Golden Agers travel to Kohler on a bus tour on April 6, 1961. The village provided help in sponsoring dinners and trips. Today, the Golden Agers are treated to an annual Christmas Party at Pershing Elementary School, with entertainment provided by the students.

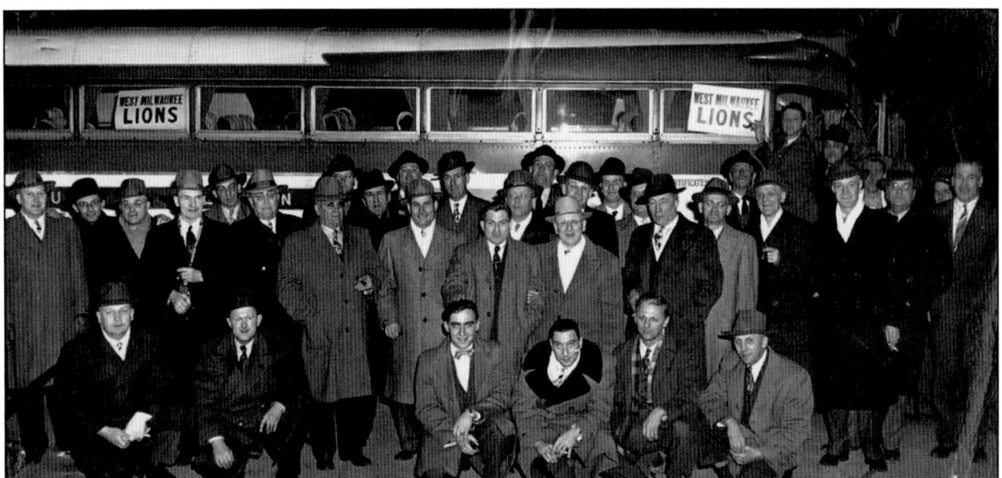

The West Milwaukee Lions pose during an outing in the mid-1950s. The local Lions Club chapter was founded in 1937 to encourage village improvements, assist the needy, and perform other charitable works.

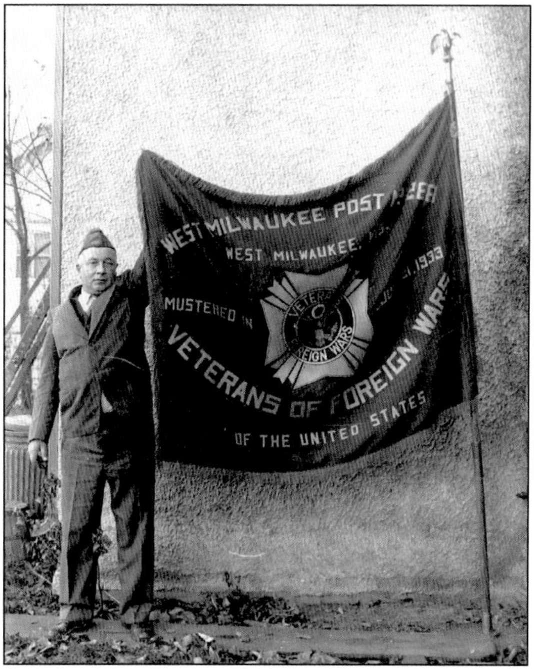

A great debt is owed to the many veterans and active servicemen and women who have contributed, sometimes with their lives, to the well-being of our country and community. Shown left is Royal Michel of West Milwaukee VFW Post 2861. Below is Kuwait veteran Jim Morrison, a former postman in the village.

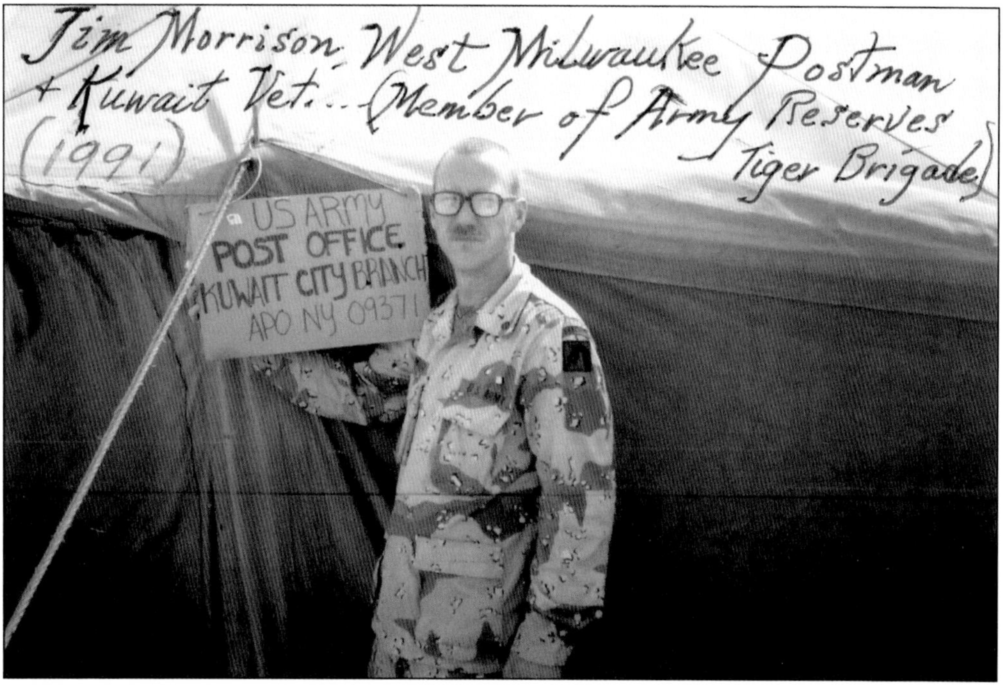

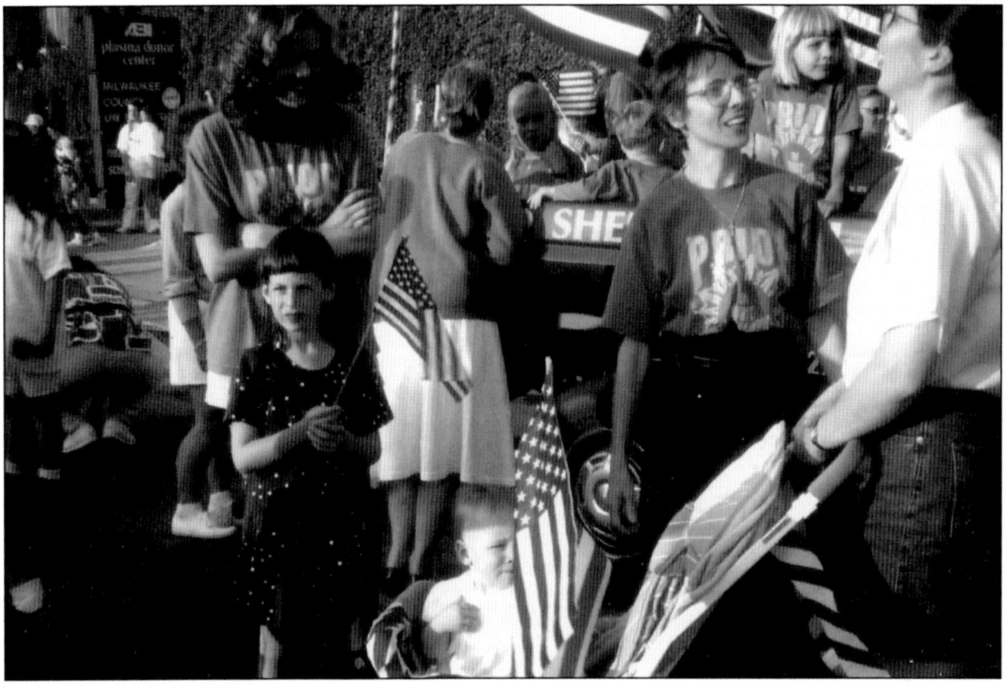

PRIDE in West Milwaukee was founded in 1993 by Diane Brazale as a means of promoting community spirit. The group has participated in picnics, evening walks, flower plantings, and as shown above, the West Allis Fourth of July parade. The acronym stands for Pride in our community, Respect for one another, Involvement in our community, Development of our Village, and a safe Environment for everyone.

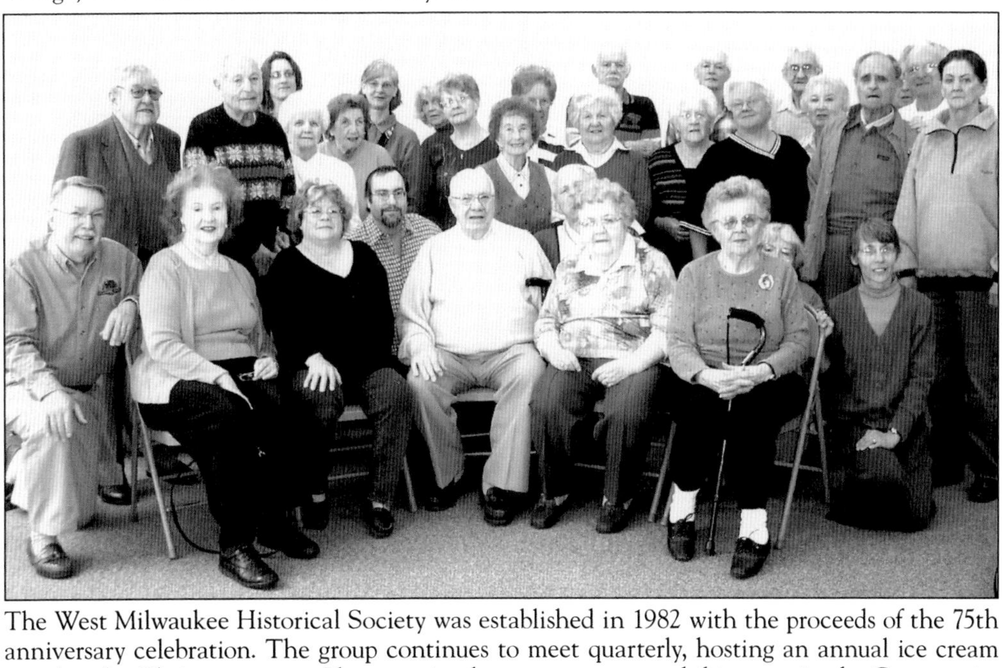

The West Milwaukee Historical Society was established in 1982 with the proceeds of the 75th anniversary celebration. The group continues to meet quarterly, hosting an annual ice cream social and a Christmas party. Plans are in place to create an exhibit room in the Community Centre to be shared with citizens and schoolchildren.

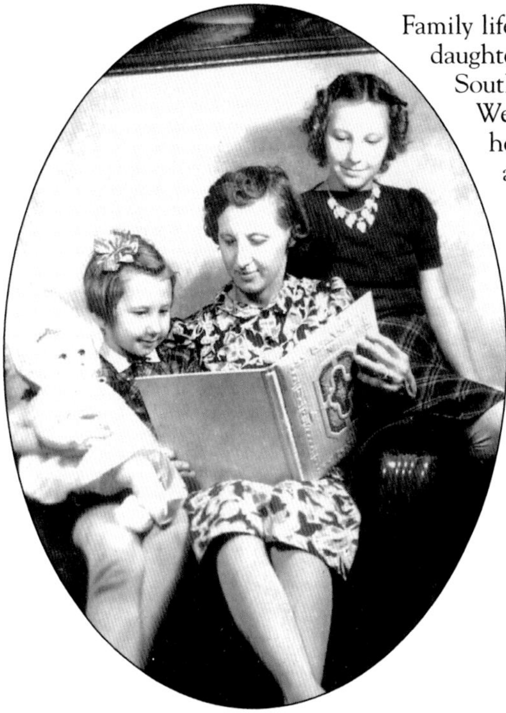

Family life is depicted here, as Helen Goran reads to her daughters Janice (left) and Shirley (right) in their South Fifty-second Street home. Janice's daughter Wendy Callahan currently lives there and still has her mother's doll. Helen's two brothers, Robert and Walter Funke, lived on the same block.

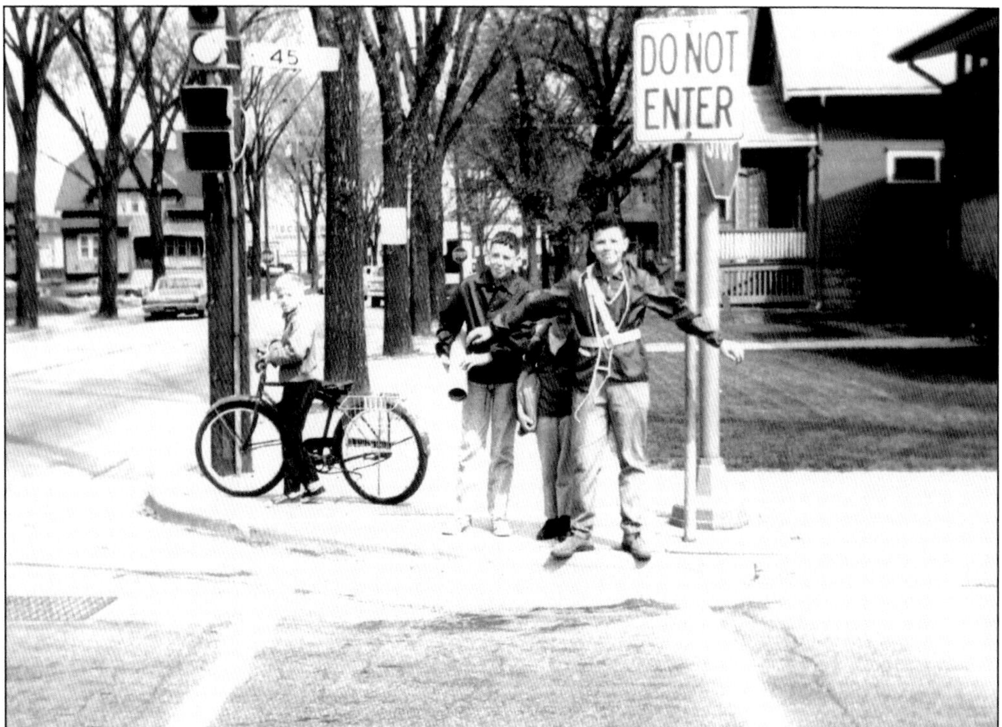

A school cadet helps children cross the street in this 1969 view of South Forty-fifth and Scott Streets, looking east. Note the bicycle the younger boy is riding, popular in the days before BMX and mountain bikes.

Six

PERSONALITIES

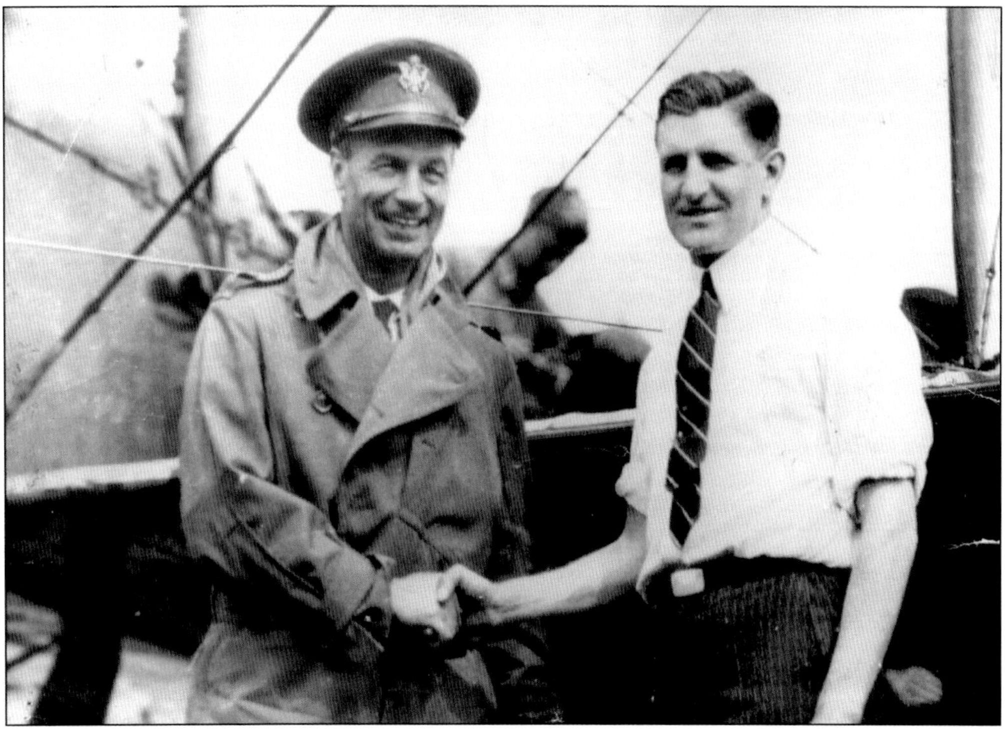

Gen. Billy Mitchell (left) and Gillis Meisenheimer, pictured here, were both pioneers in aviation connected with the village of West Milwaukee. Billy was the first of nine children of John Mitchell, whose 480-acre estate (which included a racetrack) lay just south of the village from Forty-third to Sixtieth Streets and from Lincoln Avenue to the Kinnickinnic River. Gillis was the son of E. J. Meisenheimer, West Milwaukee president from 1911 to 1914. He lived in the large home just east of the current village hall. Gillis flew for Great Britain in World War I and later managed Milwaukee County's first airport (now Currie Park).

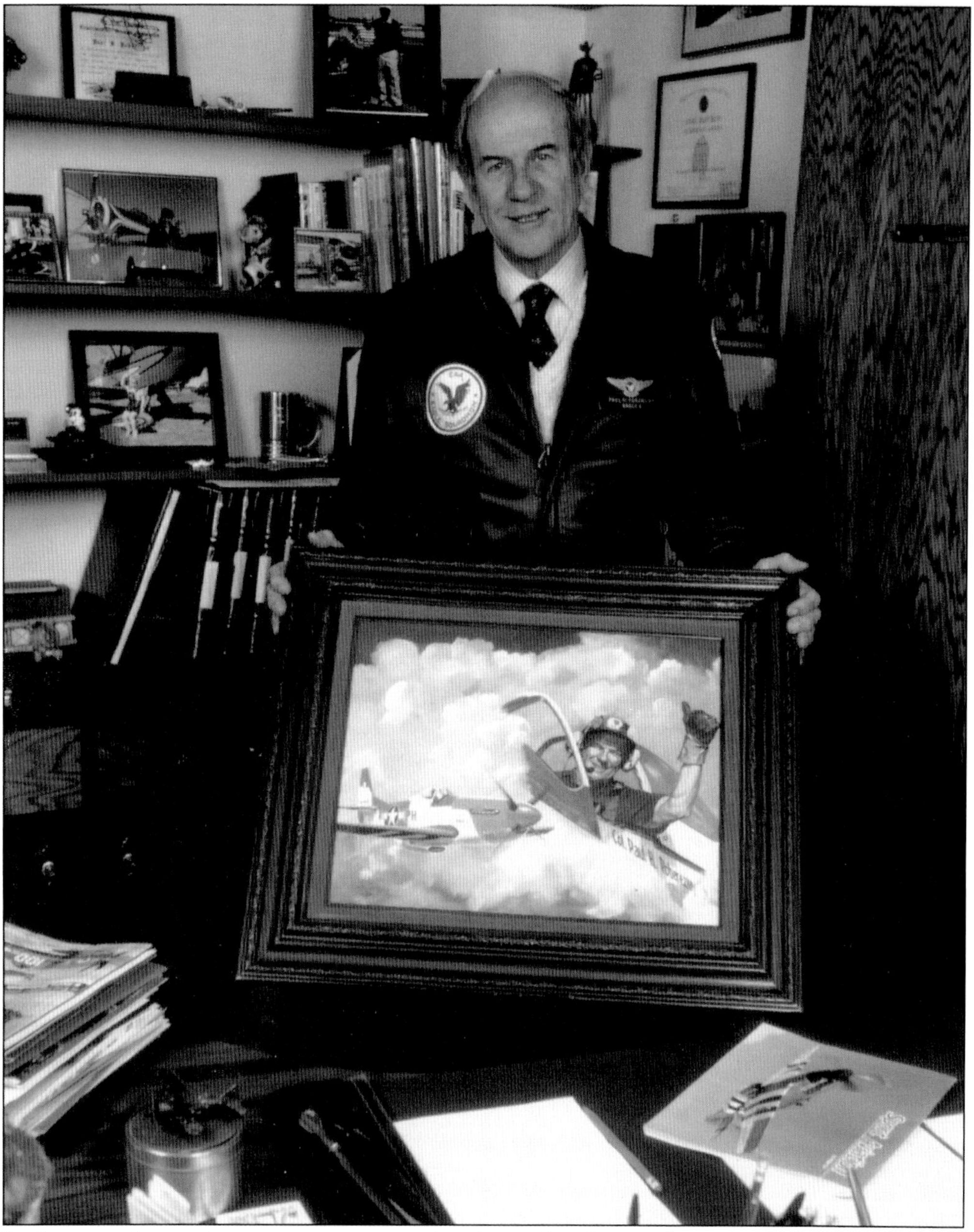

Enthusiasm for airplanes in every aspect has been the driving force in Paul Poberezny's life since childhood. West Milwaukee residents remember the time he buzzed the high school to impress his girlfriend (now wife, Audrey) but had mechanical difficulty and was forced to land in Chain Belt (now Rexnord) Field. With hard work and dedication since that time, Poberezny has accomplished much. He is known worldwide for starting the Experimental Aircraft Association. (Courtesy of Paul Poberezny.)

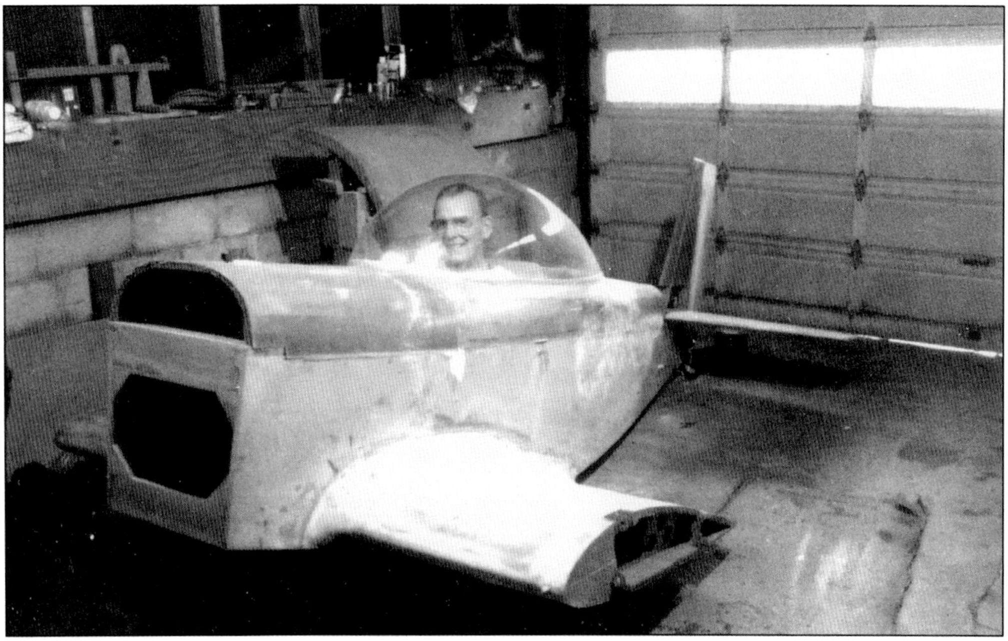

Kenneth Sturm, a 1940 West Milwaukee High graduate, married Evelyn Bublitz, who graduated in 1941. He built a single-seat, single-wing experimental aircraft (seen above, a KR-1) from the basement and garage (below) of his home on Fifty-fourth Street. The project began when he received the plans from his wife for Father's Day in 1977. An astonishing 1,540 hours were spent working on it, but Sturm died in 1994 before flying his plane. It was then donated to the Young Eagles Program of the Experimental Aircraft Association. Sturm flew many types of planes as a member of the Wisconsin Air National Guard. When the guard was activated in 1951, he participated in over 100 combat missions in Korea and was awarded the Distinguished Flying Cross. He retired as a lieutenant colonel. (Both courtesy of LynnEve Sturm.)

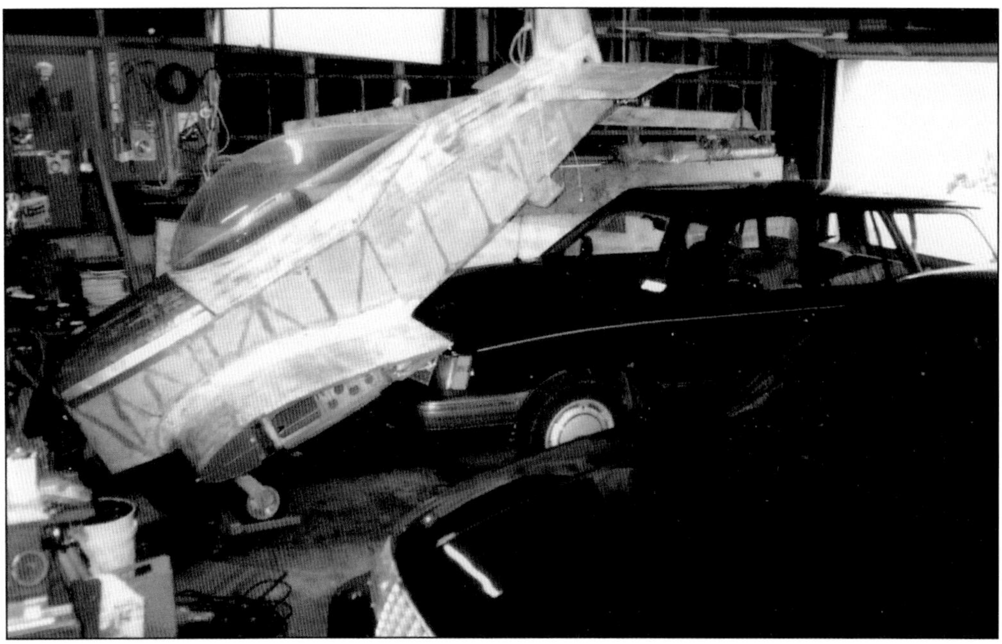

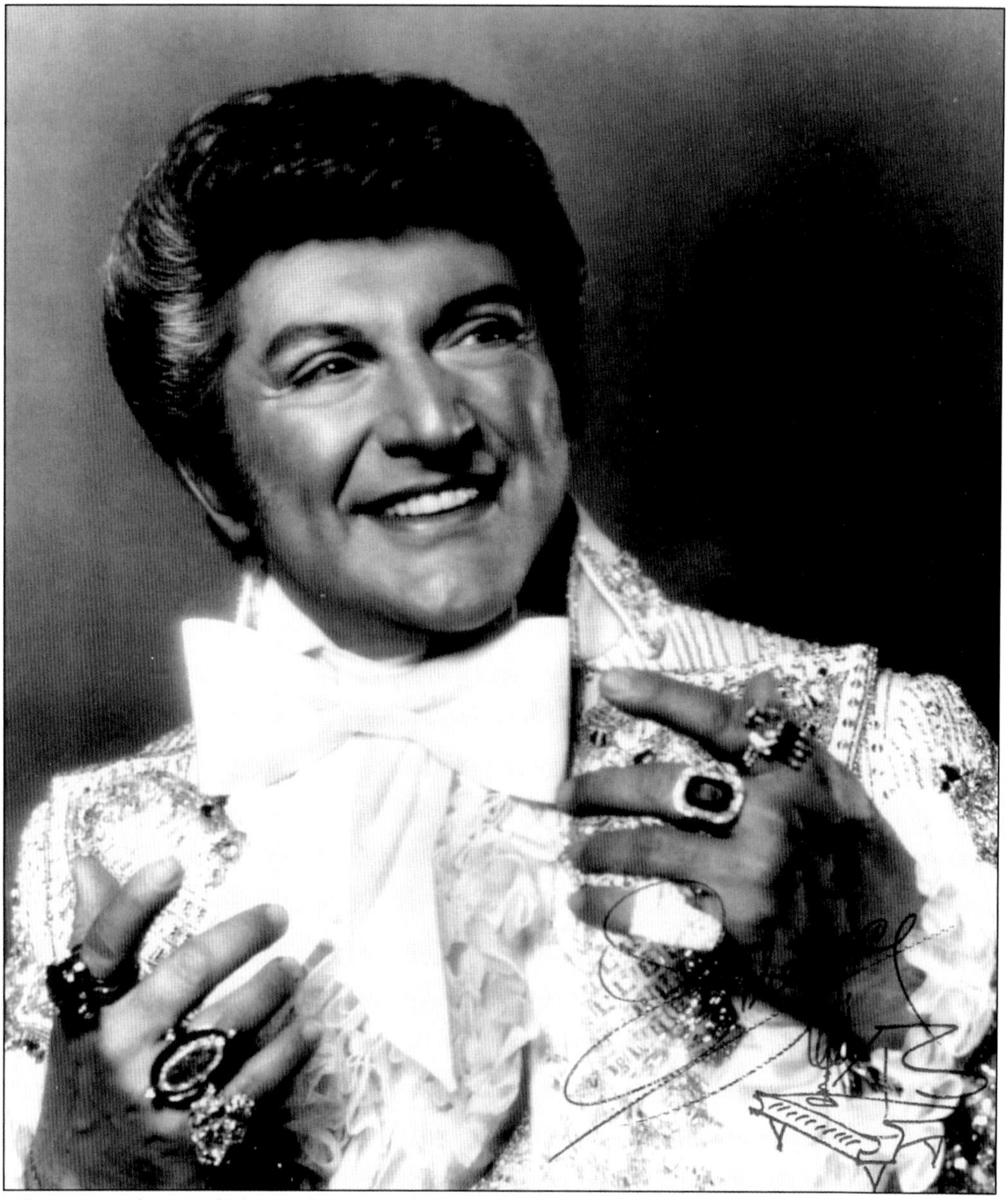

Liberace was born Wladziu Valentino Liberace in 1919, the son of Salvatore and Frances Liberace. The family moved to West Milwaukee in 1923. Salvatore was a member of the Milwaukee Philharmonic Orchestra. Frances played the piano. The family, including sister Angelina and brothers George and Rudolph, lived at Forty-ninth Street and National Avenue. Liberace was known throughout the country for his unique, flamboyant style, both on television and in concert. West Milwaukee residents knew him as "Wally."

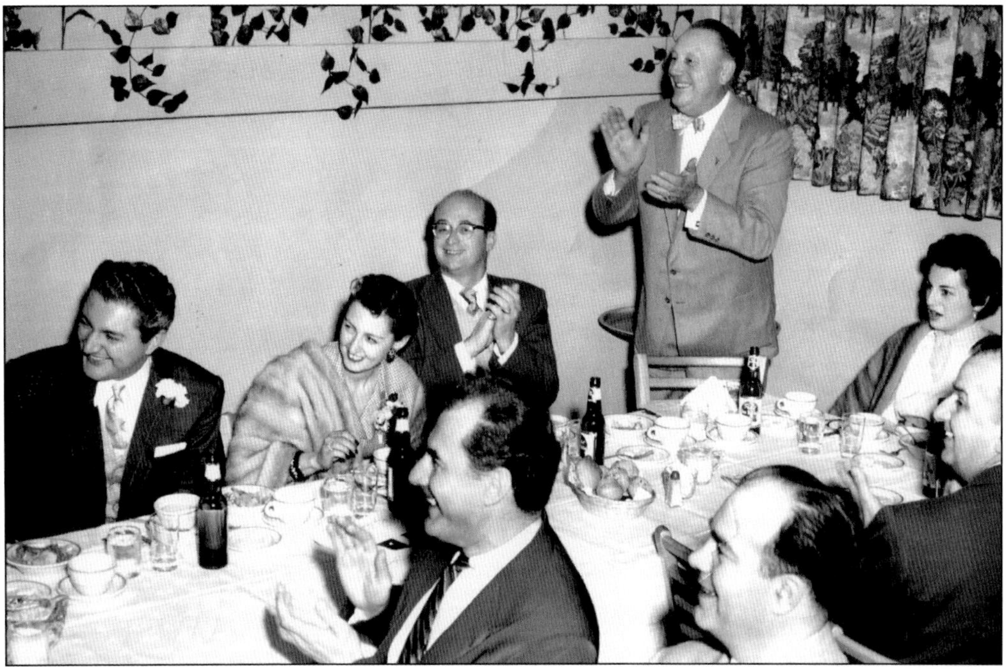

Liberace was presented with an award and made an honorary life member of the West Milwaukee Lions Club. The celebration at the Westward Ho Restaurant included the musician's sister Angie (second from left), businessman Art Knutson (standing), and funeral director Tony Verbick (far right).

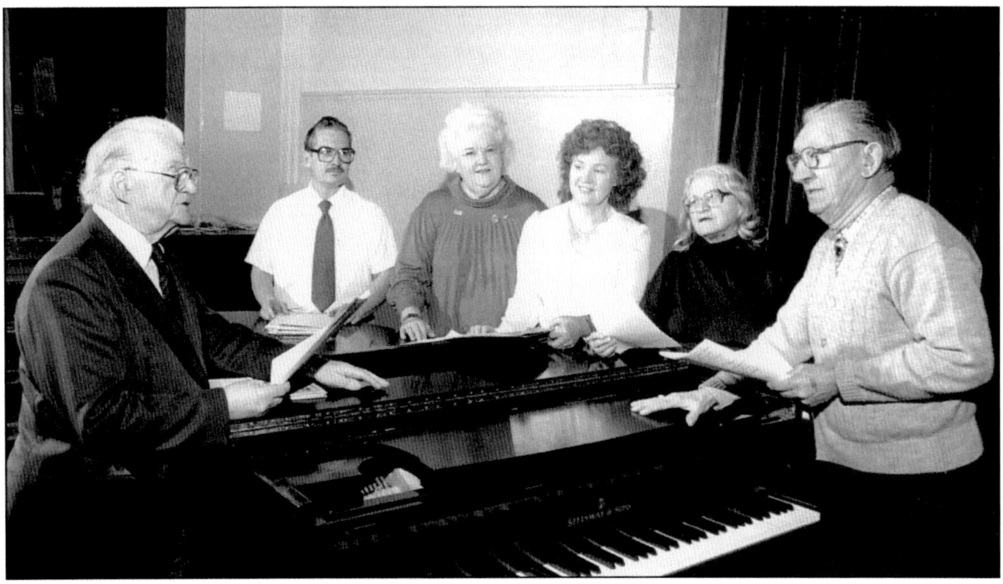

Liberace died on February 4, 1987, in Palm Springs, California, at age 67. A memorial service was held on March 8 at West Milwaukee High School. Pictured here, from left to right, are Steve Swedish (well-known Milwaukee band leader), Jack Driessen (high school principal), musical sisters Flo Bensene Selbo and Jean Bensene Cefalu, Jenny Schuler (village president), and Joey Zingsheim (friend and classmate who composed a song entitled "Liberace" for the occasion). (Courtesy of the *Milwaukee Sentinel* © 2004 Journal Sentinel Inc., reproduced with permission.)

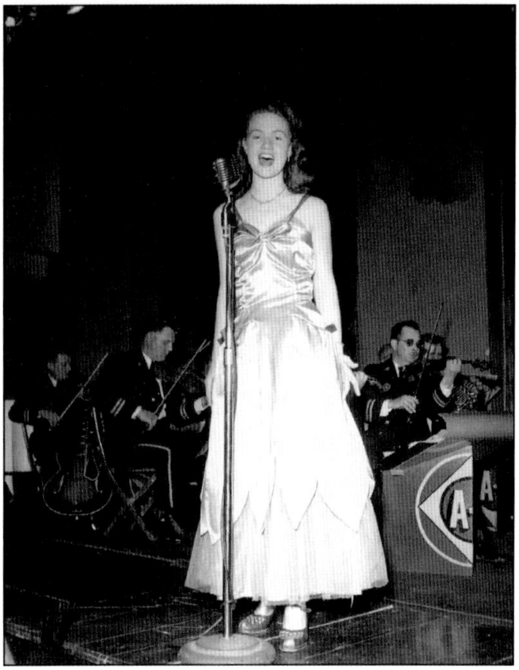

Jean Bensene Cefalu was born in West Milwaukee and attended St. Florian's School and West Milwaukee High School, graduating in 1949. That same year, she was a runner-up in the Miss Milwaukee contest. Through the years, she was a member of many theatrical and musical groups and also performed a solo at the funeral service for Liberace. She and her husband, Paul, live in the house where she grew up, at Fifty-second and Mitchell Streets. Jean continues to use her vocal talents at weddings, funerals, and concerts. (Courtesy of Jean Cefalu.)

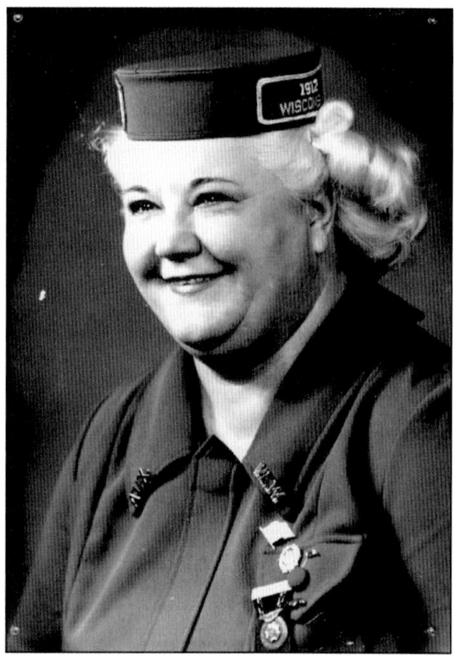

Florence Selbo was born in 1922 and moved to West Milwaukee in 1929, when her father, John Bensene, became a West Milwaukee policeman and built a home on Fifty-second and Mitchell Streets. She was a classmate and friend of Liberace. As a WAC in World War II, Flo was an entertainment specialist in the army special services. Both she and her husband, Arthur, remained active in many veterans' groups, holding leadership positions and receiving awards. Flo sang and played piano, accordion, and trumpet for many groups and events. (Courtesy of Jean Cefalu.)

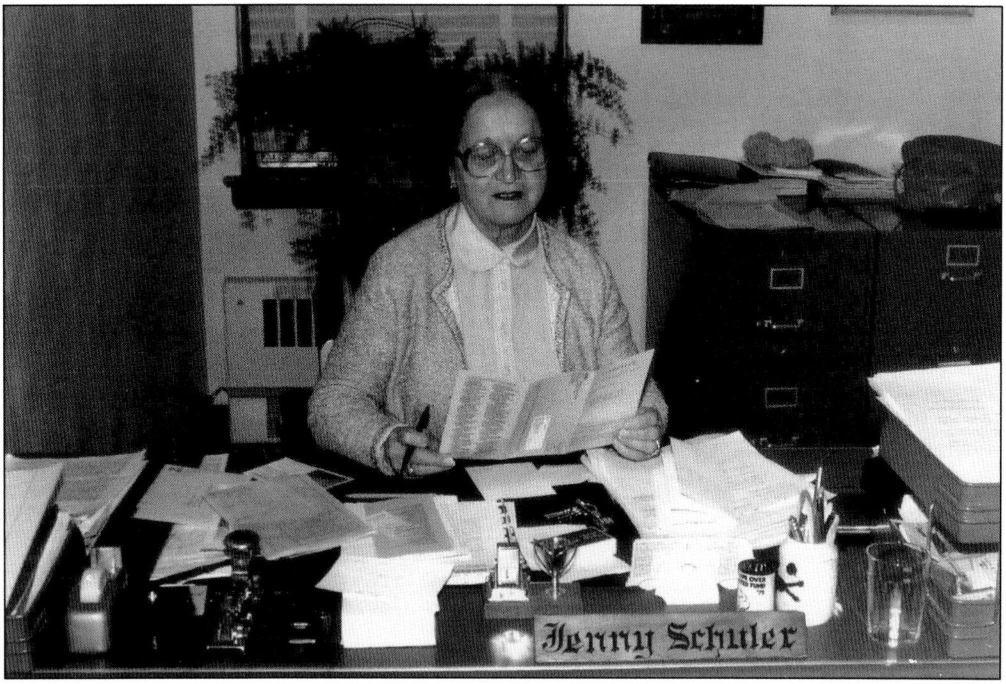

Jenny Schuler, a dedicated West Milwaukee resident, served as village president from 1982 to 1990. She was the first female municipal executive in Milwaukee County. She was also the village's first female trustee, holding that position from 1968 to 1982. In addition, Schuler served on numerous village committees with special interests in recycling and housing for the elderly. She worked at the Harnischfeger Corporation for 39 years and was for many years a board member of the Guardian Credit Union.

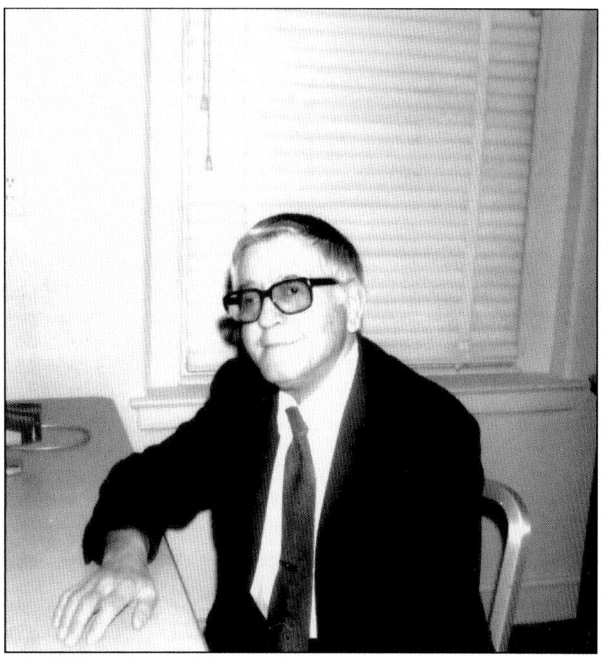

A graduate of Marquette Medical School, Frank X. Schuler worked for many years as the village health officer, conducting physical exams at Pershing Grade School. Dr. Schuler had an office at 5304 West Greenfield Avenue, but he also made house calls.

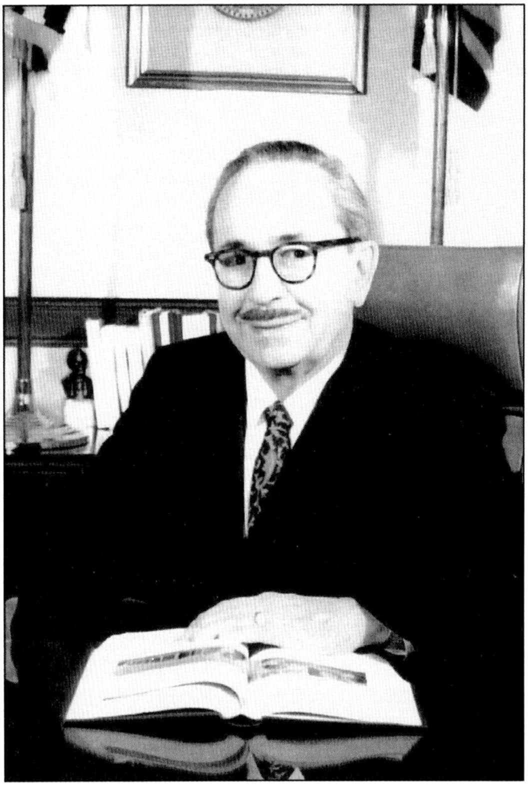

The Busby family is listed on West Milwaukee's original 1906 census. Allen J. Busby served as village attorney for 25 years. He also served 36 years in the Wisconsin State Legislature (two terms in the assembly, followed by nine in the senate). During his youth, he and brother Bert hired others to sell peanuts, Cracker Jacks, and chewing gum outside the gate to the Soldiers' Home, where many people entered for band concerts. Senator Busby, his wife, Linda, and children Tom and Judy lived at Fifty-third and Mitchell Streets. (Courtesy of Judy Coffey.)

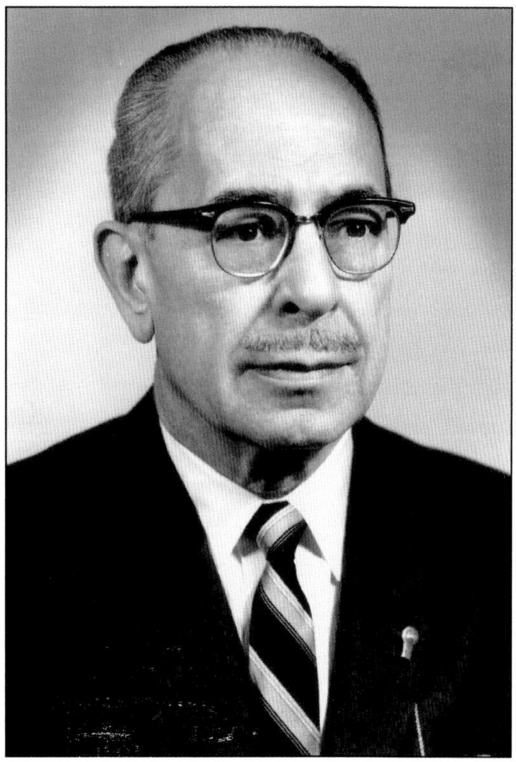

Dr. Bert Busby was a 1924 graduate of Marquette Dental School. Also a musician, he used the money he earned playing to pay his tuition. He was elected village trustee in 1933 and county supervisor in 1936, serving in the latter position until his death in 1960. He introduced a resolution in 1944 that led to the construction of Milwaukee County Stadium. Dr. Busby was married to Marjorie Webb and had two children—Burt and Barbara. (Courtesy of Barbara Belongia.)

Art Knutson, vice-president of the chamber of commerce, crowns Judy Busby Miss West Milwaukee at the village's golden anniversary celebration in 1956. Judy was 16 and a West Milwaukee High School sophomore at the time. She then presided over the week-long activities. One of Judy's prizes was a course in modeling, which became one of many pursuits over the years. (Courtesy of the *Milwaukee Sentinel* © 2004 Journal Sentinel Inc., reproduced with permission.)

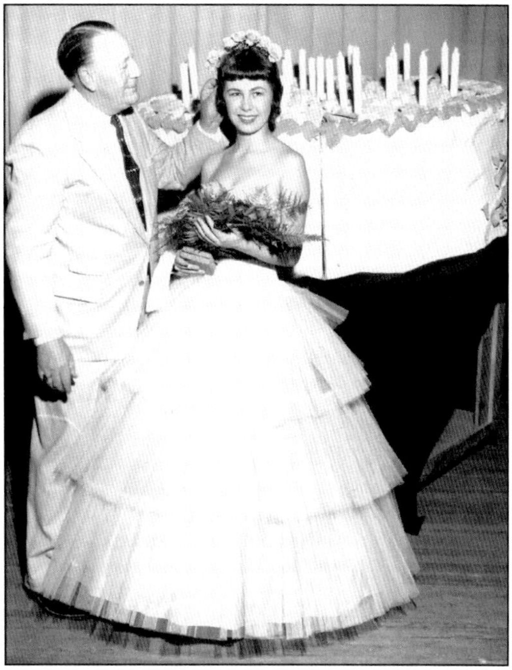

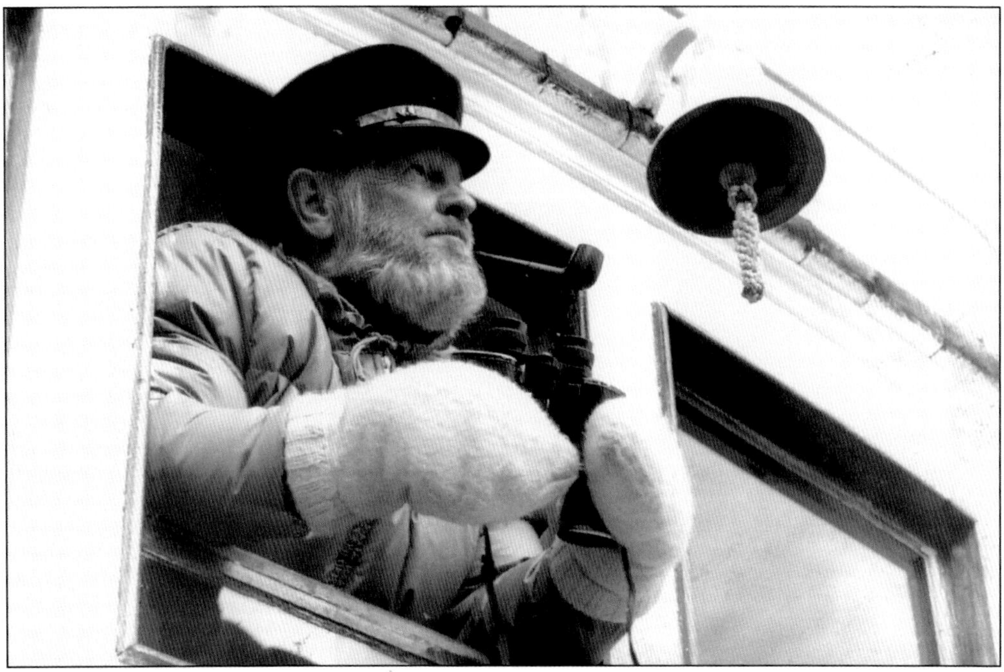

Melvin "Dick" Luckow lived with his family at Fifty-fifth and Lapham Streets until his death in 1983. The home is unusual because it has an attached museum filled with the results of his many fishing and hunting trips all over the world. Luckow hunted in North and South America, all the countries in southern Africa, Australia, New Zealand, India, Pakistan, Vietnam, and Afghanistan. A favorite photograph, seen above, was taken during a Norwegian expedition. (Courtesy of Annette Luckow.)

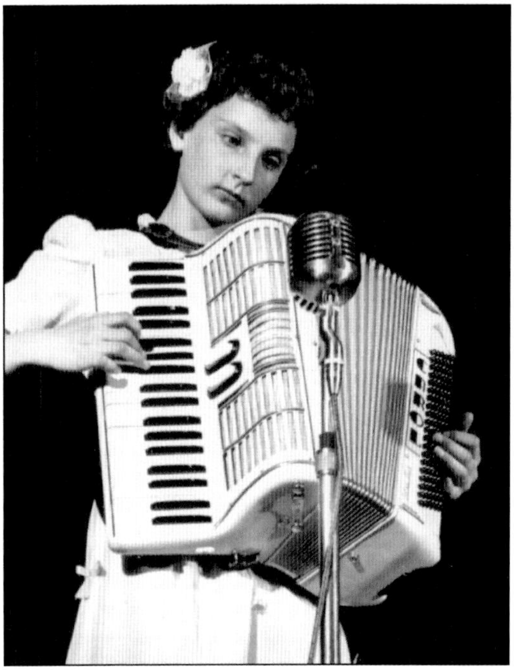

Carol Nawrocki, who has lived in West Milwaukee most of her life, is pictured here with her accordion. Carol comes from a musical family, both mother and grandmother having played the organ for a Polish national church. She took lessons, as did many other neighborhood children, from Frank Cascio on Forty-sixth and West Beloit Road and taught younger children as a junior and senior at West Milwaukee High. (Courtesy of Carol Nawrocki.)

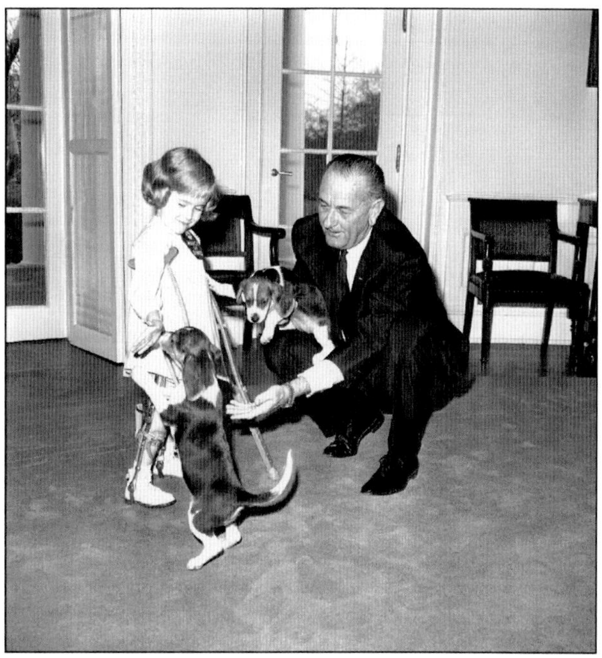

Born with spina bifida, Lori Wagner was the daughter of Mary Ellen and Hank "Skip" Wagner of West Milwaukee. She became Milwaukee County's March of Dimes Poster Child in 1965 and the national March of Dimes Poster Child in 1966. Here, she appears at the White House with Pres. Lyndon B. Johnson. Lori enjoyed singing and playing the piano and drums, as taught by her band leader father. She died at age 12 from complications of her condition. (Courtesy AP/Wide World Photographs.)

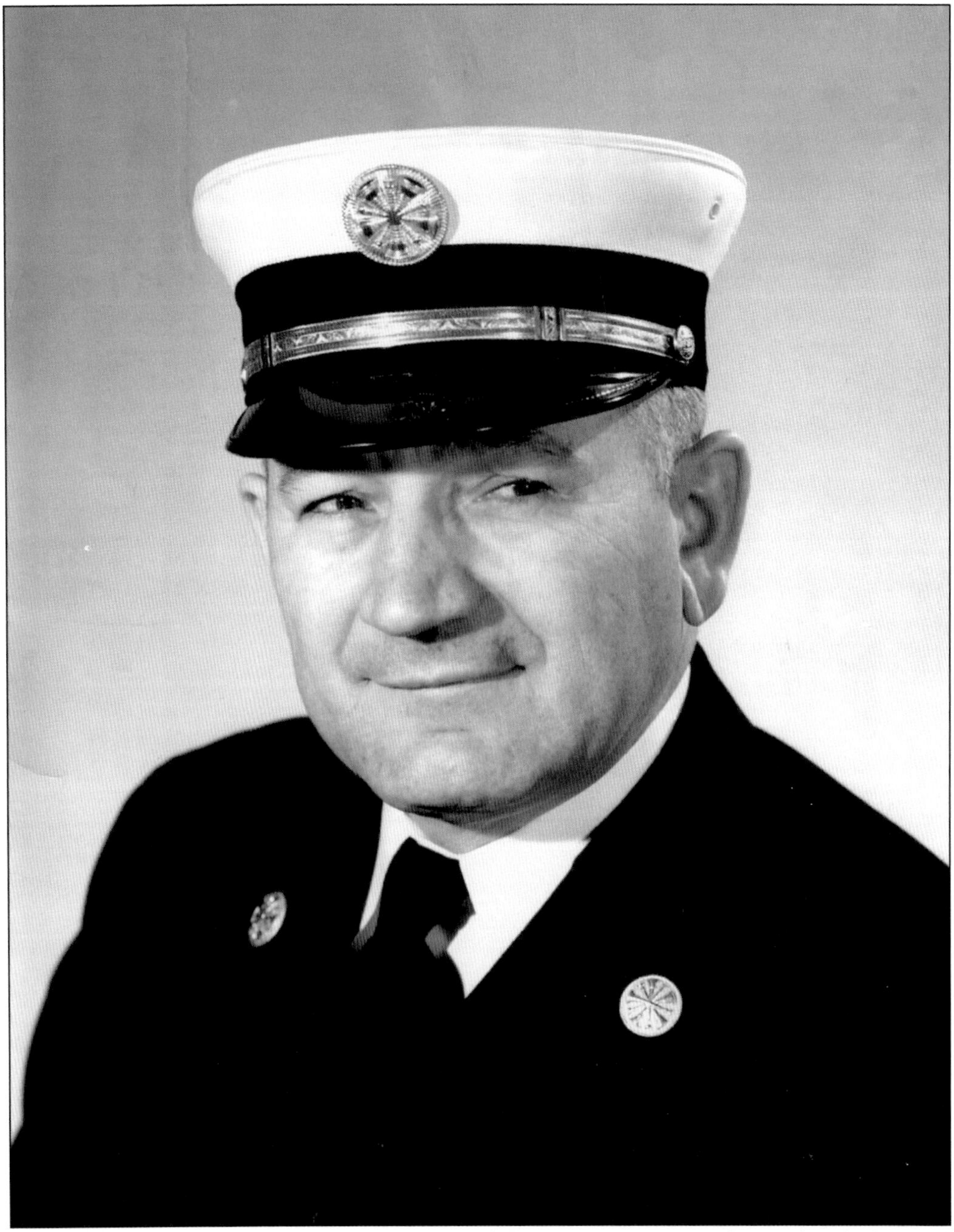

John Pavlik was, first of all, a patriot who joined the army at age 16 and served with the 32nd Division on the front lines of Europe in World War I. He served in many veterans' groups for the remainder of his life, becoming the national commander of the Veterans of World War I in 1984 and 1985. A highlight of his life was reciting the poem "In Flanders Field" at Arlington National Cemetery on November 11, 1989. Pavlik used his military background, his experience as battalion fire chief in Milwaukee, and his own personal passion to create an excellent fire department in West Milwaukee. He worked as fire chief from 1951 until his retirement in 1966.

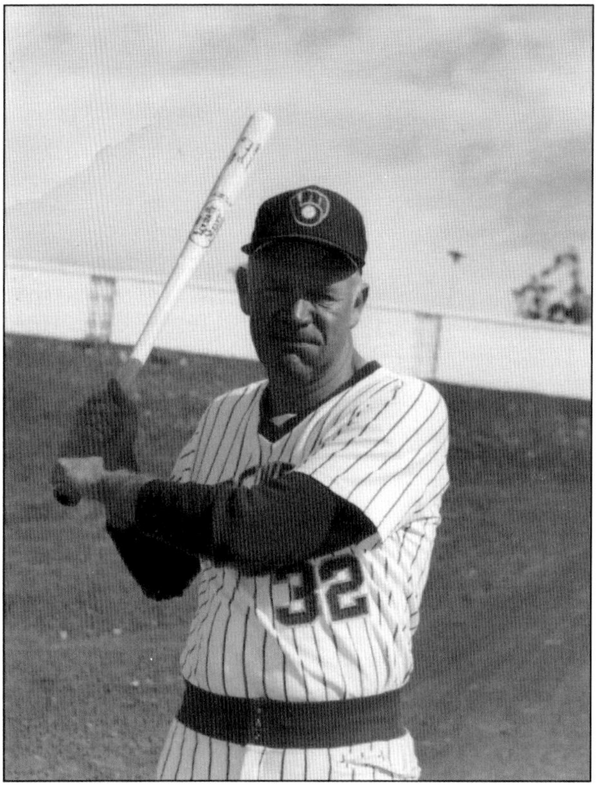

Harvey Kuenn, a major-league baseball player for many years, married Audrey Cesar, whose parents, Mitzi and Al, owned Cesar's Inn. He brought thrills and great excitement to the village. As the Milwaukee Brewers' (baseball team) manager of "Harvey's Wallbangers," he won the American League championship in 1982. Overflow crowds filled Cesar's Inn and spilled out onto National Avenue. Kuenn played in the 1962 World Series and in seven All Star games. (Courtesy of Audrey Kuenn.)

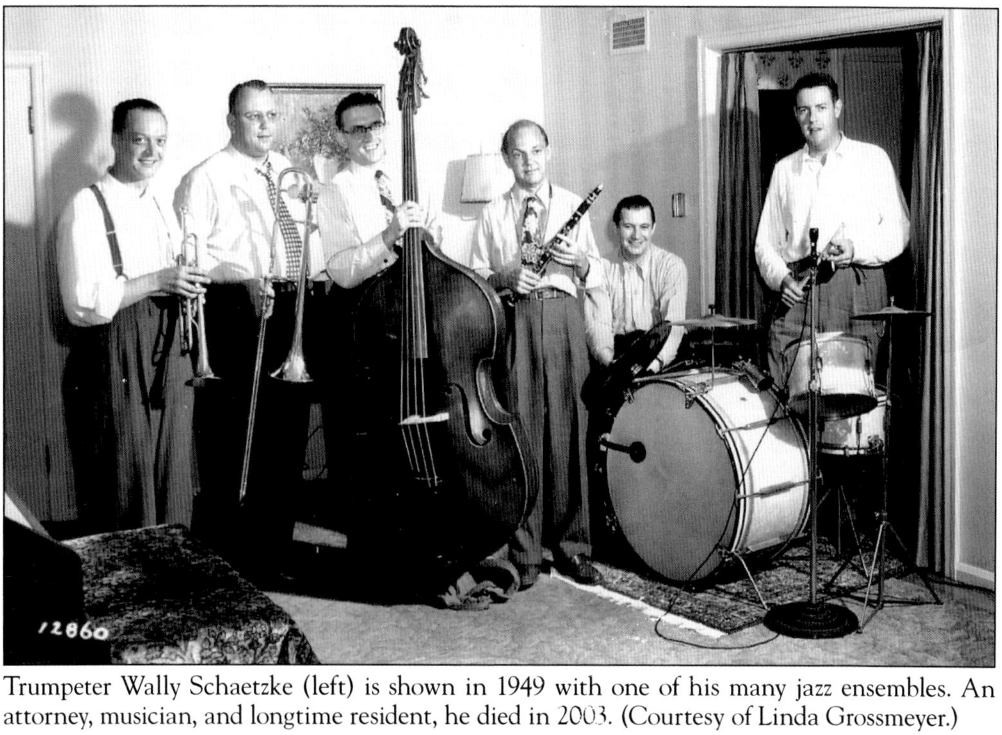

Trumpeter Wally Schaetzke (left) is shown in 1949 with one of his many jazz ensembles. An attorney, musician, and longtime resident, he died in 2003. (Courtesy of Linda Grossmeyer.)

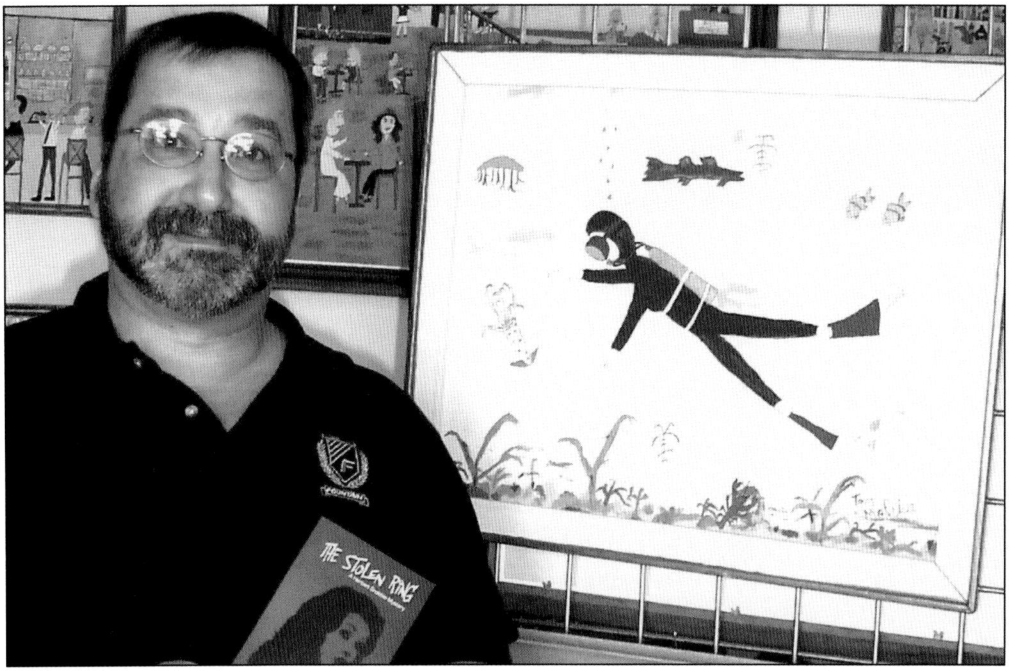

Tom Mollica is the local author of the recently published novel *The Stolen Ring*, which portrays a private detective living in the village. A third-generation West Milwaukee resident, Tom is also an artist. His studio is at the same location as his grandfather John Zawerschnik's plumbing business, at Forty-seventh Street and National Avenue. Zawerschnik was a longtime plumbing inspector for the village. He also served on the school board.

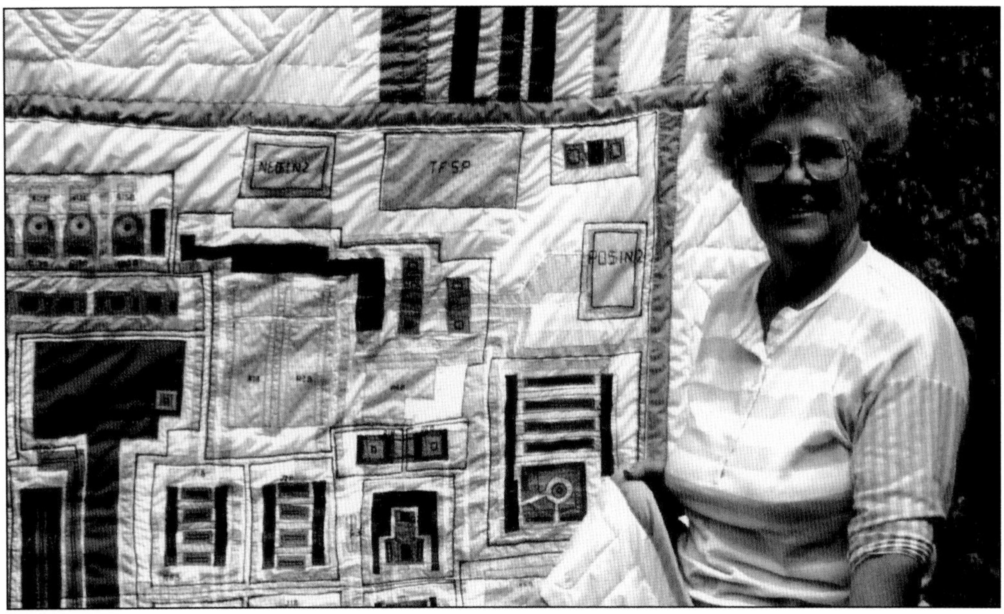

Edie Wurcer is one of the village's prominent community activists. A beautician and fabric artist, she has lent her talents to various organizations, such as the Garden Club, historical society, and St. Florian's Church. She is currently on the Centennial Committee, selling memorial pavers (engraved bricks) and shirts featuring the village logo. (Courtesy of Edie Wurcer.)

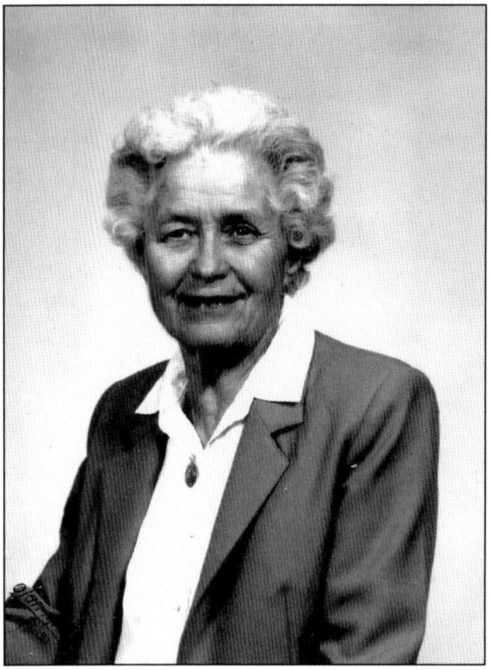

Eleanor Benda was a Daughter of the American Revolution who could trace her roots to Ethan Allen. Along with her husband, Frank, and daughter Sally, she moved into the family home on West Beloit Road in 1956. Her daughter Anne was born shortly thereafter. Eleanor worked as the historian and editor for the village's 75th anniversary booklet. With money from the anniversary and copious historical materials, Eleanor contributed to the forming of the West Milwaukee Historical Society in 1982. She served as its president until 1994. (Courtesy of Frank Benda.)

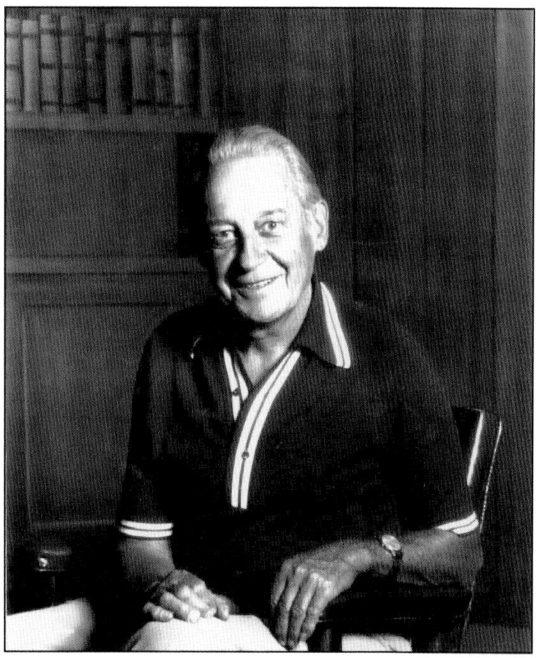

John Schnabl lived his entire life in West Milwaukee. He served on the Civil Service Commission for 39 years, participated in the Austrian Society, and for many years hosted gatherings at his home on South Fifty-second Street. Four generations of John's family have lived here. A charter member of the West Milwaukee Historical Society, he has left us the legacy of a taped walking tour of the village. (Courtesy of Janis Schnabl.)

Seven

INTO THE FUTURE

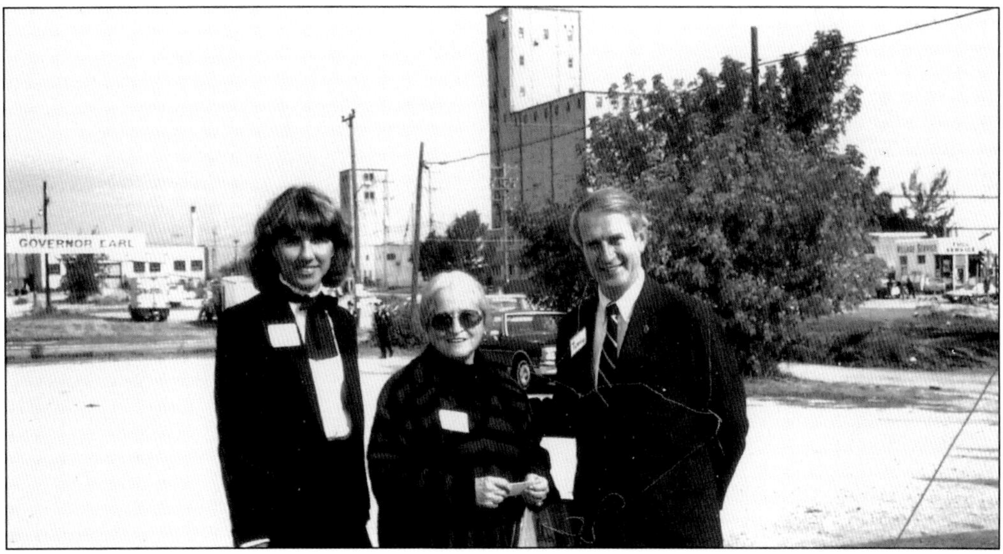

A groundbreaking ceremony for the development of the Forty-third Street corridor was held on October 11, 1986. Rep. Margaret Krusick secured over $10 million in state assistance for the project. Pictured here are Krusick (left), village president Jenny Schuler (center), and Gov. Anthony Earl.

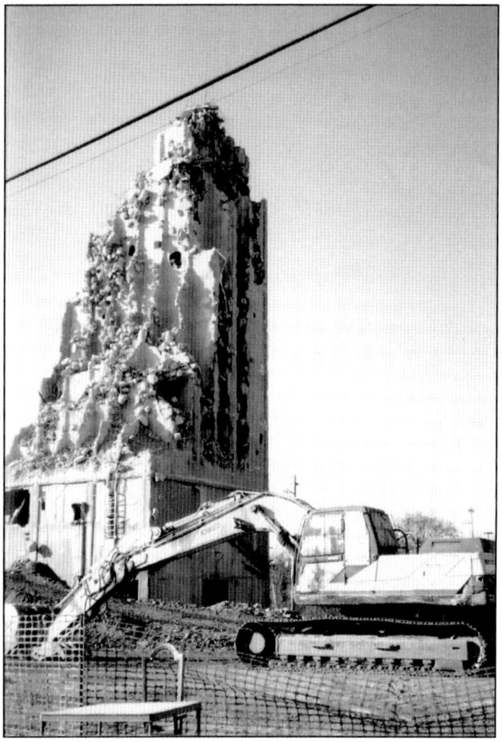

Crumbling and chipping away, this unused concrete structure, known as the Kamm Tower, was part of the West Milwaukee landscape since the early 20th century. It was demolished in 2002, signaling a new era for the West Milwaukee skyline.

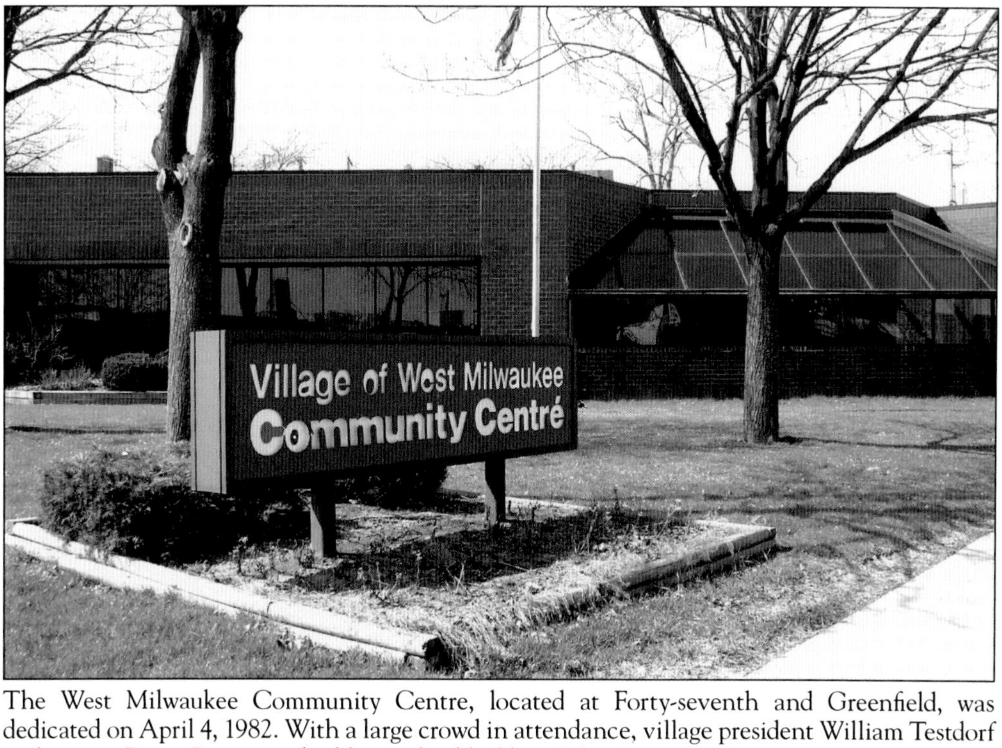

The West Milwaukee Community Centre, located at Forty-seventh and Greenfield, was dedicated on April 4, 1982. With a large crowd in attendance, village president William Testdorf and trustee Roger Parys cut the blue and gold ribbon. The Community Centre was funded by a $205,000 grant from the Community Development Grant Block Program.

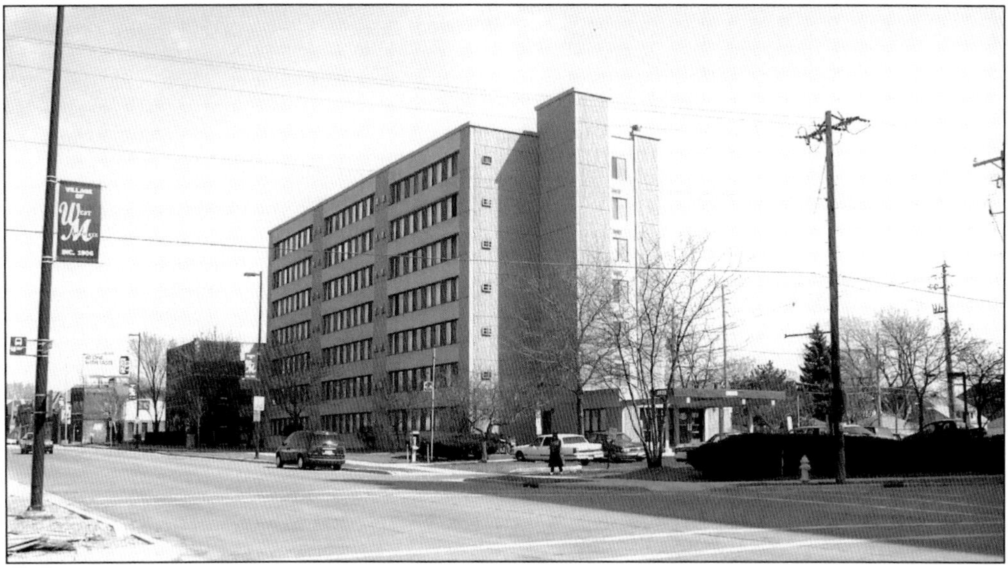

The Congress Apartments, at Fortieth Street and National Avenue, became West Milwaukee's first housing for senior citizens. Constructed in 1981 at a cost of $2.4 million, the building is seven stories high and includes 73 units.

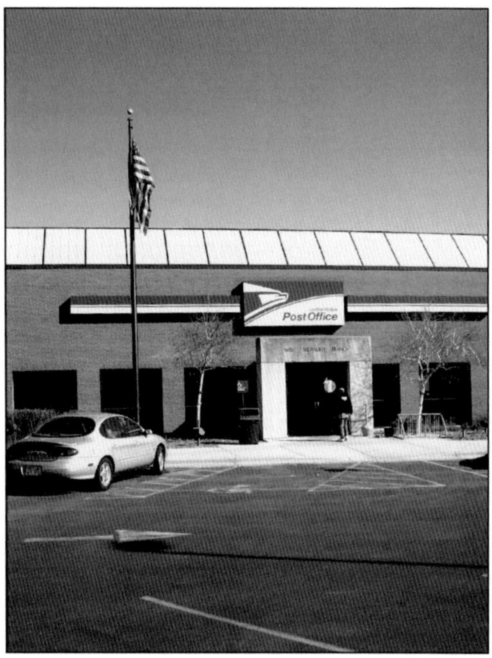

The West Milwaukee Post Office, a dream of villagers for years, was constructed on a 6.5-acre site on the northwest corner of Forty-third Street and Lincoln Avenue. The 60,000-square-foot facility was dedicated in the fall of 1991. It serves zip codes 53215 and 53219. Most of West Milwaukee has a zip code of 53214 and is served by the West Allis Post Office.

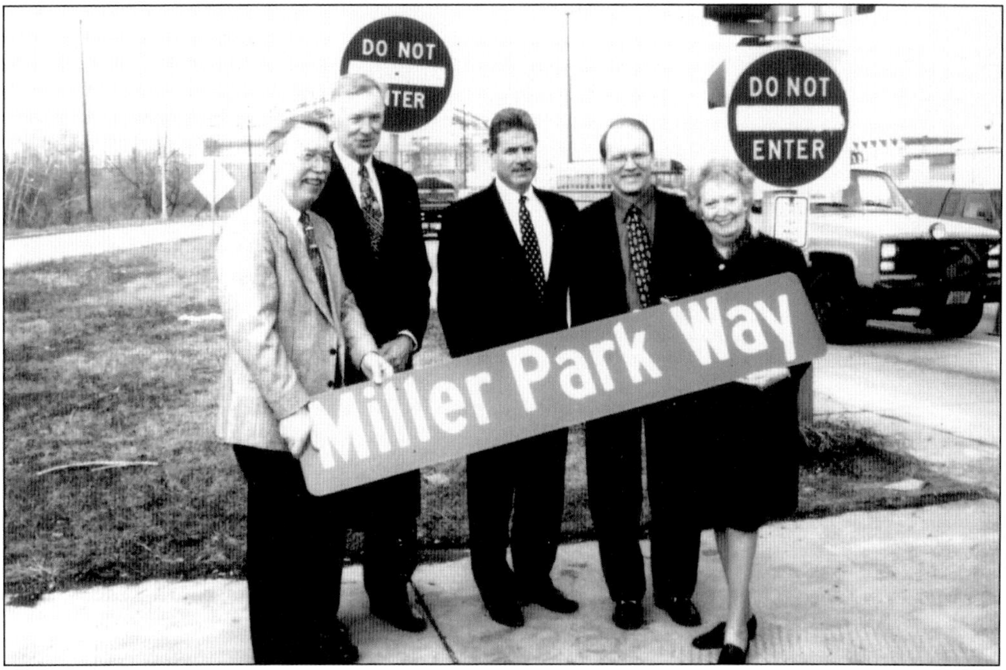

Forty-third Street was renamed Miller Park Way on March 1, 2000. The change was proposed by Judy Fell, a member of the Community Development Authority, and approved by the village board. Holding the new street sign, from left to right, are village president Ron Hayward; Mike Duckett and Frank Busalacchi of the Stadium Board; Laurel Prieb, a spokesperson for the Brewers; and Judy Fell.

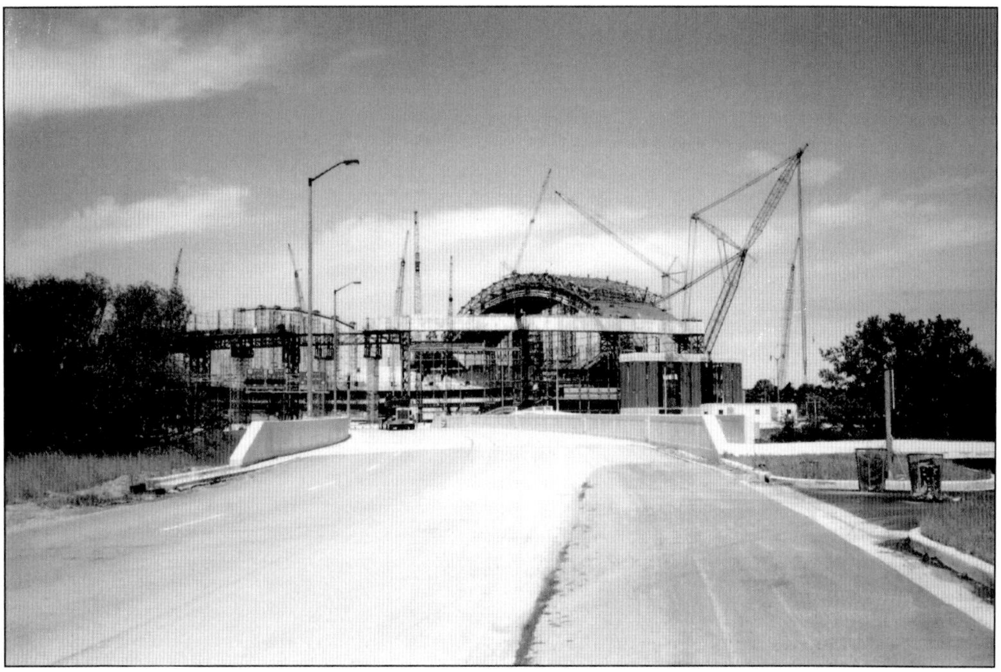

Miller Park is located just north of the village, within easy walking distance for West Milwaukee big-league fans. This image shows the stadium under construction. The infamous "Big Blue" crane, which tragically collapsed later in the construction process, is seen at right.

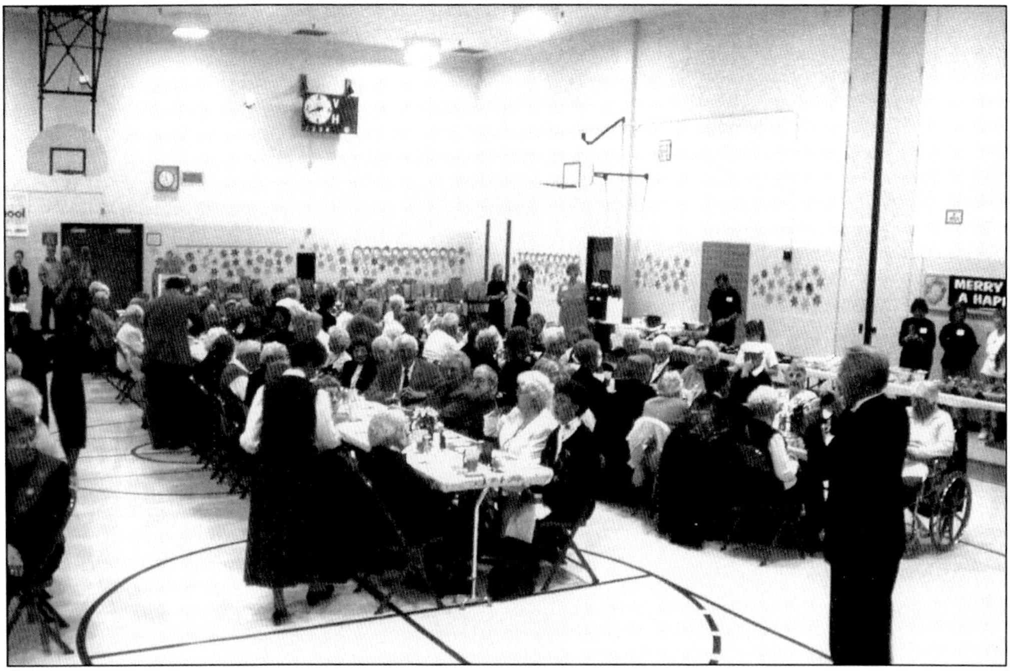

West Milwaukee Golden Agers are treated to a lovely Christmas party every year in early December. Pershing School students create place mats for the tables, provide the entertainment, and assist in any way needed. Businesses and industries have been generous in their support; GE Medical even sends Santa and his helpers. Here, village president Ron Hayward acts as master of ceremonies.

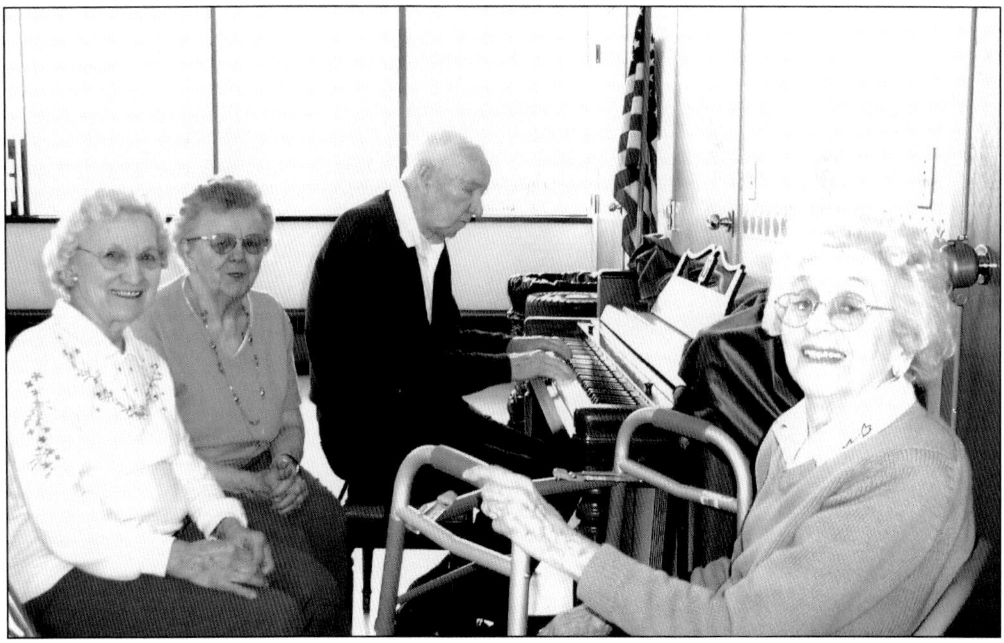

Seen here from left to right, Josephine Schmidt, Rose Kaminski, Martin Zavodnik, and Gerda Griebsch sing all the old favorites as they gather around the piano before lunch at the Community Centre (a Milwaukee County luncheon site).

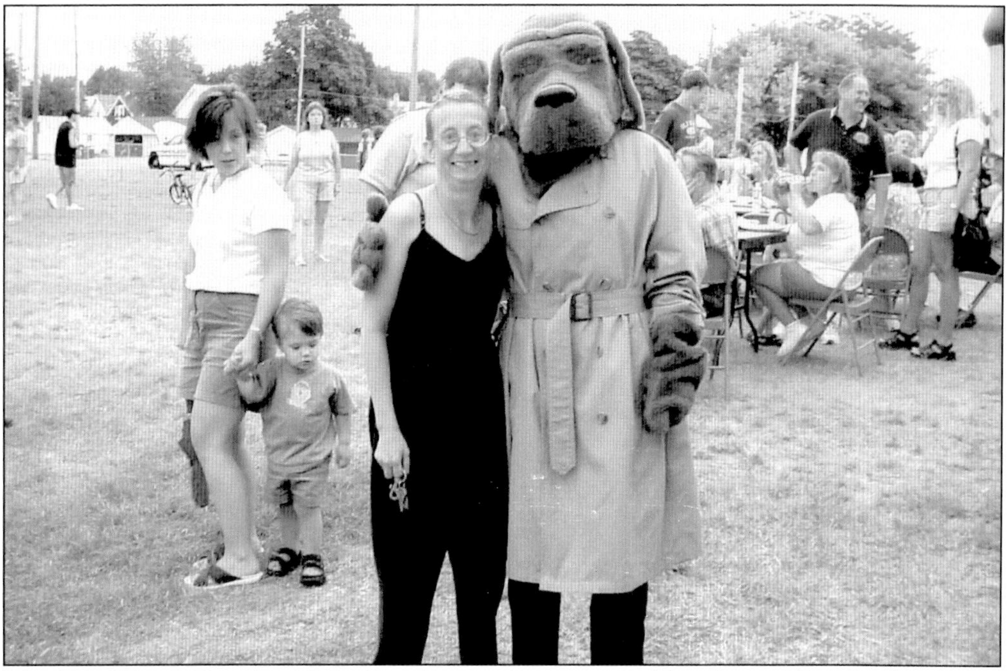

The 2004 West Milwaukee Night Out Against Crime was held at the middle school. Pictured here is McGruff, the crime dog. Also helping to make the event fun and safe were a clown, the Milwaukee Fire Department, police on horseback, and Curtis Ambulance. Milwaukee County Flight for Life workers thrilled onlookers by landing on the field and explaining their purpose and procedures. The West Milwaukee Police Department arranges the event each year. (Courtesy of the West Milwaukee Police Department.)

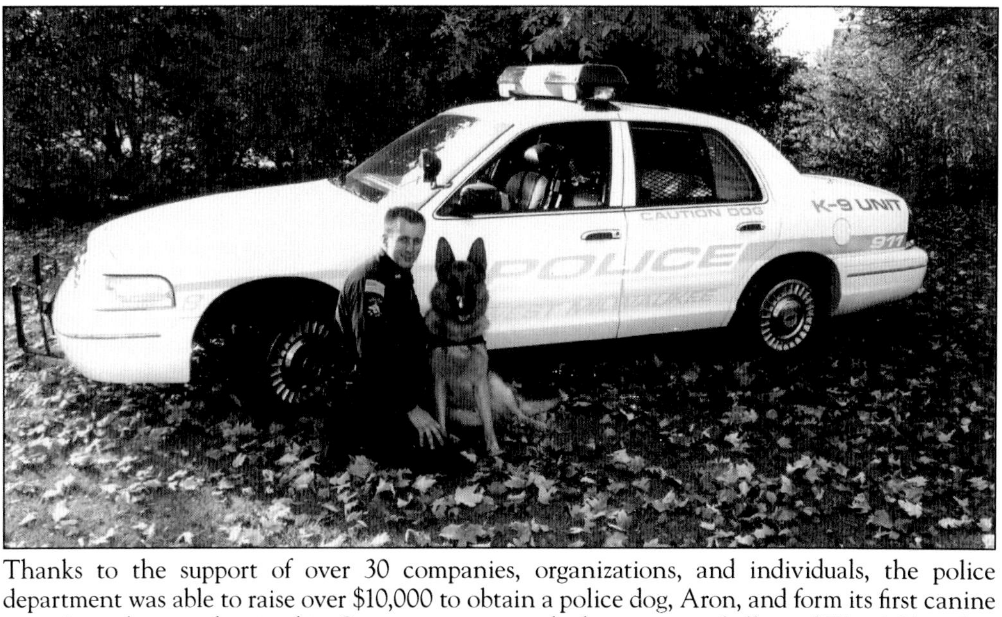

Thanks to the support of over 30 companies, organizations, and individuals, the police department was able to raise over $10,000 to obtain a police dog, Aron, and form its first canine unit. Aron, born and trained in Germany, now patrols the streets and alleys of West Milwaukee with officer Russell Blank in a squad car modified for K-9 use. (Courtesy of the West Milwaukee Police Department.)

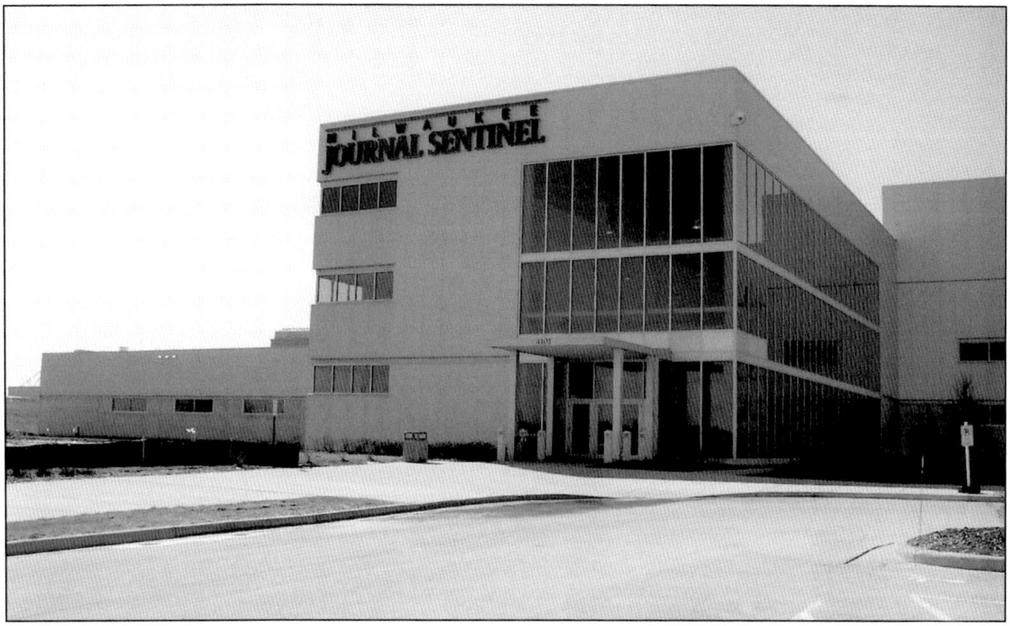

The *Journal Sentinel*'s production building opened in 2002, and printing and distribution of the newspaper were transferred here from the paper's downtown location. The structure was built at a cost of $106.6 million and boasts three new state-of-the-art presses, which are five stories high.

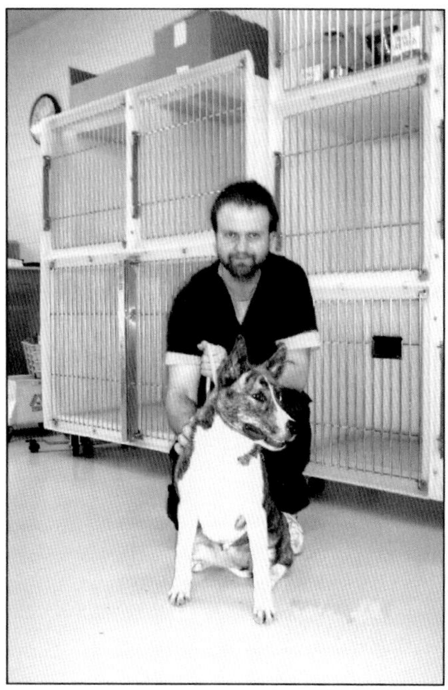

The brand-new Milwaukee Area Domestic Animal Control Commission facility, at 3839 West Burnham, opened in 1998 and now serves 19 communities. Ben Shaw, a veterinary technician, appears here with a five-month-old female Siberian Husky–Akita mix.

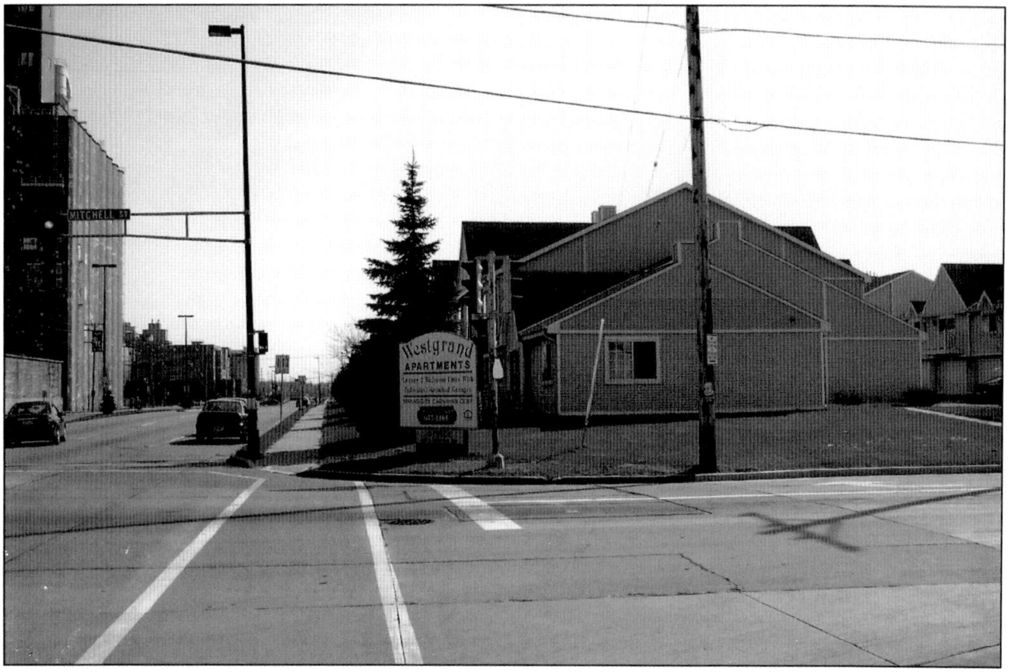

The Westgrand Apartments, seen here, and the Ogden Apartments and Condominiums anchor the north and south ends of Miller Park Way, providing a residential area in the midst of new retail development.

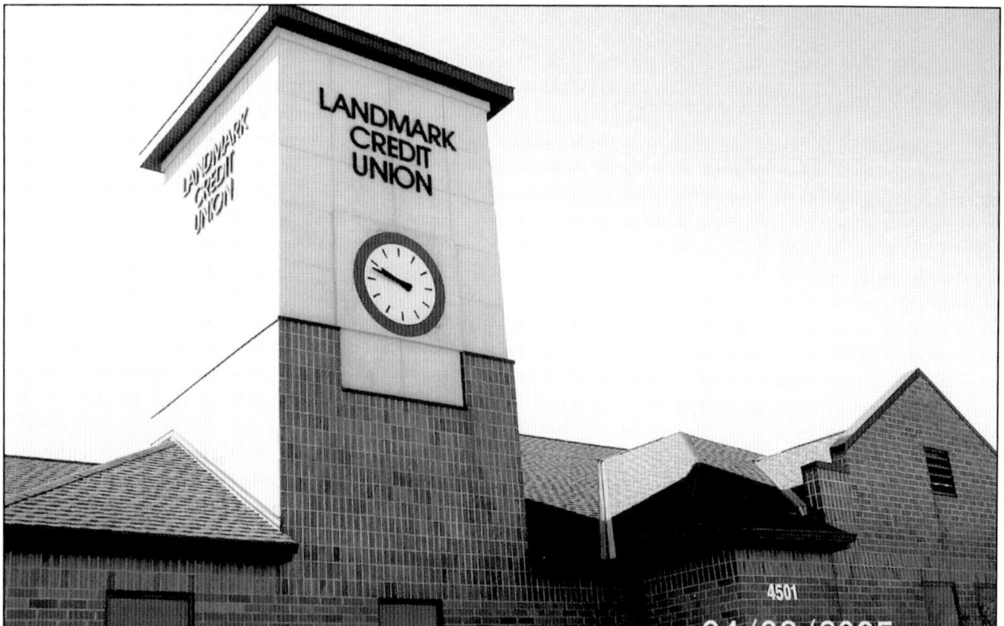

The Landmark Credit Union, located at Fifty-first and Mitchell Streets since 1969, moved into a new 6,000-square-foot facility on the southwest corner of Miller Park Way and National Avenue in 1999. The building's beautiful clock tower is noticed immediately upon entering the village from the north.

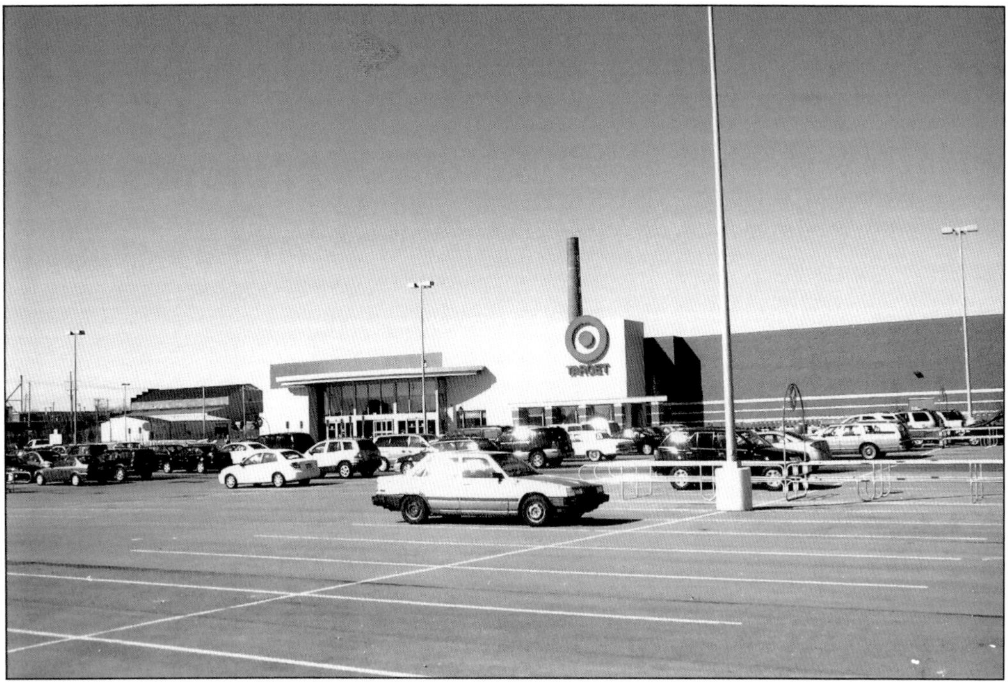

Target opened in West Milwaukee in July 2004. The 230,000-square-foot space is a retail anchor supplying a wide array of goods and including an in-store Pizza Hut and Starbucks. The site has been quite improved from its former field of weeds, where many village clean-up efforts occurred just a few years ago.

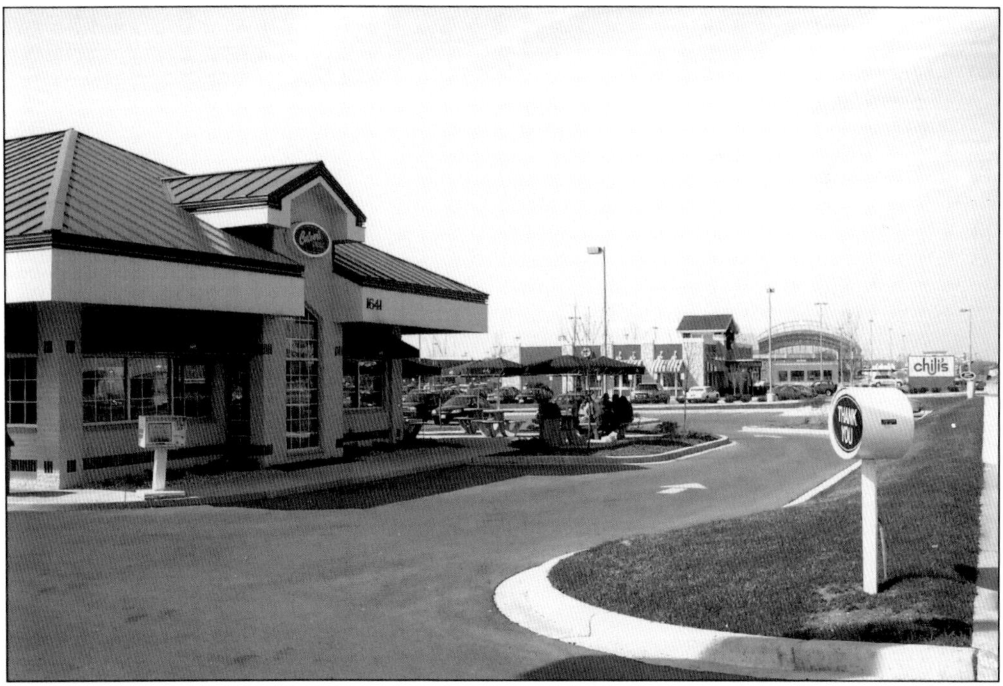

Outlots on the Target land parcel provide retail space for indoor and outdoor dining. This view, looking north along Miller Park Way, is a glance at new development all along the corridor.

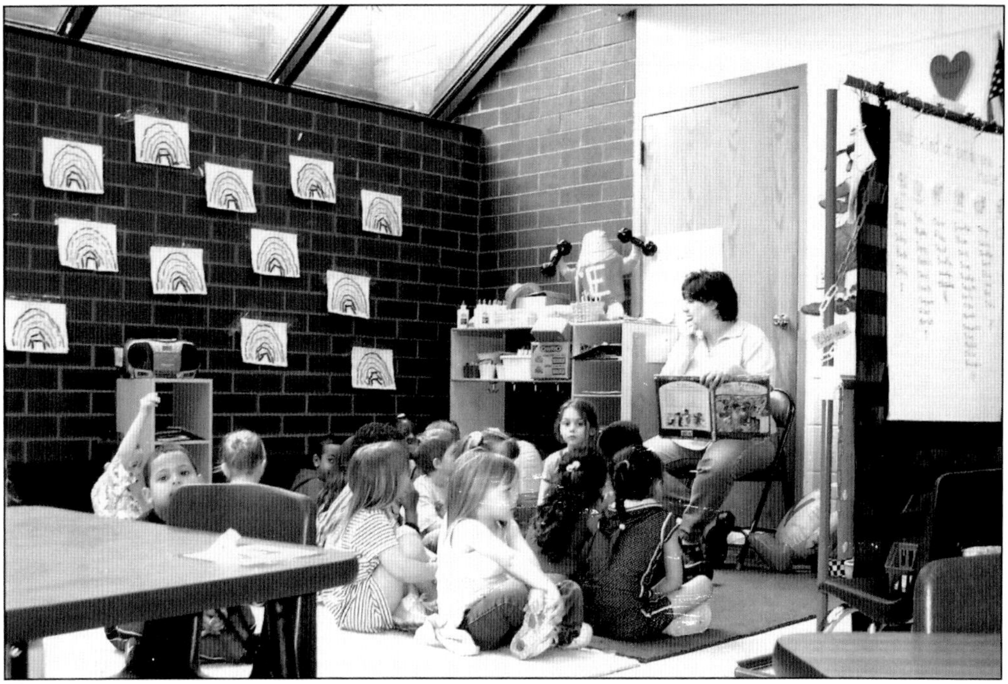

Pershing School's four-year-old kindergarten has held classes in the lower level of the West Milwaukee Community Centre since the fall of 2002. The afternoon class of the 2004–2005 school year poses with teacher Dianna Brophey (pictured). Kathleen Marx (not pictured) is the assistant.

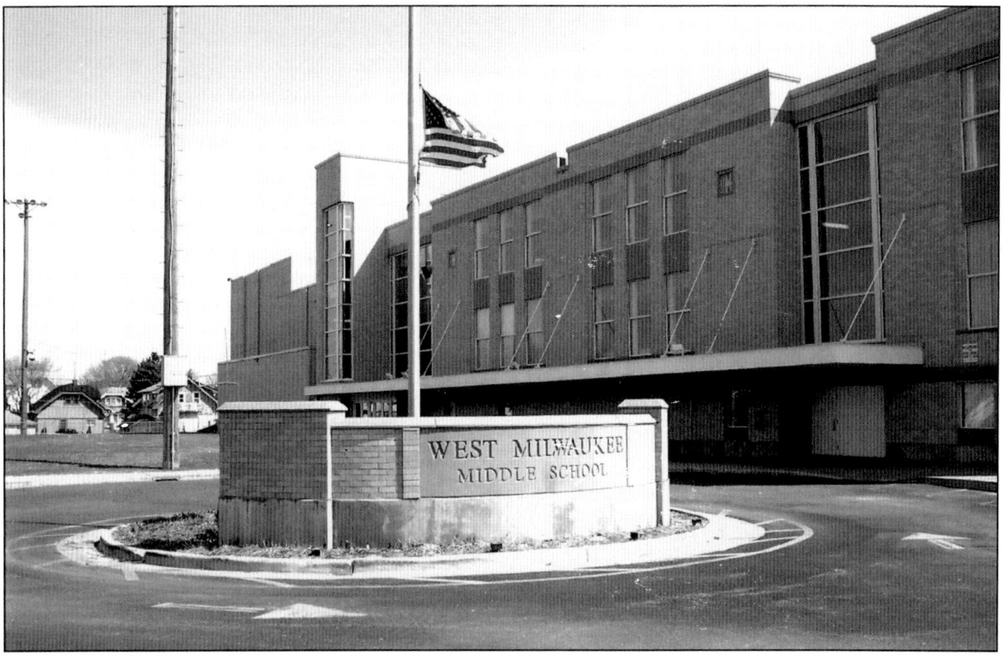

West Milwaukee High School closed in 1992; however, the building was completely renovated at a cost of $9 million and opened as West Milwaukee Middle School in 1997. The new circular drive at the rear is seen with the flag at half-mast, as ordered by Pres. George W. Bush due to the death of Pope John Paul II in April 2005.

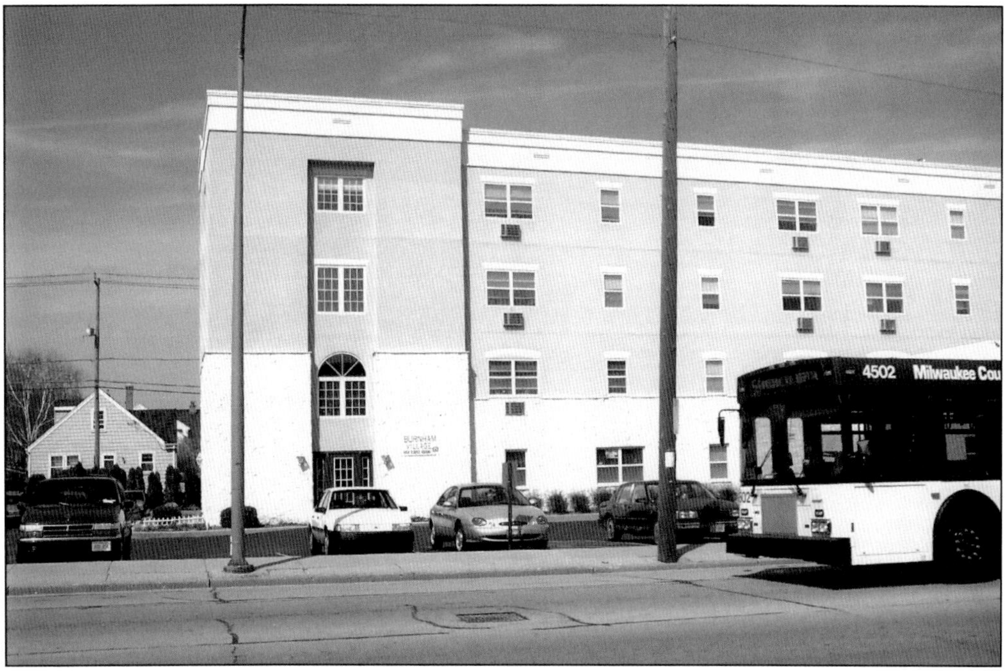

A 40-unit government-subsidized apartment building for seniors opened in 1997 between Fifty-second and Fifty-third Streets and Burnham. Developed by a group of six area churches called the Housing of Limited Income Elderly, it has allowed many senior citizens to remain in the village.

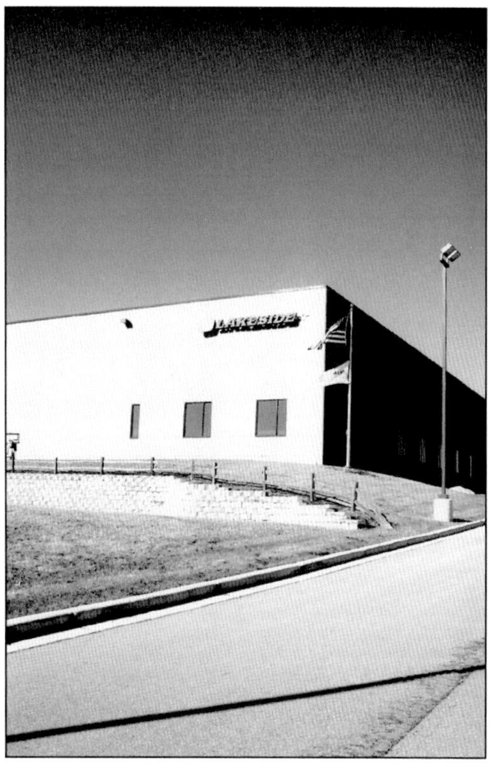

Lakeside Manufacturing, in business for 60 years and formerly located in Bay View, has been a member of the West Milwaukee business community since July 2002. The company is a leading manufacturer of stainless steel and laminated wood mobile equipment for the commercial food service and clinical health care industries. The facility is situated on Electric Avenue between Hangers and the Norandex and Reynolds Distribution Center. This is the former site of Wehr Steel.

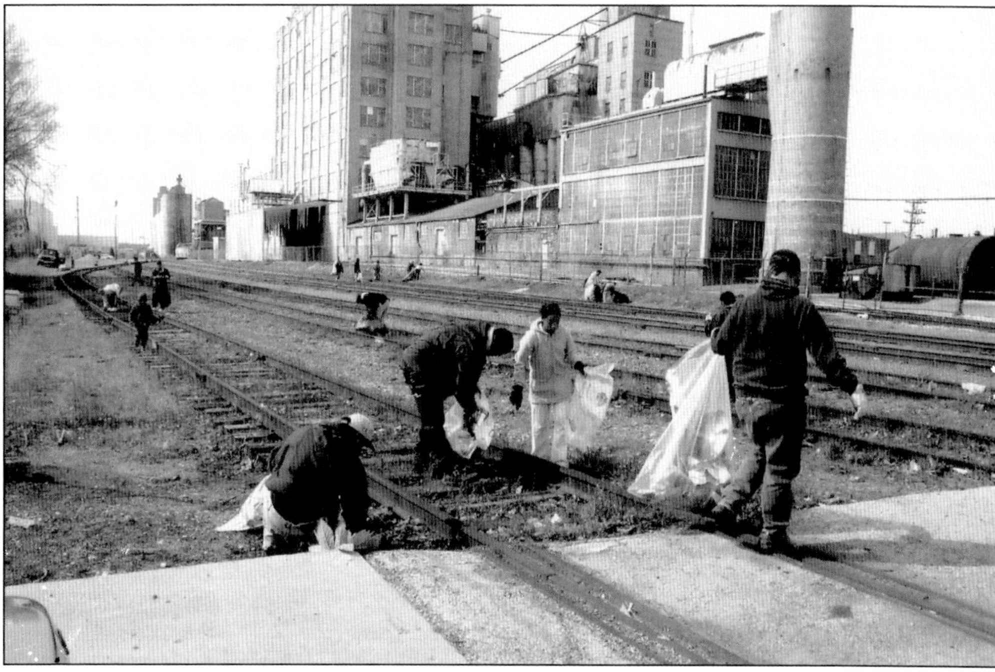

Volunteers collect litter along the railroad tracks east of Miller Park Way as part of the "Keep Greater Milwaukee Beautiful" campaign. The event is held each April on the Saturday closest to Earth Day. West Milwaukee residents turn out in force to get the job done. Local firefighters have joined in, as well as representatives from Harnischfeger, the *Journal Sentinel*, and Lakeside Manufacturing. McDonald's, Culvers, Rupena's, Starbucks, and Tony C's provide refreshments.

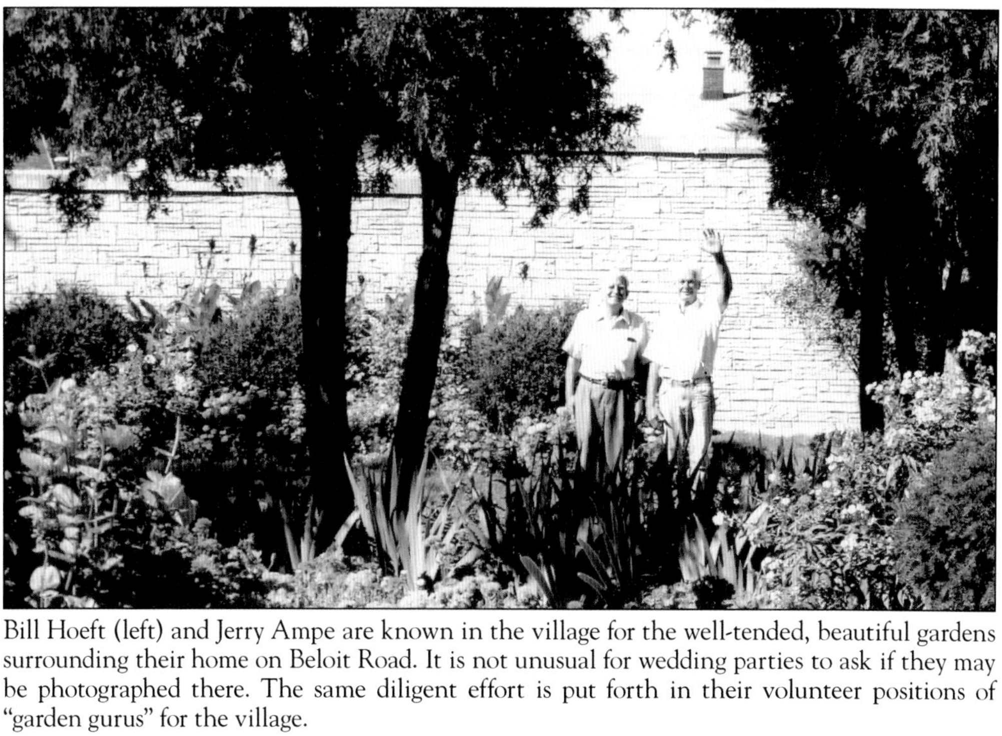

Bill Hoeft (left) and Jerry Ampe are known in the village for the well-tended, beautiful gardens surrounding their home on Beloit Road. It is not unusual for wedding parties to ask if they may be photographed there. The same diligent effort is put forth in their volunteer positions of "garden gurus" for the village.

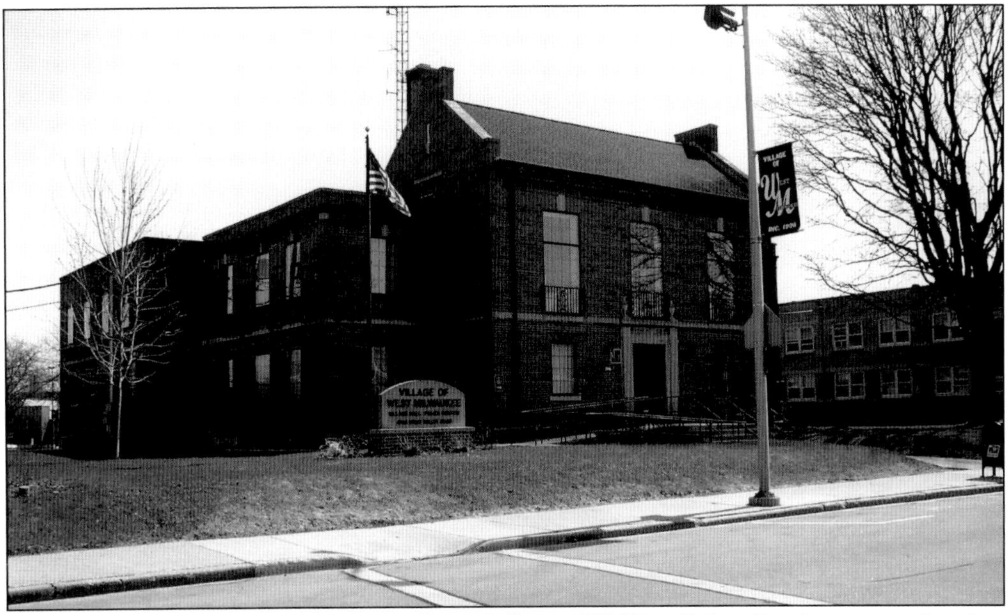

Renovation of the West Milwaukee Village Hall, at 4755 West Beloit Road, was completed in 1999 at a cost of $1 million. Originally constructed in 1928 at a cost of $35,000, the building was expanded in 1952 and 1957. The building was completely redone, but architectural features were preserved. Importantly, it was made handicap accessible. The police department and municipal court offices are housed on the first floor, and all administrative offices on the second floor. The boardroom has been moved to the Community Centre.

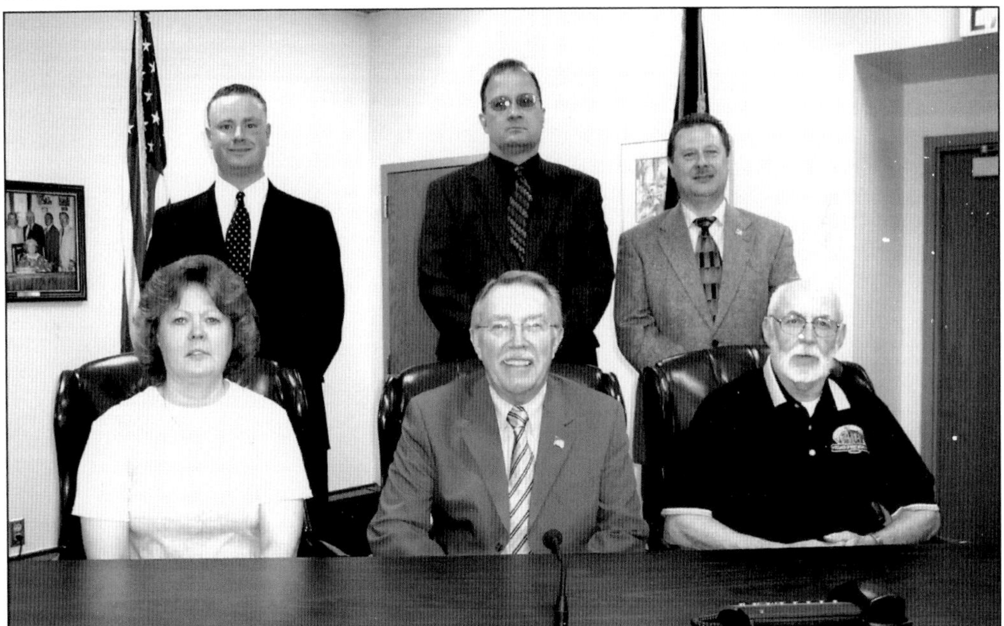

On Tuesday April 19, 2005, new board member Justin Hern was sworn in, joining the current trustees in a photograph. Pictured here, from left to right, are the following: (first row) Sharon Kroening, president Ron Hayward, and Frank Stoffel; (second row) Justin Hern, Richard Lewein, and Kurt Ritzka. William Kieckbusch is not pictured.

ACKNOWLEDGMENTS

We are grateful to the many people who have contributed their time, talents, and materials to the compilation of this book. In particular, thanks go to Sally Burke and Eva Ritzka for typing captions and text; Kurt Ritzka for scanning and restoring photographs; Ron Hayward for unlocking many doors; and Edie Wurcer for gathering information. Thanks in general to all those who have lent photographs and family stories, and to those who, years ago, wrote the first history of West Milwaukee.

A very special note of appreciation is due to Dr. Walter Funke, former village dentist, remembered for his love of community and passion for history. His legacy is the research and collection of maps and photographs that are the basis for this book and the West Milwaukee Historical Society's permanent collection.

Lastly, many, many thanks go to Elaine Ritzka, villager extraordinaire, without whose patience, diligence, competence, and good humor this book would not have been written.

—Karen Hayward, President, West Milwaukee Historical Society

This book is dedicated to all West Milwaukee residents—past, present, and future.